EQUIPPED BY THE WORD

EVERY DAY

HELMUT SCHULTZ

Foreword by Dr. Wesley Duewel

OMS International, Inc.
Box A, Greenwood, IN 46142

Printed by Evangel Press, Nappanee, Indiana

Scripture quotations are from the Holy Bible, New International
Version. Copyright   1973, 1978, 1984 by Zondervan
Publishing House

Cover photography by Helmut Schultz.
Cover design by Foster Pilcher.

Schultz, Helmut 1931-2002
        Equipped by the Word Every Day / Helmut Schultz
        ISBN 1-880338-37-8

        1.   Devotional calendars.   2. Bible-Meditations.
        3.   Christian life—Meditations.   I. Title

                        242'.2

FOREWORD

Helmut Schultz, my beloved co-worker, was deeply committed to God, to His Word, and to His cause. He loved to share with others the truths which had blessed his own heart. He preached with a burning passion as one who trembled at God's Word (Isaiah 66:2). God honored his vision, his commitment, and his passion.

In this book of daily readings, Helmut shares truths which the Holy Spirit has impressed upon him as he has meditated upon God's Word. There are autobiographical sections toward the end.

May God make this book a blessing to you.

All for Jesus,

Dr. Wesley L. Duewel
President Emeritus
OMS International

September 2003

INTRODUCTION

This book was authored by both of us. Our ministry together for the past 45 years has been a team and partnership effort. At times one of us may have been more visible than the other, but all the time we were supporting the other behind the scenes. The inspiration behind the writing was the sincere desire to leave behind for our family, relatives, prayer warriors and co-workers our witness to God's faithfulness. It is also our prayer that college and seminary students around the world will read and sense a strong urging by the Spirit to seriously consider God's call to the world.

I thank God that I had the strength to write most of the book after three operations and two rounds of chemotherapy. God has lengthened my days and made my dreams come true.

Helmut and Norma Jean Schultz

(Note: Helmut died on August 17, 2002. With a promise to Helmut and strong support by many praying people, Norma Jean finished the book by August 2003.)

Obedience

Scripture Reading: Genesis 12:1-7

Key Verse: *The Lord had said to Abram, Leave your country, your people and your father's household and go to the land I will show you...So Abram left, as the Lord had told him... (Genesis 12:1,4).*

Meditation: To begin a new year with obedience follows a pattern given to us by God in the example of Abram (Abraham), the father of the faithful. "He obeyed and went even though he did not know where he was going" (Hebrews 11:8).

To leave one place for a destination unknown is different from leaving a place with nowhere to go. Having nowhere to go indicates lostness, being abandoned, and losing contact.

To go out not knowing himself where he was to go, but trusting completely in someone who has covenanted to be the guarantor of his way indicates belief in a protector greater than himself. For an intelligent person like Abram to leave the area of his heritage for a place he neither knows nor comprehends by map or stars makes us notice carefully the character of the person he is trusting. Acts 7:2 quotes Stephen as saying, "The God of glory appeared to our father Abraham..."

Abraham recognized this Appearing Person as the Lord God himself. The God of glory was addressing Abraham. This revelation was to be obeyed. To Abram who lived in the midst of people who worshipped nature, the All-Powerful appearing to him over-rode all other considerations. He would do what he was being told to do. A great promise of becoming a special chosen nation lent great incentive, but Abram could have refused for fear of change. But he chose to obey, and by faith in the God who appeared and gave the promise, Abram started on the journey. He demonstrated his faith by his obedience. He believed God and it was counted to him for righteousness.

Thought for the Day: *God reveals Himself to each of us in His own way. When we know He is Lord we will do what He says and be protected by His resources, and rewarded by the fulfillment of His promises.*

Obedience

Scripture Reading: Genesis 17:1-10

Key Verse: *The Lord appeared to Abram and said, I am God Almighty; walk before Me and be blameless (Genesis 17:1).*

Meditation: The previous encounters with God required only being obedient, which is demanding in itself. Now God appears to Abraham with more promises, but with specific requirements. He describes Himself as the Almighty God, One who is capable of fulfilling His promises. He then makes specific promises: "I will multiply you; you shall be the father of many nations; your name will be Abraham; kings shall come from you; this is an everlasting covenant; all the land of Canaan shall be your everlasting possession; I will be the God of all who come from you."

The specified first requirement was: "Walk before me and be blameless." Another reading for blameless is "whole." "Walk before me and be whole." The same word was applied to a sacrifice, to be without blemish. But when applied to people, it meant to be "whole-hearted," to be obedient to God's commands. First, God changed their names: "Abraham" meant to be a father of many nations. "Sarah" meant Princess. Their names were an announcement of God's intention and would be a testimony to everyone that they encountered.

The second requirement was circumcision of every male person in the extended family who would be included in the chosen nation. This distinction of the members of the nation was the sign of the covenant; they had been chosen by God and were demonstrating their obedience.

In the New Testament, Paul shows us (Romans 2:28,29) that the requirement is now one of the heart and not of the body. We who become a part of the covenant of those marked by Christ's sacrifice participate in the cleansing of the heart, to be whole-hearted in obedience to Christ's requirements just as Abraham responded to the demands of God's direction in patriarchal days.

Thought for the Day: *To be "whole-hearted" requires total abandonment to the direction of God in our lives; He promises eternal citizenship to those who pledge allegiance to Christ's nation of believers.*

Partnership

Scripture Reading: Genesis 18:1-14

Key Verse: *Is anything too hard for the Lord? Sarah will have a son (Genesis 18:14).*

Meditation: Abraham had been honored with the appearance of the Lord God Almighty to him as recorded in the previous chapter. Now three heavenly beings appeared to him. Genesis 18:1 says, "The Lord appeared to Abraham" and 18:2, "three men were standing nearby." We are not told their individual identifications, but the text says the Lord spoke to Abraham. As the relationship of obedience and trust continued, God was demonstrating His "partnership" with Abraham and now, clearly, with Sarah.

Sarah was included in the preparation of hospitality to welcome the visitors who ate the food prepared for them. Then they told Abraham, so that Sarah could hear, of the miracle that would take place so they could have a child. Sarah laughed within herself, just as Abraham had done as recorded in the previous chapter when he found the idea hard to accept. But it was true and made possible only by the power of the Almighty God who was again honoring them with His special presence.

In God's plan nothing is too hard. The hard part is our adjusting our perspective to see His power. Both Sarah and Abraham were limited just as we are by our understanding only of what we have experienced or been taught to expect. When we are challenged to trust God for things that have never happened before in our realm of experience, we fall back on our own resources and fail to let God provide for us.

Thought for the Day: *I wonder what God would do for us if we could open our eyes and see the Almighty standing "at the door of our tents" waiting to give us divine provision and future promise? God needs us to be a part of the partnership.*

Partnership

Scripture Reading: Genesis 18:16-33

Key Verse: *Then the Lord said, Shall I hide from Abraham what I am about to do...(Genesis 18:17).*

Meditation: Abraham now enters a new level of his relationship with the Lord God. He has been selected to be the father of the chosen people through whom God will make Himself known in ever increasing revelations. He decides that Abraham should be included in this decision about Sodom. What an honor to be made aware of God's intentions, to be asked to share in the plans of the kingdom!

God was already answering the concern about the city, whether it was the cry of those suffering or the awful repulsion He Himself felt at the state of things there. Now, He says that He will listen to Abraham who wants to intercede should there be any "righteous" in the locale. Starting out at 50 and reducing the number to ten, by faith Abraham received God's promise to spare those who would follow Him.

After having received the promise of a son yet to be born, Abraham was bold to expect further answers to his supplications. But it was more than just an exercise in prayer. His friendship with God brought to him the privileges of partnership, being aware of God's strategy in His world. As with all privileges, responsibility follows. Abraham was exercising the responsibility of intercession for the world in which he lived. His part would be to represent the nation of human beings before the Almighty. "Abraham remained standing before the Lord" (Genesis 18:22). After Abraham had specified as far as he dared the possibility of the presence of any righteous, he "returned to his place" and the "Lord went his way."

Thought for the Day: *God is willing to hear our pleas, both for ourselves and for those about whom we are concerned. He is ever righteous even when we do not see the circumstances that surround His decisions. He is gracious to listen to us and consider our proposals, when we have entered by the covenant of His Son into partnership with Him.*

Mercy and Justice

Scripture Reading: Genesis 19:1-28

Key Verse: *The two men said to Lot, Do you have anyone else here...get them out of here (Genesis 19:12).*

Meditation: Commissioned by heavenly authority, two angels went to Sodom to carry out the rescue of "anyone righteous" in accordance with Abraham's plea, and to carry out the destruction, the judgment on the city for its wanton evil and complete immersion into vileness, repulsive to the Almighty.

The angels knew the danger they were facing as they entered the city. Lot, following the etiquette of the Middle East, invited them to stay in his home. Apparently no place was safe in the city, for men surrounded the home demanding to use the guests for their purposes. The angels would not let Lot provide substitutes for them, but struck the intruders blind in order to save Lot.

Lot had chosen to live in Sodom and apparently had gradually become used to the violence and immorality around him. Even though he tried to convince his sons-in-law, they would not take the warning seriously. The angels had to urge Lot himself to hurry, but yet he lingered (verse16) so that the men actually had to take hold of his hand, his wife's hand, and the hands of the daughters to get them outside the city. The action of mercy and salvation was all in answer to Abraham's prayer, "...for the Lord was merciful to them..." (verse16).

Again, even though the angels admonished them, "Don't look back and don't stay anywhere in the plain...or you will be swept away" (verse 17), Lot pled to stay somewhere in the plains, in Zoar. Zoar was also slated for destruction, but because Lot went there, it was spared. Still Lot's wife hung on to the pull of Sodom and so became part of the destruction.

Thought for the Day: *We do not question God's judgment on the evil city but we can be amazed at His mercy to Lot, extended to his family. God is patient with us and wants so much better for us than we can desire for ourselves.*

Mercy and Justice

Scripture Reading: Genesis 19:27-38

Key Verse: *Then Lot went up out of Zoar and dwelt in the mountains and his two daughters with him; for he was afraid to dwell in Zoar. And he and his two daughters dwelt in a cave (Genesis 19:30).*

Meditation: Someone has said, "Our choices determine our destinies." Lot made choices against the advice of the angels, one of whom was apparently the Lord himself. The angels told him to "Escape for your life! Do not look behind you nor stay anywhere in the plain." But he wanted to go to Zoar.

Abraham had pled for mercy for any righteous who might be in Sodom. Even though Lot did not fit the picture of "the righteous" because of having been stained so much by the culture of the city, God did honor His conversation with Abraham and tried to see that these relatives were rescued. Even though they had all these warnings, three of them still perished by their own choice and the other three lived in fear the rest of their lives.

Evidently Zoar was a very wicked place also, to the extent that Lot was afraid to live there. He and his daughters ended up in a cave -- very far from the ideal place he wanted to be. He had always chosen the level fields when Abraham had given him a choice. Now he had to live in the least desirable place. There he succumbed to the influence and trickery of his daughters and after drinking himself into a stupor he fathered children by his own daughters. The sons of incest were named Moab and Ammon. As Lot strayed farther and farther away from the protection of the Almighty, he began nations that would eventually be in conflict with the families that tried to save him.

Thought for the Day: *We can pray for those we love, but they have their own choices to make as to whether they will follow the divine options given to them. God promises covenant protection to those who follow Him, but destruction comes to those who disobey. God is both merciful and just.*

Direction and Deliverance

Scripture Reading: Genesis 21:8-21

Key Verse: *...But Sarah saw the son whom Hagar the Egyptian had bore to Abraham was mocking (Genesis 21:9).*

Meditation: The history of the stepfamily relationship goes back to chapter 16 where, after Hagar conceives, she very naively mocks Sarah as being a wife who cannot have a child. Sarah treats her harshly in return and Hagar flees into the desert. Here the Angel of the Lord found her "near a spring of water in the wilderness" (Genesis 16:7) and advised her to return to the home of Sarah and Abraham. The angel told her to call the name of the unborn child Ishmael and foretold he would live in hostility and be in constant conflict. While this prophecy was not something to be desired, Hagar did recognize that God had appeared to her. She was honored with His Presence, "the God Who Sees Me."

Hagar was both a victim and a guilty party. She was used both by Sarah and Abraham as a concubine which was the accepted custom of that culture. Sarah had considered her a substitute to provide the promised heir. Abraham accepted Sarah's suggestion. One wonders what Sarah expected out of Hagar once she became the bearer of Abraham's child. The Angel of the Lord told Hagar to go back and fill her role and not try to take the place of Sarah in the household.

God planned that Ishmael would be a father of many descendants that could not be numbered. Later, when Hagar's son apparently drew attention away from Isaac on the great day of the feast, Sarah wanted the stepfamily removed permanently. Now Ishmael was the guilty party and both he and his mother were victims. Even though Abraham was deeply grieved, he followed his wife's admonitions to remove this threat to the legal position to their son, Isaac.

Thought for the Day: *We are sometimes caught in the web of ambiguity, and may become the victims. God has seen the whole scenario. Like the total story of Abraham, we must expect God to work out our lives because we cannot.*

Direction and Deliverance

Scripture Reading: Genesis 21:8-21

Key Verse: *And God heard the boy crying; and the angel of God called to Hagar from heaven and said to her, What is the matter, Hagar? Do not be afraid; God had heard the baby crying as he lies there (Genesis 21:17).*

Meditation: Hagar and Ishmael were sent away by Abraham with only bread and a skin of water hooked on her shoulder. They wandered in the wilderness. It is difficult to understand why Abraham did not provide them with many more provisions. In his defense, perhaps we can say that God had promised him that Ishmael would have many descendants because of being Abraham's son. Perhaps Abraham literally turned them over to God. We do not know what was in his mind.

Hagar soon ran out of water and left the son to die, but he could still cry. God heard the cry and responded in a voice from heaven. The God who sees is also the God who hears. He is also the God who opens eyes. "God opened her eyes, and she saw a well of water..."(verse 19). God provided sustenance for them. He then continued to be with them so that Ishmael became an expert hunter living in the wilderness. God reiterated His promise to make of him a great nation.

Hagar was an Egyptian, and so she chose an Egyptian wife for him. The Ishmaelites and their descendents have been competitors with Israel through all of succeeding history. In spite of what God knew would result from Ishmael's being rescued, He honored his promise to Abraham to protect them because of the family relationship.

Thought for the Day: *God sees our vulnerability and tries to intervene for us as we open our lives to Him. None of us wants to be a Hagar or an Ishmael, yet sometimes we find ourselves in untenable circumstances. God is merciful and provides a way of escape, a deliverance that takes the form we need at the time.*

Divine Demands

Scripture Reading: Genesis 22:1-8

Key Verse: *Take your son, your only son, Isaac, whom you love, and go to the region of Moriah, sacrifice him there as a burnt offering on one of the mountains I will tell you about (Genesis 22:2).*

Meditation: We cannot imagine a more severe test than that of having your own child torn away from you in an act of violence. While the people of Abraham's day did not consider the offering of a child sacrifice an act of violence, but rather of appeasement, it was still a heart-wrenching requirement to the parents involved.

We have to assume that this test by God fit the culture of the day, but we know Abraham had gone beyond the culture in his personal experience with the personal God he had come to know. He was a friend of God, by faith following Him wherever He would lead. Abraham had already sacrificed his own homeland based on God's demand that he go to a land that was to be shown him only after he started to obey. He was in the process of following the One called the Lord God Almighty.

We would think that God had tested Abraham quite enough and that God could see that Abraham's heart was set on following Him. But God had further tests for him: He must take his only son Isaac (whom some think was about 14 years old) and go three days journey to sacrifice him at a designated place.

Having only recently sent away Ishmael, the only substitute for being the heir, one wonders what was in the mind of Abraham when the boy asked, "My father...where is the lamb for a burnt offering?" We see Abraham's unfaltering obedience and unwavering dependence on God when he answers, "God will provide the lamb for a burnt offering."

Thought for the Day: *In our obedience to God sooner or later we face demands structured to our circumstances. God wants to show us He will always supply the resources required by His demands. By God's own performance He actually gave His only Son as the sacrifice for us. Jesus is our resource to meet the ultimate demand of God.*

Divine Provision

Scripture Reading: Genesis 22:9-20

Key Verse: *He went over and took the ram, and sacrificed it as a burnt offering instead of his son (Genesis 22:13).*

Meditation: We can only imagine the churning emotions of both Abraham and Isaac as they proceeded to the designated place for the offering. Having assured his son that God would provide, Abraham appears to be reassuring himself that God would carry out His promise in raising Isaac from the dead. Certainly Abraham expected God to be faithful to carry out the covenant made years before that had started him on this journey. It was not Abraham's work to figure out how, but only to obey his Friend whom he obviously trusted without questioning.

We cannot know the thoughts of Isaac as he was bound and saw the knife raised above his body by his father whom he loved and also trusted. We only know that Abraham was giving to God in the way he thought he should the most precious thing in his life and the symbol of all his earthly hopes.

Suddenly in the bushes a ram must have caused a noise, for it was behind him that Abraham turned and saw a provision for a sacrifice. What relief he must have felt as he grabbed the ram and sacrificed it in place of his son!

God will provide! His promise was repeated by an angel who spoke from heaven: "By myself I have sworn, says the Lord, because you have done this, and have not withheld your son, your only son, I will indeed bless you...multiply your descendants, ...and by them shall all the nations be blessed..., because you have obeyed my voice." This is said to be the last time recorded that God spoke directly to Abraham.

Thought for the Day: *Abraham called the place, "The Lord Will Provide" or "The Lord Will See." We do not know how God sees our needs or how He will provide, but He has promised to honor our obedience. Our job is to trust when we do not understand.*

Continuing Covenant

Scripture Reading: Genesis 24:1-14

Key Verse: *Go to my ...relatives and get a wife for my son Isaac. Make sure that you do not take my son back there (Genesis 24:4,6).*

Meditation: Finding a wife for covenant son Isaac had to be top priority for Abraham. Following the custom of "arranged marriages" prevalent in that day and still used very effectively in many societies, Abraham directed his most faithful and trusted servant to look for the mate for Isaac. The instructions signify the great importance attached to the relationships involved. To be directed to go back to Abraham's kindred indicated sound continuity with the family "back there." Obviously Nahor, Abraham's brother, had not been given the same directive to leave the area as Abram had years ago, but Nahor's family must have been following Jehovah God to the extent they understood. Nahor's wife was Milcah and their son was Bethual, father of Rebekah and Laban.

The faithful servant naturally had questions about the task he was assigned. "What if the woman is not willing to follow me (whom she does not know)? Should I take Isaac to meet her there in her homeland?" The servant was forbidden to take Isaac anywhere near the old country. Abraham wanted Isaac in the promised territory that was his by divine decree.

To insure the selection of the right bride and to assure that servant that he would be in the right place at the right time, Abraham reminded himself and all of us that God would send His angel before and perform the search and order the circumstances for them. Accepting the assignment and the assurance of divine guidance, the servant prayed for direction through the selected girl's giving his camels water. "By this I will know you have shown kindness to my master" (24:14).

Thought for the Day: *Being aware of God's promises assures us of God's provisions. In this case, the young woman chose to follow the invitation that was proven valid and safe. Abraham chose to continue to follow the plan of God; the servant chose to follow Abraham's command and Rebecca chose to trust the servant's promise. We can trust God's plan for us.*

Commitment

Scripture Reading: Genesis 24:15-67

Key Verse: *So the servant put his hand under the thigh of his master Abraham, and swore an oath to him concerning this matter (Genesis 24:9).*

Meditation: Abraham was committed to the decision to follow God and see that his son, Isaac, stayed in the land where God had led them. He did not want his servant to take Isaac back to the land of the ancestors for any reason. He assured the servant that God would give him the protection and guidance of His angel in order to accomplish the task. Abraham's commitment was well placed.

The servant vowed to carry out the wishes of his master. He had always been the person on whom Abraham relied and was even thought to be the only other possible recipient of Abraham's estate should there not have been an heir. Emotionally he was a member of the family and he took his responsibilities very seriously. His commitment to his master was as to the Lord.

Rebekah, once she understood she was being asked to leave her family and go on a long journey to a strange country to become the bride of an unknown person, displayed the most courage. We have to read into this commitment an understanding of how God works in a person's life to love and to provide for her. She, even in her culture, embodies a tremendous commitment to the promise she expected to become a reality of her future.

Isaac, so calm and submissive to the will of his father, demonstrates a personality earlier profiled in the journey with his father to the sacrificial altar. He asked legitimate questions but did not debate the answers. After his mother's death he was meditative, and no doubt wondered how and whom God would provide for his needs. A person of miraculous conception and birth, he had ample experience to teach him to stay committed to God who worked through his father's faith and wisdom.

Thought for the Day: *God's choices are based on His perfect knowledge. How blessed we will be if we commit ourselves to His plan for our lives.*

Abraham's Death

Scripture Reading: Genesis 25:5-11

Key Verse: *Then Abraham breathed his last and died at a good old age...(Genesis 25: 8a).*

Meditation: Apparently death did not take Abraham by surprise at the age of 175 years. The key verse suggests that life was not extorted from him, but that he cheerfully resigned himself to dying. Abraham had obviously used his time wisely by *setting his house in order.* His two sons, Ishmael and Isaac, who had formerly been estranged, had been reconciled and demonstrated their harmony by both being present at the funeral to show their respect.

The original Hebrew translation is said to emphasize not his longevity, but rather his being full of life, experience, and contributing to the Hebrew nation. By faith, 100 years earlier, Abraham had left his country and most of his relatives, a significant sacrifice. But as a divine compensation for his faith-risk, Abraham began to know God more personally and is distinguished as one of the few Old Testament personalities who was called a *friend of God.* Abraham lived in a tent that showed his readiness to be available at God's command. He also indicated his vision of that "city without foundations whose architect and builder is God."

Abraham saw more than the Promised Land; he understood the eternal city as well. His death was not an end to his life, but a passage to the realization of the promises he had embraced by faith for 100 years.

Thought for the Day: *Only those who have a clear vision of the eternal city are content, like Abraham, to live a pilgrim lifestyle.*

Lessons From Abraham's Life

Scripture Reading: Joshua 24:1-10

Key Verse: *Your forefathers...worshipped other gods (Joshua 24:2b).*

Meditation: 1. Abraham had no special endearing qualities that caused God to choose him. Joshua 24 tells us, *"Long ago your forefathers, including Terah the father of Abraham and Nahor...worshipped other gods."* So, in spite of his demerits, God chose an idol worshipper to start a brand new voice. God sometimes has to start with what is available, but the final statement about Abraham is that the former idol worshipper became a "friend of God." We should be encouraged not to give up on ourselves and those whom God calls.

2. Abraham also reminds us that even the best of people can listen to bad advice coming from family members. Abraham had waited for God's promised son for ten long years, but he then succumbed to Sarah's suggestion to use her maid as a surrogate mother. Even though Sarah's suggestions were a common cultural practice at that time, God was displeased with this human attempt to carry out His plan. In fact, human efforts slow down God's timetable. The son Ishmael and his mother Hagar had to be sent away and the results stay with us today. God wanted Abraham and Sarah to wait for His plan which would have brought Isaac in His perfect timing.

Thought for the Day: *God works through our failures in a biblical sequence. We have to give up the Ishmael's of our human planning before we can get back on God's timetable.*

Lessons From Abraham's Life

Scripture Reading: Genesis 12:1-9

Key Verse: *...there he built an altar to the Lord and called on the name of the Lord (Genesis 12:9a).*

Meditation: 3. The lasting value of any life can be measured by the person's being able to keep the balance between worship and work. In Canaan Abraham built three altars at Shechem, Bethel and Hebron. These altars sanctified these places in God's eyes. The two most significant symbols of Abraham's life seem to be the tent and the altars. The tent was a reminder of his pilgrim consciousness of moving with God; the altars remind us that wherever he went he would express his thanksgiving and dependence by worshipping at a visible altar. Abraham's life was by no means perfect, but much like King David, we can say that the general trend of his life was *Godward.*

4. From Abraham's life we can learn something of what to expect from God when we obey Him. Most of what we gain will remain hidden to the human eye. But when Abraham died, all the real estate he owned was his burial place. The rest of the "Promised Land" was still occupied by pagan Canaanites. Most of us will pass from this life with some major unfulfilled hopes. But the fulfillment we can expect is that God will take the "little things" we have contributed and add them to those who went before us and to those who will come after us until God's final goal for His kingdom is reached. All of us are invited to be workers together with God. If we are faithful to use the gifts He has given us, we will discover the miracle of God working with us making our labors effective for Him.

Thought for the Day: *We should each visualize ourselves as being a significant link between the past and the future of God's plan for the world.*

Lessons From Abraham's Life

Scripture Reading: Genesis 22:1-18

Key Verse: *God himself will provide the lamb for the burnt offering (Genesis 22:8a).*

Meditation: 5. Abraham's experience shows us the meaning of sacrifice. He is the only person in the Bible called to sacrifice his son. Job lost his family in a catastrophic event, but Abraham himself was expected to be the direct agent of the death of his son. The directive to "offer up your son" seems incomprehensible to those who use the word "sacrifice" to include even small inconveniences. In retrospect we learn from the Scriptures that God really did not want Isaac's life, but Abraham's heart. However, that is not what Abraham felt at the time.

We are impressed with Abraham's response: He was actively listening for God's voice. When God called, "Abraham," he answered, "Here I am." He did not try to change God's mind. When God said, "Sacrifice Isaac on Mt. Moriah," he prepared to obey. He also obeyed promptly. He left early in the morning, probably leaving some indication for Sarah telling where they were going.

We can learn 1. God is not interested in our things, but in having our whole hearts. 2. God much prefers a "living sacrifice" to a dead one. 3. Some sacrifices always precede true worship. 4. When we give to God the best, He often returns it to us with an enhanced sense of stewardship. 5. God will provide -- "Jehovah Jireh" is a personal experience.

Thought for the Day: *Faith may call us to the edge, but God is never too late nor is He ever limited in His resources.*

Isaac, the Quiet Patriarch

Scripture Reading: Genesis 17:15-22

Key Verse: *I will establish my covenant with him (Isaac) (Genesis 17:19).*

Meditation: The Scriptures speak clearly of the God of Abram, the God of Isaac and the God of Jacob. Not one patriarch, but all three are needed as vessels to reveal to the people what God is like and what He is "up to" in the nations of the world. Without question Abraham was the true forefather, for he was the first man in history to be called upon both to forsake everything and to sacrifice his only son.

Isaac, the second patriarch, appears to be a quiet man in contrast to his father. Isaac's life is not known for any daring triumphs. Nor are there any records of God's breaking in upon Isaac's life with visions and calls to action. But in the quietness of Isaac's life there were two important communications from God.

God revealed himself to Isaac to remind him that the covenant He made with Abraham would now be extended through Isaac as well (Genesis 15:1-5). The only requirement for Isaac was that he have faith in what God promised. Then, God communicated with Isaac the second time (Genesis 26:15) to actually ratify the earlier covenant.

Like Isaac, it is important that each of us realize we are needed in God's great plan. While some may be called to be trailblazers, not all of us are. Some may be like Isaac who was a well digger. He concentrated on re-opening his father's wells. In addition to providing for his own flocks in this way, he also actively ministered to the people of the community. The people would know that the God of Abraham is still alive and working out His purposes in Canaan.

Thought for the Day: *Just as Abraham needed an Isaac and later Jacob to keep his work going forward, so no one stands alone in the fulfillment of God's purpose.*

Isaac, Example of Submission

Scripture Reading: Genesis 22:1-19

Key Verse: *The fire and the wood are here, Isaac said, but where is the lamb for the burnt offering (Genesis 22:7b)?*

Meditation: God refers to Himself as *The God of Abraham, Isaac and Jacob,* so it appears that all three persons are needed to fully reflect who God is and how He deals with people. Abraham is considered the originator of the Jewish nation through the initiative of God. What, then, do those two other patriarchs teach us, especially Isaac, almost overlooked by biblical scholars?

Isaac demonstrates submission. At this event he was probably just in his teens. He did not resist parental authority as he trudged up the steep climb on Mt. Moriah to worship and sacrifice. He asked that one question, "Where is the lamb?" He was young and strong and could have run away from his elderly father. Isaac's trustful acquiescence to being "the lamb" is most amazing and must be appreciated deeply. We also admire Abraham who, according to Hebrews 11:19, was motivated by his faith in the resurrection power of God. We can see in this act of absolute surrender on the part of Isaac a shadowing of Jesus, except that Jesus actually was our sacrificial Lamb.

Isaac received a marvelous inheritance from his father, Abraham, the gift of grace and acceptance into the family of God without having to offer himself as the sacrifice.

Thought for the Day: *God is the ultimate originator of our salvation provided for us by his Son as the Lamb.*

Jacob Grasping

Scripture Reading: Genesis 26:21-34

Key Verse: *... his hand grasping Esau's heel; so he was named Jacob (Genesis 26:26).*

Meditation: When our daughter was having her first son, she said, as she was in the throes of labor, *"Mom, we are going to name the baby, Jacob. Jacob was a good man, wasn't he?"* I, momentarily stunned by her question and by the timing, choked out, *"He **became** a good man, dear."*

That was not the best answer. He never **became** a good man, but he did become a man who recognized God as the source of life. He did wrestle with the Almighty and God had mercy on him. We all are something of a Jacob. He recognized God after many attempts to direct his own life.

Jacob came out of the womb grasping for control. He saw it demonstrated by his mother, Rebekah, in her trickery to get favors for her selected son. He saw his father let King Abimelech think Rebekah was his sister. We are often perplexed by the double-mindedness of others. Then we look into our own hearts and are appalled at our own temptation or actual practice of double-mindedness. When we are victims of deception we are angry, disappointed, disillusioned, and feel victimized.

We live in the human race first deceived by Satan. Certainly we feel the results of disobedience of our first parents, Adam and Eve. Only God can rescue us from the damage we still suffer from the inherited curse of the sinful nature in our hearts.

Thought for the Day: *How can we know what is in our hearts? Only God can show us if we are grasping for our own will or for His perfect plan for us.*

Jacob Deceiving

Scripture Reading: Genesis 25:27-34, 27:25-33

Key Verse: *Isaac trembled...and said, Who was it, then that hunted game and brought it to me? I blessed him – and indeed he will be blessed (Genesis 27:33)!*

Meditation: We love to have social interaction over food. Sharing words and edibles produce a blessed sense of satisfaction in our hearts. Someone has said that the produce of the earth is God's way of communing with us. In those types of fellowship where He is honored, no doubt He is in the midst of our talking and our eating.

However, our story of Jacob, Esau and Isaac provides an area of indiscrimination. Our appetites can blind us to the more spiritual areas of our lives. Esau was so caught up in meeting his physical appetite that he blinded himself to the deception of Jacob. Esau did not seem to care what the bowl of soup cost; he just wanted to satisfy his hunger. Isaac thought he was getting stew prepared with great love, but failed to understand the real intent behind the feast.

Jacob knew exactly what he was doing. He deceived Esau for a birthright that gave him double the land rights, political leadership and ultimate headship over the nation to come. Rebekah knew God had said the older would rule over the younger, but she tried to affect it by human methods, setting up the deception plan for Jacob. But the victims are also guilty, Esau and Isaac, caught up in the appetites of the present.

How much we need in our world to be totally in tune with God's plan for us. We must not let the good things God has given us overshadow the better things He would give us.

Thought for the Day: *Father, help us to trust you for the good things You promise us and keep us from trying to take them by our own methods.*

Jacob Running

Scripture Reading: Genesis 27:42-28:20

Key Verse: *When Jacob awoke from his sleep, he thought, Surely the Lord is in this place, and I was not aware of it (Genesis 28: 16).*

Meditation: Rebekah told Jacob to run for his life to her brother Laban's place. She knew Esau would plan to destroy Jacob for his deception. Not only would Jacob leave home and father, but also his mother whom he never saw again. Her plan to get the blessing for her favorite son deprived her of that son in the end.

God gave the mercy and grace that Jacob needed so desperately. He certainly did not deserve to be rescued or blessed in this enormously defiant, deceptive style of life he chose. Nevertheless, God planned to fulfill His pattern for the family of Abraham. He would use Jacob as the blessing had promised.

For the first time Jacob recognized the God of Abraham and Isaac. When God revealed Himself above the ladder that connected heaven and earth, Jacob responded to the revelation. He, filled with wonder, took his pillow stone and made a memorial calling the place, Bethel.

Jacob had left the protection of his parents, but now he was under the direction of a Father who would guide him the rest of his life. Jacob even promised to give God a portion of all that was provided him. Ever the negotiator, he made a case for receiving God's care.

Thought for the Day: *No matter how much God reveals Himself to us we do not become "good" by ourselves, or by our negotiation. The grace that covers us comes only from God in His mercy.*

Jacob Working

Scripture Reading: Genesis 29:16-30

Key Verse: *Jacob was in love with Rachel and said, I'll work for you seven years in return for your younger daughter, Rachel (Genesis 29:18).*

Meditation: Jacob's journey of escape planned by Rebekah took him to Laban, Rebekah's brother. His work and his future revolved around a tricky person. Both Jacob's relatives and he himself continue to practice the manipulation of deception. Jacob loves Rachel, but is tricked into becoming the groom of Leah, Rachel's older sister. He has to work seven more years for Rachel. We admire his devotion and perseverance. Finally, he has Rachel as his bride, but Leah has children and Rachel is barren.

Even though the grace of God continues for these who are becoming the people of God for the redemption of the human race, the people themselves do not show much grace to each other. Laban tricks Jacob. Jacob in turn tricks Laban and multiplies his herd and flocks. Finally, Jacob realizes he must run again. Rachel agrees and encourages him to do whatever he must do.

Again God steps in redemptively for Jacob. In Genesis 31:24 the Lord God appears to Laban and warns him not to say anything to Jacob, good or bad. So God is guiding Jacob and his family in yet another move towards the redemption of the world.

Thought for the Day: *God uses people in whom we see many flaws. We can be thankful that He blesses us, too, in spite of our flaws.*

Jacob Worshipping

Scripture Reading: Genesis 31:29-42, 32:22-32

Key Verse: *So Jacob called the place Peniel, saying, It is because I saw God face to face, and yet my life was spared (Genesis 32:30).*

Meditation: We become almost tired of the continuing saga of this complicated family. Perhaps our society is just as complex today. When we read a story like this, we wonder where the "good" people are. Jesus changed our world by making it possible for our hearts to be changed. We are forever different when we recognize Him as the Head of our household.

Jacob was running from Laban, but God was protecting Jacob. Rachel thought she would help. She could not leave behind the gods of her father. She took them and hid them without Jacob's knowledge. That is one time Jacob did not have to deceive Laban. He honestly did not know the gods were among his moving household. Rachel very cleverly concealed them during the search. Laban minded God's warning not to say good or bad to Jacob. They made a covenant with each other and parted peacefully.

Jacob learned he would have to face Esau. Now he must pray for more protection. He recalls the guidance of God to him from the time he headed for the country of Laban to the time of his present situation. He had only a staff when he started, and now he had great herds, flocks and families. Jacob admits his unworthiness before God.

Thought for the Day: *Crises in our lives turn us to God. When we turn to Him, we find He has been there all along.*

Lessons From Jacob's Life

Scripture Reading: Jeremiah 31:7-14

Key Verse: *For the Lord will ransom Jacob and redeem them from the hand of those stronger than they (Jeremiah 31:11).*

Meditation: Jacob experienced the unconditional love of God. In his dream where the ladder reached from heaven to earth with angels ascending and descending, God was extending His own presence to Jacob. God loved Jacob, not because of who he was, but because of who God Himself is.

Even when Jacob was running, God was running beside him. God gave Jacob a lot of space, but He kept tightening the distance between Him and Jacob, and finally Jacob ran into God. David later had the same experience, and in the Psalms declared he could go nowhere where God was not present.

God does not despair of us even when we despair of ourselves. Jacob, even when he received the irrevocable blessing from his father, Isaac, could not feel a personal assurance of living in a blessed state. He could not enjoy a blessing obtained falsely. God knew that Jacob did not need punishment. God knew he needed hope.

God has a purpose for His kingdom and His purpose is bigger than the individual. Jacob was thinking of Jacob, but God was thinking of Israel. (Later Israel would be thinking of Israel, but God is thinking of the Messiah who will save the world).

Thought for the Day: *We are all included in the redemptive plan of God.*

Joseph Loved and Hated

Scripture Reading: Genesis 37:2-10, 41:42-45

Key Verse: *His brothers were jealous of him, but his father kept the matter in mind (Genesis 37:11).*

Meditation: Joseph, the favorite son of Jacob, and of his own chosen wife, Rachel, had dreams given by God. He never questioned the authenticity of the dreams. He shared them freely with his father and his brothers.

We might say Joseph was naïve or too assuming. Perhaps he should have been more cautious, but God gave him these visions. No doubt God wanted him to let his family know what He Himself was trying to convey for the future. Prophets are not often welcomed in their own village, as Jesus taught many years later.

However, true to our human shortsighted nature, Joseph's brothers, and even his father, misinterpreted the intent of Joseph's prophecy. They could not see God's hand on them in a blessing that appeared to be for someone else. While God purposed to link Joseph with the plan of salvation for the family, the brothers did not see themselves as included. Intensely jealous, they looked for a way to punish their "upstart" younger brother.

Thought for the Day: *Others' treatment of us may cause great pain, but God will provide grace for the present and redemption for the future.*

Joseph the Captive

Scripture Reading: Genesis 37:12-36

Key Verse: *Come, let us sell him to the Ishmaelites and not lay hands on him…(Genesis 37:27).*

Meditation: We, who all our lives have enjoyed the freedom of democracy, are cut to the heart by Joseph being sold by the brothers into slavery. Nothing could be worse than to be put into chains and driven like an animal along a desert pathway to the unholy destination of Egypt. Joseph went from favored son to common slave, a status unknown to him, and never experienced by any in his family. How could brothers do this to one of their own?

Jealousy, greed, irrationality drive people to lose their sense of justice and balance. The brothers lost their heads in their mob rage attitude. No one of us is ever far from misinterpreting the motives of another. We can attack and punish others by words as well as by our actions. We can take away their reputations and their freedom.

We need to guard our thoughts, words and actions by biblical standards so that we never damage another's personhood.

Thought for the Day: *The human freedom of others can bring suffering into our lives. Our trust must be in God to overrule the choices of others.*

Joseph Coping

Scripture Reading: Genesis 39:1-19

Key Verse: *The Lord was with Joseph... (Genesis 39:2).*

Meditation: I have often wondered how refugees survive when jerked from their homes and forced to walk in terrible weather with their babies and elders to unknown places. I am amazed by the survivors of the Holocaust, and later of the German people in the 1950's when they trekked across Poland in the evacuation from Russia. These people demonstrated resources unrecognized by those of us who have not been challenged by those circumstances. They struggled, like Joseph, with conditions beyond their control.

Potiphar, Pharaoh's captain of the guard in the Egyptian force, bought Joseph, under God's protection, to work for him. Joseph worked faithfully, gaining the respect and trust of his owner. He easily could have taken advantage of his favored status. He could have cheated, tricked or manipulated his master. Rather, he chose to respect the domain of the people to whom God had sent him.

God engineered Joseph's circumstances. Certainly Joseph recognized that God was delivering him from a worse slavery. God gave him dignity and was also positioning him for His purpose. He learned to live with pain in the face of injustice.

I think his early dreams stayed in his heart. He knew God would fulfill those dreams sometime. God was connecting Joseph with resources for the future. Like Joseph, we follow God by faith, knowing there are unseen results waiting for us who trust completely in a God who does all things well.

Thought for the Day: *God is always thinking bigger thoughts than we are thinking.*

Joseph, Principled

Scripture Reading: Genesis 39:6-19

Key Verse: *How then could I do such a wicked thing and sin against God (Genesis 39: 9b)?*

Meditation: Joseph, reared in a home with multiple wives, knew well the tense interactions within such a family. His mother, Rachel, enjoyed the status of favored wife of Jacob. Leah and Bilhah took second and third place. But somehow Joseph carried a biblical view of man-woman relationships. This woman who now invited him to enjoy her body was a married woman. She was the wife of Potiphar, his owner and boss. But day after day, alone with the temptation, Joseph could have been desensitized to the danger beside him.

Joseph experienced the difference between being tempted and actually sinning. He knew that a legitimate desire fulfilled illegitimately went against the commands of God. No sin is done in isolation from its effect on others. Even though Potiphar's wife appeared to be acting alone, she involved her husband and Joseph in her illicit desire.

Not only did Potiphar's wife offer herself; she grabbed Joseph and drew him forcefully to her. Joseph knew the outcome if he accepted her offer. He also knew the consequences if he resisted her. But he willed not to participate in betraying God and sinning against his master.

Thought for the Day: *Our response to temptation reveals our true character.*

Joseph Betrayed Again

Scripture Reading: Genesis 39:19-40:23

Key Verse: *Joseph's master put him in prison (Genesis 39:20a) and the cupbearer forgot Joseph (Genesis 40:23b).*

Meditation: My wife asked me one time, "How long will it take for us to be vindicated in this situation?" She was very disappointed when I answered, "Probably ten to 15 years."

Joseph had resisted Potiphar's wife. We would like to see Potiphar believe Joseph and honor him for his virtue. But that is not realistic. The man is going to believe his wife. Joseph was betrayed again, not by family members, but by the lies of Potiphar's wife. Virtue does not always win in the evil world. However, God again had a plan, even though it took years. At least Joseph was not executed, but he was imprisoned.

Again in the throes of injustice and cast into prison, Joseph apparently did not allow bitterness to destroy his relationship with God. The jailer favored him, and soon he was using his dream interpretation gift for the baker and the cupbearer. The cupbearer was restored to his former position as Joseph predicted. Joseph asked him to put in a good word with the authorities, but the cupbearer forgot until years later.

Betrayed and forgotten -- how unjust. How long before Joseph would be vindicated? Joseph must have wondered, too, as he waited in jail.

Thought for the Day: *The long wait not only tests our patience, but it tests our trust in God's wisdom and power.*

Joseph Vindicated

Scripture Reading: Genesis 41:9-14, 39-44

Key Verse: *Pharaoh said to Joseph, I hereby put you in charge of the whole land of Egypt (Genesis 41:41).*

Meditation: When Pharaoh had dreams that no one could interpret, the cupbearer finally recalled Joseph, the man who had interpreted his dream correctly. Pharaoh sent for Joseph. Joseph told him of the predicted seven years of prosperity and the seven years of famine, and advised him to prepare.

God had allowed Joseph 13 years of painful preparation for a task that would save Joseph's family, those who had betrayed him. The nation would also be saved, and eventually all of us, because Jesus would be born through the nation of Israel.

Joseph's fruitfulness began in prison. He learned the language and culture of Egypt and thus gained the respect of all for whom he worked. He endured temptation to lust, to self-pity, and to bitterness. He steadfastly refused to give up hope or trust in God. He refused to let his circumstances distort his image of God. He held on to his dreams. In time, and according to God's plan that included all of us, Joseph was vindicated.

Thought for the Day: *God's time is always perfect, even if to us it seems delayed.*

Joseph, Forgetting and Forgiving

Scripture Reading: Genesis 41:46-57

Key Verse: *It is because God has made me forget all my trouble (Genesis 41:51).*

Meditation: Joseph had suffered for 15 years before he became Prime Minister of Egypt. He prepared for the seven years of famine by conserving the abundance of the first seven years. Joseph also was blessed with two sons, Manassah and Ephraim.

Manassah means "God has made me forget all my trouble and all my father's household." Joseph let his pain go and actually forgave his brothers years before he saw them again, when they came to get grain for their families. Ephraim means "God has made me fruitful in the land of my suffering." Joseph gave praise to God for using the suffering to give him a resulting ministry to two nations and many people.

Joseph learned that even his brothers could change. He tested their attitude towards their father before he revealed who he was and gave them his forgiveness. Joseph saw that God worked in changed people for good. Forgiveness gave his brothers hope.

In all the injustices of his life Joseph managed to channel the negative experiences into positive actions. He recognized that God took all the evil circumstances of his life and turned them into salvation, even for those who tried to destroy him. Joseph entered into God's forgiveness of his family and effected their deliverance from destruction.

Thought for the Day: *God takes the circumstances of our lives and uses them for our good and for the good of others. He effects a special purpose and plan for each of us.*

Divine Guardianship

Scripture Reading: Exodus 1:1-7

Key Verse: *Now Joseph and all his brothers and all that generation died (Exodus 1:6).*

Meditation: In Bible classes we often hear, "We are immortal until our work for God is done," and "God buries his workmen and carries on the work." In youth I accepted these slogans and even gained comfort in the concept of God's sovereignty over my life. I confess now that when a friend is taken early in his life I am tempted to question an idea once so easily accepted.

When Joseph, the great-grandson of Abraham, died in Egypt, some must have questioned the timeliness of his death. Joseph outlived 11 brothers who had come with their father to Egypt to escape the worldwide famine. As that generation who had experienced living in the land of Canaan died, there was no "heir apparent" to lead them back. Even more alarming, Israel seemed quite contented in Egypt, enjoying the good life in the fertile land of Goshen. From the human perspective, everything seemed to be at a standstill as far as God's promises were concerned.

Biblical history shows the period between the death of Joseph and the emergence of Moses spanned 400 years. How did Israel remember its destiny during this long period? We have no record of any new revelations or ministry of prophets in the many decades. While we do not want to give simple answers to complex questions, the story of Joseph's death followed by four centuries of silence assures us that when the important people in our lives pass away prematurely, God has a continuing plan and it is right on His schedule.

Thought for the Day*: The ultimate protection of any movement is not in man, but in God who continues the work.*

Trust in God's Faithfulness

Scripture Reading: Genesis 50:22-26

Key Verse: *...you must carry my bones up from this place (Genesis 50:25b).*

Meditation: At the age of 110 Joseph suddenly announces to his shocked family, "I am about to die." He does not rehearse his brothers' cruelty towards him. Neither does he talk about being significantly used to save the whole known world from death and extinction during the seven-year famine. He addressed Israel's future destiny in the plan of God, attempting with his remaining strength to communicate his contagion of faith.

Joseph's parting words, filled with profound confidence in God's faithfulness, extended beyond his present time to future generations: "God will surely come to your aid and then you must carry my bones up from this place." Joseph was so sure God would do it that he even extracted an oath that they would not bury his casket in Egypt. For the next 400 years the Israelites saw the epitaph, "Do Not Bury Me in Egypt." When the time of the exodus came, Moses, the new leader, remembered and felt personally responsible that the bones of Joseph be taken to the land of Canaan.

In Hebrews 11 the recurring phrases are "by faith they died" and "dead yet speaks" to describe the many Old Testament saints. For 400 years Joseph's body lay in an unburied coffin, but his faith in God and his obedience record kept speaking even to the ensuing generations.

Thought for the Day: *True faith focuses not on our human circumstances, but on God who already sees all the unseen future.*

Joseph, Dead but Still Speaking

Scripture Reading: Hebrews 11

Key Verse: *...I am about to die... (Genesis 50:24).*

Meditation: Important lessons from Joseph's life include:

Every movement started by God will continue until His divine purpose has been realized. Human leaders may fail and people will die, but there is a goal in God's planning that will be reached. Pharaoh discovered this at a great personal and national loss to Egypt. Each time we pray the Lord's prayer, we are affirming the truth that ultimately God's plan will be done on Earth as it is in heaven. All of history is moving towards God's pre-ordained goal. In spite of human appearances, God is in control. As Christians, our prime responsibility is to identify with God's work and become "workers together with Him."

God's timing of important events and our human calculations do not always harmonize. Joseph never tried to squeeze God into his human calendar. As Joseph was about to die he did not despair that Israel was still in Egypt. Neither did he feel that his life had been a failure because the exodus did not happen in his lifetime. Without a word of regret he simply announced, "I am about to die." Joseph was resting in the assurance that God, not man, was the primary actor in Israel's history.

Thought for the Day: *While we may not always be able to discern clearly the purposeful movement of God in human history, in retrospect, we will see surely God was in control and followed His preordained schedule.*

Joseph, Dead, Yet Speaking

Scripture Reading: Genesis 15:13-16

Key Verse: *...He is patient with you, not wanting any to perish, but everyone to come to repentance (II Peter 3:9b).*

Meditation: The death of Joseph teaches us there are often divine mysteries behind delays. These mysteries, however, may be understood only with the passing of time when we gain a new perspective of the reason the delay was necessary. We may be given a glimpse of the reason in prophetic scriptures that are actually a preview of history before it actually takes place. Both of these factors, mystery and prophecy, play important parts in the postponement of the exodus.

The numerical strength of Israel at Joseph's death was about 300 of Jacob's family. They would not have been able to dislodge the Canaanites who occupied the land; nor could they occupy 11,000 square miles of territory. Time was needed to expand the population to at least one million persons before the venture could be undertaken safely.

Another reason for the delay was the prophetic word God had spoken earlier to Abraham; "the sin of the Amorites has not yet reached its full measure." While we do not know how sinful these inhabitants of Canaan were, we can determine from archaeological artifacts that their worship was polytheistic; it included child sacrifice and also the practice of religious prostitution and divination. Yet God was patient and just, waiting for their sin to reach its full measure before exercising judgment.

Thought for the Day*: Today we should not presume God is under any obligation to suspend His judgment on sin except for the purpose of affording time for repentance.*

Joseph, Dead, Yet Speaking

Scripture Reading: Exodus 14:17-22

Key Verse: *Moses took the bones of Joseph with him because Joseph had made the sons of Israel swear an oath (Exodus 14:19a).*

Meditation: The fourth important lesson from Joseph's life is that he had to live and die with an unfinished task. Joseph's dream of the "Promised Land" remained until his death just a dream. Ninety-three years earlier, at 17, his jealous brothers had sold him. Yet, after all those long years of waiting, he was not permitted by the circumstances of his life to return home again. What does this say to us?

Probably we, too, will be asked to serve at an unfinished task. Someone has observed, "At conversion we all received an unfinished task and at death most of us will leave a half-finished task." We wonder at Joseph's being able to persevere all those years full of setbacks and delays. What about us? What will keep us going?

First, we must be certain that what we give our heart and soul to has its origin in the will of God. Only with this conviction can we keep faith alive and be confident God's sovereign purpose will finish what He started, even if it takes another 400 years.

Next, we can learn that while we may not complete our God-given task, yet we can make a significant contribution in moving it to the next stage or to the next level. Joseph literally became God's instrument in saving Israel both from starvation and from extinction. It can be said that if Joseph had failed, then perhaps it would have been necessary for God to make a brand new start with men as he did in the days of Noah.

Thought for the Day: *No matter how anonymous we may be made to feel at times, we are all individually a part of God's total plan.*

God Is In Firm Control

Scripture Reading: Exodus 1:6,7

Key Verse: *Be still before the Lord and wait patiently for him (Psalm 37:7a).*

Meditation: Look at Israel in Egypt both from their viewpoint and from God's perspective: After 300 years Israel was still in Egypt and actually quite contented. Numerically they had grown from 300 to one million. The overflowing Nile River each spring assured them of a bumper crop each year, adding to their prosperity. They adopted a "settler mentality" and gradually lost touch with the "pilgrim consciousness" which had so deeply motivated their ancestors. Little by little they interpreted their election by God to be that of "privilege" rather than "responsibility," as God had originally intended.

From God's perspective, the situation was radically different. According to His divine timetable, Israel's exodus from Egypt was closer than the people realized. The amazing population explosion was a direct blessing from God to enable Israel to conquer and inhabit Canaan. As they entered their fourth century in Egypt, God's prophetic word regarding His judgment on the progressive iniquity of the Canaanites was about to happen. Everything was coming together except Israel seemed bogged down in Egypt with no leader on the horizon to lead them out.

What usually happens in history when God's people seem content but God's time for action has come? God either intentionally engineers human circumstances to make them uncomfortable or He sovereignly raises up a leader as *"a voice in the wilderness"* to awaken them to God's claim on their lives. God is very creative in putting "a burr under our saddle" of contentment. We will watch to see how God pries Israel loose from Egypt.

Thought for the Day: *No earthly power or human situation can delay or cancel the purpose of God once He has undertaken to fulfill it.*

God's Sovereignty and Evil

Scripture Reading: Exodus 1:8-22

Key Verse: *Then a new king who did not know about Joseph came to power in Egypt (Exodus 1:8).*

Meditation: From the examples of Job, Paul and others we learn we should not attribute all of our human circumstances to the intentional working of God. However, if we accept the fact of God's sovereignty, then we must acknowledge God has at least permitted what is happening to us. According to Romans 8:28 Paul also encourages us to believe our sovereign God can rescue good from those things that did not originate with Him. Joseph, in Genesis 50:20, underlines this principle of sovereignty, "You intended to harm me, but God intended it for good...the saving of many lives." Observe how God "works good" out of the evil intentions of Pharaoh and gradually pries Israel lose from the grip of Egypt.

Simultaneous with the inauguration of a new king, the past good fortunes of Israel seemed to plummet immediately. A whole sequence of stringent measures were immediately leveled against Egypt that turned their hopes into a nightmare, but ultimately turned their attention back to the land promised to their ancestors.

Stage One of Egypt's planned oppression was to suddenly strip the Israelites of their status as legitimate landowners to that of alien slaves. The taskmasters expected maximum output of bricks from increasingly limited resources. Then, as the new king observed the tremendous Hebrew population explosion, he became paranoid and started Stage Two of his oppressive measures. He instructed the Hebrew midwives to kill all male children at birth. When this effort failed, he decided to enlist the entire Egyptian population in a program of national genocide of all Hebrew male children.

Thought for the Day: *Divine sovereignty means that God, not man, has the last and final word; ultimately nothing is lost or wasted.*

Divine Providence

Scripture Reading: Exodus 1:8-22

Key Verse: *But the more they were oppressed, the more they multiplied and spread... (Exodus 1:12).*

Meditation: When our circumstances suddenly worsen, we wonder "why is this happening to me and why now?" When the new Egyptian king unleashed his repressive measures, the Hebrews were asking those same questions. They were the "chosen people" and the prospects of being obliterated as a distinct people in one generation threatened them. What if all male children were killed at birth? How would this impact God's messianic promises?

Even when God appears to be silent, He is always at work. We can rely on God's being active when His people are suffering. Even though we do not discern His hand in history today, yet He is actively at work. The scriptures affirm God is the Alpha who brought the whole order of creation into existence and the Omega, the one who will bring its glorious consummation. God's sovereign purpose works in an invisible, but unbreakable line from the beginning to the end. While evil kings and satanic power may try to break that line of God's purpose, they will all fail as demonstrated in this chapter.

The king of Egypt's plan to limit the growth of the Hebrews failed. His attempt to use the midwives to kill all the male children also failed. Then his third attempt to enlist the nation also failed, for even the king's daughter opposed her father's plan and actively became a vital link in preparing the next leader of Israel.

Thought for the Day: *The sovereign God continues to be at work in the midst of our trials, and He will also consummate our future victory.*

The Overturning Providence of God

Scripture Reading: Exodus 1:15-22

Key Verse: *Every boy that is born you must throw into the Nile, but every girl lives (Exodus 1:22b).*

Meditation: Moses, the author of Exodus, writes chapter one and part of chapter two with no names mentioned except the midwives. The names of his own parents, his older sister, Pharaoh's daughter (his foster mother) and even the name of the new king is not listed. Apparently Moses wants us to understand that while people are significant, yet the primary actor in history is not man, but God Himself. This whole section highlights the fact that God is actively at work overthrowing and overturning the wicked intentions of Pharaoh who is actually a front for Satan's purpose. Exodus illustrates a real contest being played out between Pharaoh, an evil pretentious deity, and the Lord, the true God.

In these short two chapters at least four instances are recorded of how God overturned the intentions of Pharaoh and demonstrated His own sovereignty: Pharaoh's chosen place for destruction, the River Nile, believed to be the origin of an Egyptian deity, served as an instrument of salvation for the baby Moses. The Israelite daughters who were spared from the policy of genocide became the very ones to oppose Pharaoh because they decided to fear God. A member of Pharaoh's own family becomes an accomplice in the saving of the very person whom God has ordained to lead Israel out of slavery. An Egyptian princess listens to the advice of a young slave girl who talks her into letting the mother of Moses care for him while being paid out of the king's treasury. This insured that the first instruction of Moses would be from his godly parents rather than from pagan Egyptian teachers. But the adoption of Moses would also make it possible for him to receive the best training in the courts of Pharaoh for his future leadership of two million Hebrew people.

Thought for the Day: *The Jewish midwives could not be passive in their obedience to God's will, and neither can we. Either we must choose or our circumstances will choose for us.*

Moses: Preparation for Leadership (1)

Scripture Reading: Acts 7:17-22

Key Verse: *At that time Moses was born and he was no ordinary child...(Acts 1:20a).*

Meditation: Most people in leadership will tell you that the single factor that most shaped their lives was their home life, including their parents. Without question, the daring faith of Moses' parents laid the groundwork for God's subsequent dealing with Moses himself. The parents bequeathed their lasting legacy to Moses whose final stage in training would take place away from the safeguard of home in a very hostile environment. God again demonstrated His protective care over Israel's future leader by allowing him to learn from his parents first before he would be exposed to pagan Egyptian teachers.

The biblical record does not give us many details about Amran, the father, or his mother, Jochebed, except they were descendents from the tribe of Levi, from whom the priestly line was ordained. Aaron, the older brother, later became the high priest over Israel. From one humble slave home there emerged in the darkest hour of Israel's history two significant leaders: Moses, who shaped their political destiny and Aaron who would guide their spiritual course of events.

How did Moses' parents prepare him for those years in the courts and schools of Egypt? What history did his mother rehearse repeatedly to him? God's divine protection during the months of hiding and the many deliverances in his young life; the parents' mutual inspiration to make the little basket ark in which he was placed, protected and directed to the very place where the princess was bathing; the regular visits to Joseph's unburied coffin and his last words, "Do not bury me in Egypt." Perhaps Moses even said "When I get to be a big man I will carry his bones out of this land" (see Exodus 13:19).

Thought for the Day: *God is at work in us today preparing us for what He wants to do through us tomorrow.*

Moses: Preparation for Leadership (2)

Scripture Reading: Hebrews 11:23-27

Key Verse: *By faith Moses refused to be called the son of Pharaoh's daughter (Hebrews 11:24).*

Meditation: We are given only a few details about the life of Moses between his official adoption by Pharaoh's daughter and the end of his training period of around 28 years. At his adoption he was given an Egyptian name *Moses* meaning, "I drew him out of the water." This name may also have contained a prophetic element that some day he would also "draw his nation out of slavery." For the moment, at least, Pharaoh's power, though frustrated in little ways, appeared unchallenged by anyone.

Without question, the daring faith of his parents during those formative ten years of his life at home paved the way for God's subsequent direct dealings with Moses himself. No doubt his parents were often anxious about him. Would he keep his Hebrew identity? Would the Egyptian worldview, the theory of many gods, gradually eclipse the Hebrew revelation of the One God over all? Would his training to succeed the present Pharaoh tempt him to walk away from the truth of God's will and call on his life?

We now know the answers to these questions that his parents must have asked again and again during those 28 years. Most of us who are parents or grandparents can resonate to these same concerns as our children leave home to be under many other influences. What truths can we grasp to keep us hopeful? When we dedicate our children to God and try to model the best we know, we can be assured (1) God's special presence will go with them, (2) God's special overarching protection over their lives, including times of personalized intervention, and (3) God's special redemptive overtures drawing them to Himself.

Thought for the Day: *The greatest legacy to our children is the assurance they are special and they are loved by us and by God.*

Moses: Preparation for Leadership (3)

Scripture Reading: Hebrews 11:24-28

Key Verse: *...rather than enjoy the pleasures of sin for a short time...(Hebrews 11:25b).*

Meditation: Many Bible colleges were started in the 1900's in rural areas to isolate students from the temptations of the city. One old recruitment ad read, "Come to our fine Christian college located six miles from sin (the nearest city)." The emphasis was clear; we seek to avoid sin by staying away from the world. Many biblical precedents for isolating ourselves exist in the lives of Abraham, Lot, Demas, and others. This makes the story of Moses, who spent 28 years in a very pagan court, all the more amazing.

God took a risk when He chose not to isolate his next leader for Israel, but sent Him to live right in the middle of unbelief for the next 28 years. Many powerful temptations bombarded him almost daily: He was tempted morally by loose sexual standards. He was tempted religiously by polytheism that permeated the worldview of the Egyptians. The ten plagues were a judgment from God on their many deities. He was tempted by his social position for he was being groomed to possibly serve as the next emperor. He was tempted to feel intellectually superior for his schools were the equivalent of Oxford or Harvard.

But after 28 years Moses resolutely turned his back on everything that was his to purposefully identify with the Hebrew people and God's will through them. We ask, How could Moses do that? What is the message for us who live in our "post-Christian world?" While God may not isolate us from the world, He can insulate us against its alluring powers. If God protected Moses in the Old Testament before Christ's crucifixion and resurrection, He can surely keep us today.

Thought for the Day*: God's call to be holy includes both coming out of the world and then going back into the world to serve Him.*

Moses: Preparation for Leadership (4)

Scripture Reading: Hebrews 11:24-29

Key Verse: *...He regarded disgrace for the sake of Christ as of greater value... (Hebrews 11:26a).*

Meditation: Two important ingredients are present in most life-changing decisions. Moses, like us, has to say a firm "No" to one option before he can say a wholehearted "Yes" to the other. He has to also reject the riches of Egypt, *the lust of the eyes.* Finally, he has to refuse to be called the son of Pharaoh's daughter, *the pride of life.* But Moses did more than merely say "No." After saying "No," he decisively pursued the other option, God's will.

Moses understood the pleasures of sin could only be engaged in the present. Once sin was committed, the pleasure would soon fade and only guilt would remain. If sin were not repented of, it would lead to eternal ruin and separation from God. If Moses remained at Pharaoh's palace and openly indulged in sin, he would have been guilty of one of the most serious charges of all, the sin of apostasy. He would have willfully rejected divine truth.

Moses determined to follow God's road because of the eternal reward awaiting him. He understood that by identifying with Israel he would be participating in the spiritual destiny God had purposed for the entire world through the coming of the Messiah. Moses became an important link in the destiny because of that faith-choice to relinquish his known present for the future reproach of Christ. No wonder that on the Mount of Transfiguration thousands of years later Moses was called to talk with Jesus.

Thought for the Day: *The most important decision in life is to give up the "passing" for the "eternal."*

Moses: Preparation for Leadership (5)

Scripture Reading: Hebrews 11:22-28

Key Verse: *...because he was looking ahead to his reward...*
(Hebrews 11:26b).

Meditation: Someone has said, "The most important question we can ask and answer is not about death, but about life." What are we going to put between our living today and our dying tomorrow? That answer will inevitably decide both our future and our eternal destiny.

Moses had to choose, or life and circumstances would make the choice for him. No safe or neutral path could be found. Stay at the palace and out of God's will, or identify with Israel's people in slavery where God chose for him to be.

In Christianity, contrary to other religions, the past is not as significant as the present. Then, in comparison to the present, Christianity makes the future more important. The concept of God's future being the most important shaped Moses' decision. Moses did not worship the past and his protection from danger. Nor was he bound to the present, his place in Egypt as the son of the daughter of Pharaoh. But he did cherish the future and was looking ahead to his eternal reward.

Moses firmly believed that by identifying with Israel he was also aligning himself with the people through whom the Messiah, the Deliverer, would come.

Thought for the Day: *If we demonstrate our faith by choosing the reality of the unseen future, our reward will be great.*

Moses: Preparation for Leadership (6)

Scripture Reading: Acts 7:20-29

Key Verse: *When Moses heard this he fled to Midian...(Acts 7:29a).*

Meditation: Apparently Moses continued to sense the God-given compulsion for leadership and realized he must now act decisively. God had intervened to rescue him 40 years before, and now he would fulfill the prophetic position as Moses the deliverer. He would willingly invest that valuable training he had received in Pharaoh's court for the single purpose of freeing his people. Humanly speaking, the God-chosen leader was finally ready to begin his life work.

Not long afterwards, as Moses was walking among his own people, he saw an Egyptian beating a defenseless Hebrew. Enraged by the injustice, Moses, in anger, resorted to his martial arts training and killed the Egyptian with one powerful blow. Instead of one dead, there were now two dead people. Even though it was involuntary manslaughter, he had killed an Egyptian.

Certainly his initial sense of injustice being done to his own people is understandable. But Moses stepped over the line when he gave in to his anger by killing the Egyptian. Pharaoh, too, felt betrayed by one who had been a part of his household for 38 years, and he now pursued Moses with the intent to kill him. Moses forfeited his first attempt at leadership and became an exile for the next 40 years.

Thought for the Day: *Some people are too strong or resort to carnal weapons that disqualify them for service.*

Moses: Preparation for Leadership (7)

Scripture Reading: Exodus 2:11-15

Key Verse: *...who made you to be ruler and judge over us...(Exodus 2:14)?*

Meditation: Ice hockey players are sometimes put in a penalty box for breaking the rules of the game. The "box" is a small rectangular area on each side of the rink in full view of the audience. The length of the penalty is determined by the seriousness of the offense. The most serious consequence falls on the team that must play short-handed. Many strategic games are lost by careless mistakes that benefit the opposition.

The consequences of Moses' misconduct extended over the next 40 years. His time "in the box' was not spent alone nor was the time primarily punitive. God, like a compassionate coach, was with him, rescuing good from his failure and teaching him God's way of working.

Moses started his mission of emancipating the Hebrew people with two serious miscalculations. He expected something dramatic to happen the very moment he openly declared his intention to set the people free, such as a national uprising against the taskmasters. He may have expected also that God would give some supernatural sign to visibly authenticate his leadership. We learn from the context that neither happened.

In fact, the very opposite occurred: The Hebrew slaves failed to rally around him and God did not come to his rescue with supernatural displays. His own people completely rejected any imagined authority Moses thought he had from his Hebrew background or his place at Pharaoh's court. He had no choice except to run for his life.

Thought for the Day: *The responses of people can be very fickle even when you do something sacrificial for them.*

The Sovereign Grace of God

Scripture Reading: Exodus 2:15-22

Key Verse: *...why did you leave him? Invite him to have something to eat (Exodus 2:20).*

Meditation: Moses was God's chosen leader, but he was not yet ready to lead. His reckless zeal not only contributed to the postponement of his mission, but it also jeopardized his life. Moses just barely escaped the pursuit of Pharaoh. In the midst of human folly and failure we can clearly discern the overarching sovereign grace of God.

God intended for us to remember He does not easily give up on His chosen people. For as serious as was the sin of Moses, it did not put him outside God's ultimate purpose for his life. While his wrong acts certainly carried consequences and required the corrective hand of God, yet they did not annul God's plan for him. The evidence of the ultimate triumph of God's sovereign grace is the Lord speaking directly to Moses face-to-face as a man speaks with his friend. Moses experienced an intimacy with God enjoyed by relatively few people in the Bible.

In Bible College we were often exhorted to seek God's perfect will and not settle for His permissive will. Equally challenging and anxiety producing was the inference that God's second best would leave the pre-ordained work undone in His kingdom. While this emphasis motivated me, yet it diminished both God's sovereignty and His grace. God is not dependent on my perfect performance to fulfill His plans. The serious failure of Moses did not stop God's purpose for Israel. We can count on the triumph of both God's sovereignty and His grace. The principles in Romans 8:28 are still operating in our circumstances, even in our failures.

Thought for the Day*: God's corrections are not intended to be punitive but purposeful.*

The Sovereign Guidance of God

Scripture Reading: Exodus 3:1-3, 18:1-12

Key Verse: *...Jethro, his father-in-law, the priest of Midian... (Exodus 3:1).*

Meditation: God providentially guides Moses even as he runs from God. Of all the different directions his unrehearsed trip might have taken, Moses suddenly finds himself safe in the land of Midian. Having just experienced disappointing rejection by his own people and the near death pursuit by Pharaoh, he must have been overwhelmed by the hospitality of strangers.

Jethro seemed so impressed with Moses that he offered him his daughter Zipporah in marriage. Two sons were born. The first, Gershom, means, "alien in a foreign land." The original language also seems to suggest "sojourner," one who has no plans to settle permanently. Moses was teaching his family that their future would not be in Midian. Apparently he was holding in his heart the dream of the *Promised Land.* His second son was named Eliezer meaning, "God is my help." His relationship to God remained active and now had become more personalized. He was not just the God of Moses' ancestors, but the God who is helping him personally.

Not only were Moses' social and emotional needs met through his new family, but also his religious needs. Jethro was also the priest in Midian and traced his ancestry back to Keturah, Abraham's slave mistress. It appears Jethro was a monotheist, a believer in the God of Israel. After the exodus he visited Moses at Mt. Sinai and offered a sacrifice of thanksgiving for their safe deliverance from Egypt.

Thought for the Day: *God knows what we need and may be ordering our steps even when we are least aware of His workings.*

Learning God's Time and Ways

Scripture Reading: Exodus 18:1-4

Key Verse: *…My father's God was my helper (Exodus 18:4).*

Meditation: Between Moses' arrival in Midian and the birth of his second son, a perceptible change seems to have taken place in his attitude. Even in the choosing of names for his sons this progressive change is evident. Moses is moving from his attitude of being in charge to a more restful trust in God as the one in charge of his sojourn to the Promised Land. His childhood faith in God is being transformed into a growing personal relationship with God who he now acknowledges as his Helper. It took another 40 years, however, to bring him to the place of maturity.

Church history is replete with tragic stories of people like Moses who did some bizarre things while apparently believing the idea actually came from God. Had Moses lived today he might have been tempted to rationalize his failures thinking that the purpose behind his misdeed was God-directed. Some people manifest unacceptable behavior because they followed some "voice" telling them to act. Families are left in chaos, suffering embarrassment and humiliation.

During the 11th and 13th centuries, inspired by a sermon of Pope Urban II, the church set out to emancipate the Holy Land from infidels. "God wills it" became the battle cry of the Crusaders and the primary motivation was religious. But the motives were soon tainted by politics and ethnic hostility. Victories were followed by slaughter of innocent people. Those unchristian efforts by the Crusaders continue to serve as historical barriers to evangelizing Muslims today, 800 years later.

Thought for the Day*: Let us discipline ourselves to test the spirits, for God never hastily pushes us into actions that are sub-biblical.*

Training for the Future

Scripture Reading: Numbers 11:4-15

Key Verse: *...the Israelites began wailing and cried, If only we had meat to eat (Numbers 11:4).*

Meditation: God meticulously prepared Moses for his future leadership role. Although the needs of the suffering Hebrew slaves appeared to be great, God did not hurry to graduate Moses from this university of the desert. For Moses to fail this second time would be to court disaster, so God kept him on the divine curriculum made just for him. Since God had the vantage point of seeing the future, He knew both what Moses still needed to relearn and what he needed to learn for the first time.

Formerly, Moses had worked with the elite. Now he needed to learn to relate to common people without a sense of superiority. The people would quickly perceive false humility. Moses learned genuine humility by going from the palace to the bleak pastures of Midian for 40 years.

He also learned to practice service in the desert, understand the travel routes and the watering places and shade trees. For the care of two million people, his preparation had to be all encompassing.

During this 40-year gift of solitude, Moses learned to communicate with God, enabling him to find inner strength he would need for his future responsibilities. On the way to the Promised Land deaths and funerals and detours awaited him. Dealing with people with selective memories who would recall only the good times of Egypt and murmur and complain would tax his patience. Finally, Moses would have to accept God's decision to prohibit him from entering the Promised Land personally even after 40 years.

Thought for the Day: *God's ultimate purpose of our training today is to teach us to be completely dependent on Him for a future assignment that we do not yet fully understand.*

The Fullness of Time

Scripture Reading: Exodus 2:23-25

Key Verse: *During that long period, the king of Egypt died...*
(Exodus 2:23a).

Meditation: Someone has said wisely, "Apart from the study of the Old Testament we would have an incomplete and impoverished understanding of God." Most missionaries have experienced in their evangelism only a weak response to the *good news* unless an understanding of the nature and demands of God as revealed in the Old Testament has been taught. In contrast to idols which are primarily projections of natural man on inanimate objects, the God of the Bible is alive and at work in human history.

In verse 23 two significant events are simultaneous. Both events signal the beginning of God's fullness of time for Moses to act in response to God's activity. Pharaoh's death removed the greatest barrier to the return of Moses. The Hebrew slaves now groaning under oppression and crying for deliverance indicates a critical intervention point for God. Moses would recognize that God had been actively at work in Egypt even though He appeared to be silent in Midian.

God **heard** the groaning of the slaves. God now intended to act. God **remembered** His covenant with Abraham, Isaac and Jacob. God intends to act. God **saw** the people of Israel, not just with His eyes, but with active compassion. God describes His actions with verbs of intent: He heard, He remembered, He saw. The chronological passing of time had now changed to **kairos**, the time for divine intervention, the time of fulfillment.

Thought for the Day: *God is never uninvolved in history, but His divine activity is often hidden to the human eye.*

The Importance of Duty

Scripture Reading: Exodus 3:1-3

Key Verse: *...and he led the flock to the far side of the desert (Exodus 3:22).*

Meditation: God's call to Moses at the burning bush came as a total surprise. Moses did not appear to expect anything religious to happen that day. Apparently God had not challenged him to be in preparation for a revelation. He was not even involved in a physical setting that would evoke a religious mood; no temple was nearby, only endless tracts of bare and unproductive desert sand known as wastelands.

On that day Moses was doing his duty: He was herding his father-in-law's sheep, as he had done for 40 years. This spiritual renaissance would ultimately impact both the Hebrew people and the entire world. God was teaching us that since all of our religious experiences come primarily by God's initiative, it is God's prerogative to choose the person, time and place. Most of our significant spiritual events are not announced in advance, but experienced as we respond to the call of duty, the equivalent of herding sheep. If we are doing our duty believing that God is engineering our human circumstances, then God's call can always override our call to duty.

As a young person I wanted every day to be full of spiritual adventure. But in college an elderly professor admonished us, "Young people, prepare yourselves for the fact that 95% of life is following your duty routinely. Only about 5% will be dramatic and exhilarating. If you do not do the 95% faithfully you may miss even the 5%." Naively I thought I could reverse those percentages. Now from years of perspective, I have to admit he was correct.

Thought for the Day: *I will seek to maximize God's purpose for my life by organizing my routines around His priorities.*

Immediate Attention to Small Things

Scripture Reading: Exodus 3:1-3

Key Verse: *...I will go down and see this strange sight (Exodus 3:2).*

Meditation: God's call came to Moses while he was doing the routine task of herding sheep for his father-in-law. Doing our duty faithfully builds strong character. God does not automatically impute good habits or a mature Christian behavior when we are born again. He gives us the inner resources for victorious living, but we have to practice to become consistent in our living. What distinguishes a Spirit-filled Christian from a shallow hearer of the gospel may not be in the initial experience, but in the personal disciplines and habits of the devotional and church life. Good things will happen to those faithful in carrying out their duties. As for Moses, so they can happen to us.

When God speaks to us in the line of duty, we must respond immediately. Moses could have easily rejected God's unannounced coming as an intrusion into his life. Moses had to decide quickly whether his loyalty would be with Jethro or transferred to God. He could have been tempted to stay with his employer of 40 years. He took the risk of faith to obey God.

He could also have dismissed easily the miracle of the burning bush for a desert mirage. In the hot sun he had probably had many illusions of reality. The tree was not at all impressive. Nothing had happened in 40 years. Why should he become excited about a burning bush now? The experience of Moses makes me wonder what it would take for God to get my attention today. What would it take to get the church on its knees before God today?

Thought for the Day: *We will miss many small burning bush experiences in life if we think bigness is God's only size and miracle is God's only name.*

The God Who Calls (1)

Scripture Reading: Exodus 3:4-6

Key Verse: *...God called to him from within the bush, Moses! Moses! (Exodus 3:4).*

Meditation: Sometimes Christians are so enthralled with being "called" that they spend little time becoming acquainted with the One who is calling. Moses, after his abortive attempt at leadership, is much more tentative about future assignment. He takes time to carefully verify the credentials of the One sending him. Moses now expects explicit answers. His persistent questioning and God's patient answering encourages us that we, too, can come boldly to God.

God is a personal Being with whom we can have dialogue. He is not One who simply sets the universe in motion and leaves it to run alone. Nor is He the *Unknown God* of the Athenians. God is a deity who can be known; He is actively at work in our world through His acts of providence, judgment and redemption.

The God to whom Moses related actually called him by name. God used his name twice to underscore the urgency of the mission assigned to Moses. Moses started his life born in the home of a slave. God put him in the home of Pharaoh's daughter. Moses lost that status for having killed an Egyptian. Finally, after 40 years God redeems and restores him to a special place of importance.

Thought for the Day: *Being called by God is both awesome and personally validating. A called person's commitment should be more lasting than those who merely choose their own work for God.*

The God Who Calls (2)

Scripture Reading: Exodus 2:23-25

Key Verse: *And God heard their groaning... remembered his covenant...and God looked on the Israelites because he was concerned about them (Exodus 2:24).*

Meditation: The next lesson Moses learned must have been very reassuring. He discovered in those long years of silence God had in fact been listening to the prayers of Israel. We also tend to equate God's silences with a lack of concern. In those *dark nights of the soul* we must remind ourselves not to misconstrue His *silence* with *disinterest.*

We may never witness the supernatural burning bush or the parting of the waters, but we keep trusting in His faithfulness and in the integrity of His covenant of love. During these waiting times we expect that God is always at work in history moving it inevitably toward His pre-ordained purpose. Let us firmly believe that when His moment of divine fulfillment comes, He will finalize what hardly seems to be in process today. God works in unobtrusive ways through people who do not feel the need to be in the spotlight.

Moses also discovered that the passing of time does not erase God's prior covenant promises. God's faithfulness extends from one generation to another, even bridging the gaps of the people's unfaithfulness and unbelief. God's abrupt appearance to Moses came because of His previous commitment to Abraham, Isaac and Jacob.

God has actually kept his promise to Abraham. Long centuries of Old Testament expectations have at last been fulfilled. The new covenant has been made possible through the sacrifice of Jesus. All who repent of their sins and turn to God will know the personal fulfillment of Jeremiah 31:34b: "For I will forgive their wickedness and will remember their sins no more."

Thought for the Day: *Our Bible is divided in half, into Old and New Covenants. In both covenants God Himself keeps the main responsibilities.*

The God Who Calls (3)

Scripture Reading: Exodus 3:3-7

Key Verse: *So I have come down to rescue them... (Exodus 3:8).*

Meditation: God, through all the years of Israel's history, had actively been involved in the life of the Hebrew people. He clearly heard, saw and remembered everything that transpired since He made his covenant with Abraham 800 years earlier. God now reassures Moses that His faithfulness to past generations would be extended to him until everything He had promised would be fulfilled.

Now Moses would experience God's decision to manifest Himself visibly and to audibly talk in our space/time world. God actually presented Himself to Moses and spoke out of the fire. While God could observe from the perspective of heaven, it seems that in order to bring about change on earth, He must come to earth Himself. God not only called Moses; He was also committing Himself to work through Moses. God even accommodated Himself to allowing Moses the help of Aaron, although that was not God's initial plan.

God came down to deliver Israel *from* Egypt and to *bring them* to the Promised Land. One aspect of the Abrahamic covenant would remain unfulfilled for the next 1,500 years. One greater than Moses would come (Christ) who would save the people from their sins. The deliverance by Moses only prefigured faintly the greater deliverance Christ would provide from the power of sin into the service of God.

Thought for the Day: *At Pentecost, Christ, through the Spirit, reenacted in His disciples all He provided on the cross for the full freedom of His people to serve God with singleness of heart.*

The God Who Calls (4)

Scripture Reading: Exodus 3:4-6

Key Verse: *...And God called to him from within the bush (Exodus 3:4).*

Meditation: God as the Lord of Glory will condescend to use attention-getting devices to draw us to Him. For Moses to see a scrubby desert tree ablaze but not consumed certainly was a striking phenomenon. The tree seemed to be actually reflecting God's awesome Shekinah glory as God's actual presence, much like the pillar of fire that would later guide the people to the Promised Land.

God's approach to us may not be as dramatic or sensational, yet we can be certain that God is still trying to get our attention. We can identify special times and places when God unmistakably spoke to us. Sometimes He effects a multiplication of similar circumstances that point us to Him or to His answer to our prayers.

At another time God will direct another Christian to say something directional for us. The spiritual gift of discernment on the part of another can facilitate the decision we may be considering.

Again, in the tragic happenings of our lives, God can redeem the incident to bring us a greater understanding of His grace and power. As we wipe the tears from our eyes we can see God's face, and learn His future purpose for us.

Thought for the Day: *I will discipline myself to stop and observe the burning bushes God has providentially placed in my busy paths of duty.*

The God Who Calls (5)

Scripture: Exodus 3:1-4

Key Verse: *When the Lord saw that he had gone over to look, God called to him…(Exodus 3:4).*

Meditation: Moses learned that God's greater revelations come to those who have responded in obedience to the commands they have already received.   All revelation has implied responsibility, but the clearer the revelation, the greater the responsibility. The initial natural revelation, the tree ablaze, Moses saw. If he had refused to stop, he would still have been accountable to God. He would have missed the full potential of the encounter with God. The actual liberation of the Jewish people started, not at the Red Sea, but here in the desert when Moses stopped to examine the tree that was burning but was not consumed.

Moses also learned that God is the ultimate initiator of all religious experience.   Moses was not seeking God, but God was looking for Moses.   Moses was not seeking a call, but God needed a worker. Moses was herding the sheep when God appeared. We can realize that becoming a Christian did not begin with our decision, but with God's effective call upon our lives. The fact is, when that call first came, we were still dead in our trespasses and sins, hardly a fit candidate for making a decision. Most of us resembled Saul of Tarsus who was still resisting God, but received the revelation in spite of his protests.

Thought for the Day: *In salvation it is not my merits that count, but the acknowledgment of my demerits.*

The God Who Calls (6)

Scripture Reading: Exodus 3:4-6

Key Verse: *Do not come any closer ... take off your sandals (Exodus 3:5).*

Meditation: God showed Moses that He is holy. God's holiness does not preclude closeness or intimacy with Him. Moses took off his sandals recognizing his unworthiness in God's presence, but he was not restricted in his proximity to God. In his subsequent conversations with God, Moses seemed completely free to ask anything of a personal concern such as more information about God's name and identity, his own speech handicap, his doubts and honest fears and finally, a request to be excused. Amazingly, God not only initiated the encounter, but He also facilitated one of the most direct dialogues in the Old Testament. God actually affirms Moses as a valuable participant in His plan to liberate His people.

Before Moses dared to come close to the bush, he first took off his sandals to demonstrate humility and reverence. Moses was not to misinterpret physical closeness with flippancy before God. His sandals had unholy dirt on them, indicating we need to put off anything tainted by uncleanness before we approach God. When we stand barefoot we feel both humble and transparent. Nothing can be hidden any longer.

In the west most people prefer to keep their shoes on in buildings, even in churches. Part of that is cultural, but we also may be sending a signal that we are afraid to be transparent and that we prefer distance to intimacy with God. With our shoes on we can easily substitute business for worship. Perhaps we would try to handle the Pharaohs in our lives in our own strength, thus repeating our past failures.

Thought for the Day: *The only appropriate posture before the awesome holiness of God is transparency, symbolized by Moses' taking his shoes off, and his face in his hands, symbolizing unworthiness.*

Learning God's Timetable

Scripture Reading: Exodus 3:1-3

Key Verse: *There the angel of the LORD appeared to him... (Exodus 3:2).*

Meditation: Moses' experience at the bush demonstrated the truth that most of the memorable events in our journey with God may have very humble beginnings. Moses followed a prescribed route as he cared for the sheep. But one day God appeared because it was His time for Israel and for Moses. Dennis Kinlaw, past president of Asbury College, said upon witnessing a spontaneous revival at the college in 1970, "Give me one divine moment when God acts and I say that moment is far superior to all human efforts of man through the centuries." God was both speaking and acting at the burning bush, and it was really there that the hope of Israel and the hope of the Messiah were reborn.

As we retrace God's interventions in our own personal lives, we are struck by how little we actually had to do with making the events happen. In Wilmore, Kentucky, the college and seminary town, John Wesley is often quoted. His statue stands on the seminary campus to remind us of his teachings and of his founding of the Methodist Church. Even a street there is named Aldersgate where Wesley in England had his heart-warming experience.

This transforming experience for Wesley happened in a humble meeting place that he reluctantly attended one night. Wesley had failed in his missionary endeavors in America: "I went to America to convert the Indians, but who shall convert me?" he cried. But that night at Aldersgate while a layperson read Luther's **Preface to Romans,** Wesley suddenly felt his heart *divinely warmed.* He later attributed his life-long call to evangelism to that divine moment at Aldersgate.

Thought for the Day: *Lord, give me that teachable curiosity of Moses so that I will not miss anything You are doing in my world today.*

God's Sovereign Grace

Scripture Reading: Exodus 2:23-25

Key Verse: *So God looked on the Israelites and was concerned about them (Exodus 2:25).*

Meditation: According to today's actuaries, the life of Moses had already peaked when God called him by the burning bush. The first third of his life was spent as the adopted son of Pharaoh's daughter learning to be the future leader of Egypt. The next 40 years were spent as a fugitive from justice in Midian, 'unlearning' many of the Egyptian ways. From a human perspective those 40 years as a shepherd seemed to be wasted.

Forty years is also a long time to reflect over one's failure. "If only I had not lost my temper and killed a man." On the other hand, it may have taken Moses that long to forgive the man who reported him, or to forgive himself and to accept God's forgiveness. Many people carry the spirit of unforgiveness to their graves. But the fact remains that God cannot trust us with leadership as long as we carry the burden of unforgiveness in our hearts. The repressed emotion will erupt in circumstances unrelated to the original source of anger.

In God's encounter here with Moses, He does not rehearse past failures. Moses' sin, no matter how serious, does not put him outside the purpose of God. While we should never soften the Scriptures' hard line against sin, neither should we stumble over the richness of God's grace and mercy to the sinner. If the God of the Old Testament dealt in sovereign grace with sinners, how much more should we, who have received that grace?

Thought for the Day: *Help me, God, to realize that Your overflowing grace is available to everyone who does not trust in his own merit.*

Initial Obedience

Scripture Reading: Exodus 3:1-3

Key Verse: *"...I will go over and see this strange sight..." (Exodus 3:3).*

Meditation: What are the signs that Moses is ready to respond to the challenge God is about to give him? The first evidence is that Moses actually stopped at the bush to observe something he could not explain rationally. How could a bush burn and burn without oxidizing and turning into ashes? Moses was not cynical or anti-supernatural in his worldview. He was not closed to the possibility of a divine intervention in his time/space/world. For someone who was once affected with a messianic complex to even stop at a tiny bush assures us that Moses had internalized, not resisted God's hard lessons of humility.

At seminary a teacher gave me this helpful advice, "The only way to keep encouraged in ministry is to observe the little things God is doing in the lives of people. Affirm the small changes and the persons will develop into the strong people you hope for." Moses' stopping was a small step, but it led to successive revelations of God to Moses. The Bible teaches us that every authentic encounter with God must have two parts. God speaks and reveals Himself, and man must respond with willingness to be a part of the answer. While Moses does not yet fully grasp who God is or the extent of His agenda, yet Moses stops and quickly answers, "Here I am, Lord."

Thought for the Day: *Each new revelation of God is an invitation to join Him in what He is about to do.*

General Versus Specific Obedience

Scripture Reading: Exodus 3:7-11

Key Verse: *"...Who am I, that I should go to Pharaoh and bring the Israelites out of Egypt?" (Exodus 3:11)*

Meditation: Moses found it much easier to respond to a general invitation than to a specific request. God put specific names of people like Pharaoh and specific geography like Egypt into the call. Moses began to squirm and feel threatened.

During my years at Bible College I was generally "mission-minded." I attended missionary prayer meetings and excitedly listened to those from the fields who spoke to us. I enjoyed reading Paul's missionary journeys and even tried to identify with him. I thought had I lived in Palestine in those days I would have been a part of Paul's church-planting team. Later, when an elderly mssionary pointed his finger at me at a youth rally and asked, "Will you go to Japan?" I had to face the specific call of God. Soon a letter came from OMS saying, "You can be on a team with seven Japanese workers planting churches all over Japan."

Like Moses, I tried to negotiate with God. Perhaps God was just testing my willingness to go. But can a person pretend to be willing without really being willing? I decided to go to a friend for advice, hoping he would discourage my embarking on such an adventure. I simply asked what he would think if I told him I was going to Japan. Before I could tell him any more details, he responded, "Helmut, if you are going to Japan count on me for your first month of support."

Thought for Today: *Postponed obedience can easily lead to disobedience.*

True Humility Versus Inverted Pride

Scripture Reading: Exodus 3:10-12

Key Verse: *"...Who am I..."(Exodus 3:11).*

Meditation: We can relate to Moses' question, "Who am I, that I should go to Pharaoh and bring the Israelites out of Egypt?" Moses rightfully saw the assignment as very difficult. He knew first-hand the might and cruelty of Egypt. The Jewish slaves were forced to build Pharaoh's grandiose expanding empire. Moses also remembered the slaves losing their personal identity to accept their lot in life and become reluctant to revolt.

Looking at himself, Moses humbly recognized his lack of leadership credentials. He did not speak eloquently. He had no authority in Egypt. He was a fugitive of 40 years. We can empathize with his sense of insecurity.

True humility never negates the reality of difficulties and human limitations. However, there is a fine line between true humility and inverted pride. True humility will not question God's wisdom or calling even if it exceeds our human giftedness. True humility will always make room for God's supernatural intervention. True humility trusts God's calling to include God's enabling and spiritual empowerment. Inverted pride, on the other hand, while being honest about inabilities, is very reluctant to accept any responsibility for what cannot be done alone. Inverted pride does not want to do anything for which we have to be 100 percent dependent on God.

Thought for the Day: *Lord, teach me the difference between the pride of working for You in my own strength and the humility that depends on You for what I cannot do.*

Human Partnership in Divine Planning

Scripture Reading: Exodus 4:10, 11

Key Verse: *"...O Lord, I have never been eloquent..." (Exodus 4:10a).*

Meditation: The revelation of God's holiness awed Moses, but it did not stifle his dialogue with God. My German pietistic background causes me to marvel at Moses' boldly speaking to God without inciting His anger. Moses even argues with God and God patiently listens.

This honest encounter by Moses with God should encourage all of us to be more open with God. God will not destroy our true uniqueness. He seems to want us to express our individuality. God does not view Moses as a passive recipient of His plan, but gives Moses permission to be assertive up to a point, as to the "how" of his participation. God even seems to respect his opinions.

God accepts changes in the details of His presented plan in order to keep Moses as a participant. For instance, since Moses felt his tongue disqualified him for leadership, God accommodated Himself by providing Aaron as an interpreter. God's Plan A became Plan B and Moses lived with the consequences of his insistence that he most likely lived to regret. At a given time, God works with the best available to Him.

Thought for the Day: *Even if we have the right to choose, it is always safest to let God choose for us.*

Who Are You, Lord?

Scripture Reading: Exodus 3:11-15

Key Verse: *"...I am who I am" (Exodus 3:14a).*

Meditation: Moses followed his first question, "Who am I?" with a second, "Who are you? What is your name?" Given the past skepticism of the Hebrews and the precarious nature of his assignment with Pharaoh, we can certainly appreciate the need for Moses to be armed with a ready answer.

God had apparently been silent without any new revelations or voices of prophets for the past 400 years. Moses had last heard about God from his parents at age ten. Some reinforcement came from Jethro, his father-in-law, and a priest of Midian. His 40 years in Egypt were filled with examples of Egyptian idolatry that challenged his child-faith and worldview of God as the sovereign Lord of history. The Israelites' concept of God's name did not allow them to say it aloud. All of these concerns must have factored into Moses' sincere question, "Who are you, Lord?"

In Egyptian worship Moses learned that all idols had personal names. The name served as a passport into the presence of that deity and promised the worshipper answers to their requests. Now Moses is sincerely asking God for some identification of Himself. God accommodates Himself to the request by answering, unlike the gods of the Egyptians, *I am who I am*, the self-sufficient One, the covenant-keeping God, whose faithfulness spans the generations, even generations of unfaithfulness.

Thought for the Day: *In John's gospel, Jesus completes the revelation of God's identity in the 22 'I AM' references. Now we can obey God with a fuller knowledge of Who He is.*

Facing Our God-Sized Task

Scripture Reading: Exodus 4:1-7

Key Verse: *"...What is that in your hand?" (Exodus 4:2)*

Meditation: Moses requested specifically a miraculous sign confirming God's call.   By using the rod in Moses' hand, God performed three successive miracles to encourage him to accept his demanding assignment.   Most of us will be confronted with some overwhelming demand.   Can we ask God for confirmation?   God will gladly honor our sincere request when we follow some guidelines:

1. Ask for a sign of confirmation only if you are willing to obey. Signs are not for information, but for obedience.
2. Let God choose the sign of His infinite wisdom and creativity.
3. Be alert and flexible for God's answer, as it may not be what you expect.
4. Do not insist on your timetable or give God a deadline. If people are involved, give God time to get them in line with His purpose for you.
5. Do not force the answer. If it does not come, look for another opening that God may be trying to get you to notice.
6. Do not insist on more guidance than you need for the first step. Divine guidance is like car lights at night. They do not show us what is around the curve until we actually get there.
7. Ask God for a promise to reinforce the concern you feel. Emotions may change, but God's word is sure.

Thought for the Day: *Most of God's promises have a future reference rather than an immediate one.   They require long-term commitment.*

Following God – Finding a Dead End

Scripture Reading: Exodus 14:5-13

Key Verse: *Moses answered the people, "Do not be afraid" (Exodus 14: 13a).*

Meditation: Most of us have followed our "hunch" sincerely thinking it is a shortcut, only to discover a dead-end road. But what complicated that discovery for Moses at the Red Sea was the fact that he had faithfully followed the guidance of God! Now they were trapped on three sides with Pharaoh in hot pursuit from the rear with 600 chariots and thousands of soldiers. Fear and anger took over with the Israelites blaming Moses, and indirectly, God, and second-guessing this whole venture which now appeared to be suicidal.

Look at the words God told Moses to speak. Apply them to your present situation where life seems to be out of control. *Do not be afraid.* God warned them not to allow the natural emotion of fear to turn into panic. Moses did not ask them to deny their fears or the reality of their threat. Fear is a God-given natural emotion. Someone has said, "In the beginning there may not be such a big gap between fear and faith as we might think." If we could discipline ourselves immediately to look to God and pray, we could neutralize most of our fears and transform them into trust.

To deal with our fears constructively we must affirm God's guardianship and sovereignty. Some of our worst moments of fear come if we feel unguarded by God. The biblical worldview assures us God is in control and even if disaster should strike, His sovereignty will rescue something positive even from a negative situation.

Thought for the Day: *Help me, Lord, in every cul-de-sac of human impossibility, to first look upward.*

Following God – Finding a Dead End (2)

Scripture Reading: Exodus 14:13, 14

Key Verse: *"Stand firm and you will see the deliverance the LORD will bring you today" (Exodus 14:13b).*

Meditation: Some of us grew up with the belief that if we are really good Christians only good things will happen to us. When we find ourselves facing serious problems we are tempted to wonder whether we had somehow missed God's guidance, or put ourselves outside God's will.

Moses had not made a mistake in discerning God's guidance, yet he finds himself hemmed in with no safe place to turn. God's second word, *stand firm,* seems humanly more demanding than the first instruction not to fear. God wants us to "stay put" in a crisis situation and avoid the natural impulse to run. We must wait until our human spirit becomes quiet before God. Crisis time is not the time to make decisions about our future. We must stand long enough to gain God's perspective of our situation and make allowance for His interventions, which usually come before our "eleventh hour."

Martin Luther stood condemned by the Emperor before the Diet for declaring that we are saved by faith in Christ alone. Although he was declared a heretic, he responded, "My conscience is captive to the Word of God; here I stand, I cannot do otherwise."

Thought for the Day: *The most significant thing in life is not the number or nature of the crises we face, but whether we remain standing firmly on God's Word to the end.*

Following God – Finding a Dead End (3)

Scripture Reading: Exodus 14:13, 14

Key Verse: *"...see the deliverance of the LORD..." (Exodus 14:13).*

Meditation: The third directorate for Moses was the imperative *see the deliverance of the LORD*. The word "deliverance" always includes in Exodus a retrospective and a future dimension. God never intended to merely get Israel out of Egypt, but also to fulfill a higher purpose. Moses asks Israel to look back and remember the miraculous acts of God in order to galvanize their hope in His future deliverance and further purpose for them as a nation.

To *stand still* certainly does not mean to remain passive in a crisis. Neither does it suggest that prayer for God's intervention is not necessary. But it does mean we should recognize it is ultimately God's battle. We should not attempt to use human wisdom or a human weapon to bring down the Pharaohs who pursue us.

In Ephesians 6, Paul emphasizes the importance of the believer standing firm, and also recognizes we are fighting a very real battle with an enemy requiring supernatural weapons. If we underestimate our enemy we shall see no need for God's armor. If we overestimate the enemy we will panic and lose our ground. All our Christian life we must remember that spiritual warfare means we have a spiritual enemy for whom we need spiritual weapons.

Thought for the Day: *Remembering God's intervention from our past crises gives us a renewed trust in God's purpose for our future.*

Following God – Finding a Dead End (4)

Scripture Reading: Exodus 14:13, 14

Key Verse: *"The LORD will fight for you; you need only to be still"*
(Exodus 14:14).

Meditation: A grandfather give his grandson five items of advice about broken things: Some broken things just cannot be fixed; some will fix themselves with time; some have to be fixed by others; some must be fixed by me and some only God can fix. We are relieved to learn that we are not expected to fix everything that is broken around us. It is, however, very easy to get in God's way as He is in the process of repairing something. If Moses had interfered with God at the Red Sea when God was working out the details for Israel's deliverance, the whole nation may have perished.

Perhaps the psalmist had this situation in mind when he exhorted, *Be still, and know that I am God* (Psalm 46:10). There are times when we just need the discipline to let God fight for us. Most of our lost battles in life were never intended for us to fight on our own. Pharaoh appeared very threatening to Israel, but he was no match for God. When Israel stood still, God placed the cloud between the approaching Egyptians and Israel in order to protect them. Egypt could not see the Israelites and were also blinded as to what God was doing on the other side of the cloud. While they waited, a strong wind parted the waters and two million slaves marched to freedom. The Egyptian army tried to follow, but the Egyptian deities could not change God's plan. As the soldiers drowned they cried, "The God of Israel is fighting against us!" (Exodus 14:25).

Thought for the Day: *I will be silent before God so as not to hinder Him from opening my Red Sea before me.*

God's Ten Rules for Living (1)

Scripture Reading: Exodus 32:15, 16

Key Verse: *...the writing was the writing of God, engraved on the tablets (Exodus 32:16).*

Mediation: Before the collapse of the Soviet Union, a Christian publishing group was given permission to have a table at the Moscow Book Fair. After much negotiation, they were given the right to distribute a limited number of New Testaments. Soon the supply was exhausted. A man who had been in line refused to leave without a Testament. He pointed to a box that had held the Bible and said, "Well, just give me the box, please." They tried to convince him there was no Bible in the box. With tears in his eyes he said, "At least let me have the box that held the Bible." To that man the Bible was of such great value that he cherished even the container that had touched the book.

We believe the Bible is divinely inspired and of inestimable spiritual value. In addition, there is something special about Exodus 20 that makes it particularly significant. **In Genesis**, many dialogues took place between man and God, but God Himself originally wrote the words of chapter 20. Words literally chiseled into granite stone by God's own supernatural hand demonstrate eternal value. Unlike the Russian man who had only an empty box, we are looking at a whole chapter written first by God.

For the next ten days we want to look not at what Moses said, but at what God actually wrote. Since the Ten Commandments are addressed to **you** as a singular pronoun, none of us can escape the personal responsibility of God's requirements.

Thought for Today: *We all must meet the God of the Ten Commandments first before we are ready to respond to the Christ of the Gospels.*

God's Ten Rules for Living (2)

Scripture Reading: Matthew 22:34-39

Key Verse: *"...love the Lord...love your neighbor..." (Matthew 22:37, 38).*

Meditation: In spite of the fact that God wrote the Ten Commandments with His own hand, fewer and fewer people view them as absolute truth today. Many think them excessively legalistic, if not obsolete. Others rationalize, thinking they have been displaced with Christ's emphasis on love and forgiveness.

Christ's answer to the lawyer who asked, "Which is the greatest commandment?" confirms Jesus' teaching that keeping the law is continually important. Christ synthesized the Ten Commandments into two summary statements: Love God supremely and love your neighbor as you love yourself.

While each of the Ten Commandments does begin with "You shall not..." there are no undue repressive constraints in what is being forbidden. Negative commands help to define clearly the borders of behavior that are acceptable to God. These clear prohibitions show us what is acceptable to God. We need not live with anxiety about pleasing God. Many parents are reluctant to say a clear "no" to their children with the result that their children continue to push beyond the limits that are best for their protection. Like children, we need to know the acceptable boundaries between God and us and between our neighbors and ourselves.

Thought for the Day: *God allows us the freedom of choice, but we must bear the consequences of our bad choices.*

God's Ten Rules for Living (3)

Scripture Reading: Exodus 20:1, 2

Key Verse: *"I am the LORD your God..."* (Exodus 20:2).

Meditation: The Israelites are now safely out of Egypt. After having no freedom for 400 years and then suddenly to be without regimentation would be a very scary experience. God meets His people at this very important juncture in their journey to becoming His chosen nation.

God certainly realized that Israel's destiny would require definitive laws and spiritual guidelines. But God did not suddenly thrust Himself on them with His divine demands. Before making a single command, He introduces Himself in terms of His prior relationship with them. He begins His divine disclosure by giving them His title, I AM. He asks Israel to remember and acknowledge Him as their Creator-God, the Self-sufficient One. In the words, YOUR GOD, He reminds them of His identification with Israel and His desire to have an on-going relationship with them. Since He uses the singular pronoun, *you,* He expresses His intense desire for a personal interaction with each one.

Israel must never forget that God delivered them not only from the Egyptians, but also from their bondage. They must also remember God accomplished their deliverance by ten intentional interventions. They were free to be God's people. The Ten Commandments were intended not to represent a restrictive code of behavior, but to define the limits of negative behavior harmful to themselves and to each other.

Thought for the Day: *God's demands on His people are always preceded by His covenant promises.*

God's Ten Rules for Living (4)

Scripture Reading: Exodus 20:1-3

Key Verse: *You shall have no other gods before me (Exodus 20:3).*

Meditation: Perhaps the one most dominant theme of the Bible is the sovereign continuous activity of God. In contrast to idols, which have eyes, ears, mouths and hands but cannot see, hear, speak or act, the God of the Bible lives and acts purposefully. God reminded Moses and Israel that He cared for them as their Creator and delivered them from Egypt. The ten commands sprang out of 800 years of caring for His people.

"You shall have no other gods before me" reinforced Israel's uniqueness. They were the only nation with a one-God faith. All other nations around them recognized many, many "gods." In missionary work I encountered fear of "gods," even of ancestral spirits. The spirits were credited with "bad luck" because the people who feared them had not properly appeased them. People were drawn to Jesus, but were afraid of the wrath of the ancestral spirits, and so were reluctant to make a public commitment.

The Scriptures never ascribe power to idols, yet Satan can mask himself behind idols and exercise his influence over people through fear. Satan's power is limited; his doom has been pronounced, yet not fully implemented. We can be bold with the assurance of God's universal presence and His absolute victory and power over every other force in the world.

Thought for the Day: *The backside of the first commandment is the assurance that God alone is supreme and transcends every other god in the universe.*

God's Ten Rules for Living (5)

Scripture Reading: Exodus 20:1-4

Key Verse: *You shall not make for yourself an idol… (Exodus 20:4).*

Meditation: A little boy was drawing a picture in Sunday school class. When asked, "What are you drawing?" he replied, "I am drawing a picture of God." His teacher responded, "But no one has ever seen God." Johnny answered, "They will when I get finished."

Exodus 32 demonstrates grave inherent dangers to trying to make a visual representation of God. When Israel asked Aaron to make a God they could see, they were not asking for an idol nor were they consciously trying to displace God. They even sacrificed their golden jewelry to help Aaron.

How could Aaron possibly have turned the concept of God into a golden calf? Perhaps it was his inherent depravity. Natural man tends to distort the representation of God. Or perhaps Aaron imitated his pagan neighbors' religious festivals and symbols. Living animals were often worshipped in Egypt, and the bull symbolized the ultimate power of fertility in the Canaanite worship.

Whatever man chooses to be his god will be inferior to the Creator God. Man tries to manipulate his gods for his own personal benefit. Men will become more and more like their idols and gradually will worship the substitute rather than the real God.

Thought for the Day: *The essence of idolatry is worshipping something God has made rather than the Creator Himself.*

God's Ten Rules for Living (6)

Scripture Reading: Exodus 20:7

Key Verse: *You shall not misuse the name of the Lord your God…(Exodus 20:7).*

Meditation: The Japanese people help you to meet others by giving you a business card. On the back they write your name and a few words of commendation. You take the card to another person who will then trust you for business or friendship on the recommendation of the first reference card. These pleasant openings for future relationships come because a friend trusted you with his name.

God shared His name with Moses at the burning bush. Moses realized immediately that God's name and God's character were intimately related. Moses took off his shoes in acknowledgment of God's awesome presence. In the Bible the character of God, the presence of God and the name of God are synonymous. When you say or acknowledge one aspect you have all three.

Jesus, in the Lord's Prayer, said, "Hallowed be your name." People must be awakened to the presence of God by the way we talk about Him. Jesus says, Not everyone who says *Lord, Lord*, will be honored in His presence. God's name is not a magical formula for success. Our use of His name must be accompanied by a personal relationship with Him and a commitment to His character and presence.

Thought for the Day: *God's name is our passport into the intimacy of His awesome presence.*

God's Rules for Living (7)

Scripture Reading Exodus 20:8-11

Key Verse: *Remember the Sabbath day by keeping it holy (Exodus 20:8).*

Meditation: First God wants to be worshipped alone and have no competing deities.   Second, we are to worship God directly with no props to assist us.   Third, we must be wholly sincere and not use God's name in any way to reflect on His integrity.   In this fourth commandment God speaks of our need for a rest from the tyranny of our schedules to focus on Him and on eternal realities, *time for our souls to catch up with our bodies.*

God ordained the need to rest before the labor unions suggested the concept.   Doctors have concurred; our bodies need time to replenish energy and our minds need to be released from the stress.   The Sabbath started with God in Genesis where He rested from his work of creation. He paused to celebrate and take pleasure in His accomplishment.   Most nations have observed a seven-day work week except those based in Judeo-Christian traditions.   May we continue to cherish this God-given day and remember the Giver lest we become like the nations around us and focus on the idols of things and activity rather then the God who created His world and us.

The Old Testament Sabbath has been replaced by Sunday.   We must avoid the pharisaical extreme of focusing on negatives for observing the day of rest.   On the other hand, we must guard against turning the holy day into a constant holiday and deprive ourselves of our deepest need, to transcend our daily pressing cares by participating in worship and viewing our lives from God's perspective.

Thought for the Day: *I will intentionally discipline my weekly schedule to anticipate the Lord's day for the purpose of physical and spiritual renewal.*

God's Ten Rules for Living (8)

Scripture Reading: Exodus 20:12

Key Verse: *Honor your father and mother (Exodus 20:12).*

Meditation: Commandment Five makes the transition from our relation to God to our relationship with our neighbor. The commandments in themselves cannot empower our actions; they can only guide our actions. Commandments cannot make us do the right things. Right relationships with our neighbor follow a prior personal relationship to God.

God places our relationship to our parents in top priority. The concept of both parents being featured here departs from that culture's emphasis on male dominance. The word, *honor*, in the Bible is reserved for God, meaning to venerate or revere. Yet in this commandment God Himself consents to share that kind of honor with parents.

Some commentators suggest that God is extending to parents the distinctive role of being go-betweens for Him. Serving as God's bridge to children gives parents great responsibility and significance. From parents children learn their understanding of God. Someone has said, "Parents serve as skylights through which we gain our first glimpse of God." We learn reverence and acceptance and unconditional love. In the context of family we discover the significance of others as well as our own self-worth.

Thought for the Day: *The family is God's centerpiece for society.*

God's Ten Rules for Living (9)

Scripture Reading: Matthew 5:21,22, Exodus 20:13

Key Verse: *You shall not murder (Exodus 20:13).*

Meditation: Our Judeo-Christian traditions are founded on the Scriptures that teach all human beings are created in God's image and must be treated with dignity. This *divine image* distinguishes mankind from the rest of creation and calls for reverence for the life of every person. We must keep sensitized to the sacredness of life as we wrestle against those voices demanding the "right" of physician-assisted suicide and other related concerns. Otherwise we may be sending a false signal to society that anything less than a perfect, trouble-free life is not worth living.

Mother Teresa and her sisters, motivated by the conviction that every person has the right to die with dignity, ministered to people daily in the slums of Calcutta, India. They picked up a man, washed him, sang to him and comforted him in his dying. He looked up at them and said, "All my life I have lived like an animal on the streets; now I am dying like an angel."

As a nation we must remember that all men are created in God's image and might does not always make war right. While there may be "just wars," we must go to war only as a last resort when other methods to settle controversies have been exhausted. Otherwise, we would be shedding innocent blood, which like Abel's blood in the Old Testament, will cry out against us for not allowing them to live out their God-ordained destiny. We must not tamper with this precious gift from God without serious consequences.

Thought for the Day: *Only God who gives life has the ultimate prerogative to take it on His time schedule.*

God's Ten Rules for Living (10)

Scripture Reading: Exodus 20:14, Matthew 5:27-30

Key Verse: *You shall not commit adultery (Exodus 20:14).*

Meditation: A five-year-old boy was having fun driving nails into his parents' furniture. They were not happy, and scolded him strongly. He tried to undo what had offended his parents so profoundly. He started pulling out the nails one by one only to find that each left behind an ugly hole in the beautiful wood. The sin of adultery is something like that, except it involves sensitive human relationships and ultimately destroys our relationship with God. Some one wisely observed, "When the seventh commandment is broken all the other nine commandments are also torn down. No amount of remorse or even godly repentance can repair fully or perfectly the damage done nor remove the scars of unfaithfulness.

The word for marriage in Hebrew comes from the same root as the word consecration and sanctification. This high view of marriage calls for exclusive dedication to one spouse and the separation from all other competing loves. Paul's teaching on marriage is based on God's ideal in Genesis 2:22-24. Marriage is God's idea, and its purpose is to complete what is lacking both in man and in the Garden of Eden. The fall of man has dimmed God's ideal, but the undergirding principles of biblical marriage have not changed.

Jesus reiterated these three principles in Matthew 19:1-9 that call for:
1. An exclusive commitment
2. Separation from parental domination
3. Physical and sexual cleaving with the potential of reproduction.

Thought for the Day: *Christian marriage is lifelong, monogamous, and heterosexual commitment.*

God's Ten Rules For Living (11)

Scripture Reading: Exodus 20: 15, Ephesians 4:28

Key Verse: *You shall not steal (Exodus 20:15).*

Meditation: A number of years ago a picture on the cover of the Saturday Evening Post showed a nicely dressed woman buying a Thanksgiving turkey from a smiling butcher. As the turkey was being weighed on that old-fashioned scale, the artist captured something both comical and serious. While the eyes of both buyer and seller were focused on the sale their hands were elsewhere. His thumb was on the sale pressing it down and hers was under the scale pressing it upwards. Each one was unaware of the other's actions, but both were mutually guilty of breaking the eighth commandment.

The backside of this commandment is also a positive reminder that God approves personal ownership of property and desires for us to be industrious. The Hebrew people viewed possessions as a sign of God's blessing and indirectly as an extension of themselves. Thus they had strict rules against theft and rather demanding guidelines to compensate the injured person up to and beyond the value of the loss. If a thief voluntarily confessed, he was still expected to add one-fifth beyond what was taken plus bringing a trespass offering to the Lord. If he stole something he could not restore, he was expected to pay four-fold with "goods in kind."

The Old Testament prophet Malachi lifts stealing out of the normal interpersonal context into our stewardship to God. The sin of Israel and of many current Christians today, is thinking our possessions to be our own with right of decision about their use. We violate God's law when we do not give God His portion, at least, the tithe.

Thought for the Day: *God gives us all we possess to use as faithful stewards under His direction.*

God's Ten Rules For Living (12)

Scripture Reading: Exodus 20:16, James 3:6

Key Verse: *You shall not give false testimony against your neighbor (Exodus 20:16).*

Meditation: The tongue does large-scale damage. Even from a distance the tongue is capable of doing extensive damage. One careless, unproved rumor dropped at one end of a town will inevitably work its way across town gathering additional material with each report. By the time it reaches the subject, the rumor is hardly recognizable leaving only deepened suspicions, hurt and defamation of innocent people in its wake. An old proverb says, "There is nothing so impossible to kill as a rumor, once unleashed it can never be snuffed out." Perhaps that is why James refers to the tongue as a fire fed by hell from within our unsanctified human nature.

I have a close pastoral friend who served in a church given to the spreading of unverifiable rumors about pastors and people in the church. This besetting sin often clings to people who are very orthodox in their beliefs. My friend determined that he would always confront this self-destructing tendency. He and his wife had barely finished unpacking when one of the brethren came by saying, "Pastor, I don't know if you heard or not, but..." Before the church member could finish his feigned litany of grief over the "offense," my pastor friend stopped him in his tracks with, "Who told you?" The pastor then asked the man to immediately get into his car and they would together go to the source and test the truthfulness of the rumor. Picking up people along the way, the car was packed by the time they got to the first person that had started the story. They found the end tale was so distorted that it completely misrepresented the original story.

Thought for the Day: *The eagerness we display in listening to and in repeating unverifiable rumors is a measure of the depth of human depravity still hidden in us.*

God's Ten Rules For Living (13)

Scripture Reading: Exodus 20:17, Genesis 3:1-7

Key Verse: *You shall not covet...(Exodus 20:17).*

Meditation: Satan successfully employed the first temptation to covetousness when he tempted our first parents to partake of that which was forbidden by God. He skillfully planted the desire in Eve's heart to be like God. Then he bewitched her to believe that God was withholding something from her that was her "right" to enjoy. Our consumer-driven culture provides a convenient "front" for Satan to plant the seeds of discontent in the hearts of even the most sincere Christians. He also used the stratagem of discontent to cause Demas to become a dropout from missionary work. Perhaps the saddest words Paul ever wrote about a former coworker were "...Demas, because he loved the world, has deserted me." John Mark once also left Paul, but only temporarily, but there is no record that Demas ever returned.

The Scriptures teach three progressive stages in the temptation to covetousness, especially as it played itself out in the fall of the first parent of the human race. First, a pleasing thought is suggested to our emotions. At this stage it can be stopped. However, if we choose to entertain the suggestion, we will slip to being subconsciously set up for the third stage, where our human will joins the fantasy and we will act out our thoughts when the first opportunity occurs, or we will make the occasion to act on the decision to take what is not ours.

Thought for the Day: *The sign of God's silent judgment on our surfeited materialistic culture is not only our greed to get more, but the growing inability to enjoy what we already have.*

Christ's Call to Counter-Cultural Living (1)

Scripture Reading: Matthew 5:1,2

Key Verse: *Now when he saw the crowds, he went up on the mountainside and sat down... (Matthew 5:1).*

Meditation: Bible scholars agree on two reasons Jesus went to the mountain: He wanted to withdraw from the multitudes in order to teach his disciples. He also was drawing a parallel between Moses' reading of the Ten Commandments on Mt. Sinai and his position on the mountain. The teachings are not the same, but the beatitudes portray eight distinguishing marks of Christian character and conduct that were counter-culture in the time of Jesus, and even more so today.

Jesus uses the word "happy" or "blessed," but He is not describing a subjective emotional state that the person might expect. Jesus is saying what God thinks of the person, and in the second part of each beatitude, He gives the reason God is making the pronouncement. Unlike spiritual gifts that the Holy Spirit distributes to members of Christ's body in order to equip us for different ministries, here the Holy Spirit desires to work each of those eight graces in every Christian.

The beatitudes rank as the best known teachings of Jesus. Some may even glibly say, "I live by the Sermon on the Mount." But most often they know that they are suggesting an idealism that they do not expect to practice in the real world. Since Jesus **sat down,** taking the authoritative position of a rabbi, it suggests the seriousness of His teaching. The beatitudes cannot be relegated to mere idealism, but the statement of a brand new lifestyle that He Himself would model for them. Furthermore, Christ's forthcoming death and poured-out Holy Spirit on the Day of Pentecost would make it possible for men to live this counter-culture lifestyle.

Thought for the Day: *Whenever the words of Jesus are obeyed, He gives them the inherent power to transform human behavior.*

Christ's Call to Counter-Cultural Living (2)

Scripture Reading: Matthew 5:1-5

Key Verse: *Blessed are the meek, for they will inherit the earth (Matthew 5:5).*

Meditation: The ultimate source of pride of the Jewish rabbi in Jesus' day was his learning; for the Greek it was his superior intellect; and for the Roman it was his power. Jesus confronts these sources of human pride as wrong and suggests that it is the meek that are finally going to win it all, even to inheriting the earth.

As a rule, our western society, too, has little time to give to the person preaching meekness or gentleness. To the majority of people, even many in the church, it is the self-made persons, the self-sufficient, even the male-macho kind that characterize our heroes. For we, too, instinctively equate meekness with weakness. The subsequent danger for the church is that one carries over this self-sufficient attitude into our relationship with God.

According to the model Jesus himself left for us, the meek person does not demand retaliation for the wrongs done against him. Jesus did not use His access to power for His own protection. He even rebuked Peter for trying to use a sword to protect Him in the garden when the religious rulers came to arrest Him. As a recipient of God's promises Christians, too, must be patient, knowing that we will inherit the earth and reign with Jesus. We must hold on to this promise with great patience, for it often appears that evil people are rewarded and prosper. However, God is in complete control and someday He will establish His righteous kingdom on earth. We are confident that His kingdom has been inaugurated and it is now advancing, while not yet consummated. Already, through the ministry of the Holy Spirit, we have tasted the powers of the age to come, the futuristic glorious freedom of being God's children.

Thought for the Day: *Meekness is the first fruit of the Holy Spirit and cannot be produced in any other way.*

Christ's Call to Counter-Cultural Living (3)

Scripture Reading: Matthew 5:1-4

Key Verse: *Blessed are those who mourn, for they shall be comforted (Matthew 5:4).*

Meditation: It is important for us to accept the fact that Jesus did not state the specific reason for mourning. It is safe for us not to supply the object of mourning such as "mourning for sin" lest we narrowly limit the object of mourning to one thing only. However, it should be noted that the word Jesus chose is one of the strongest in the Greek language and suggests some "tragic loss" or a "very disappointing turn of events in a person's life."

The same word is used in describing Jacob's deep grief when he first believed his sons' report that Joseph was killed. To compound Jacob's sense of loss he was reminded again of Rachel, Joseph's mother, whom he deeply loved, but lost at the birth of Benjamin. Hear and feel the deep emotion in these words, **"In mourning will I go down to the grave to my son"** (Genesis 37:35b).

This state of mourning may have a number of different sources. King David expressed deep sorrow over his sin of adultery that he realized was not just against Bathsheba and her husband Uriah, but even more seriously, against God, the very God who called him and placed him on the throne. This mourning can also coexist with happier emotions. The use of the Wailing Wall in Palestine is a model we can follow. Most of the Jewish males go to the Wailing Wall expressing their loneliness for God and for the lost temple where God's manifest presence was concentrated. Their sorrow is deep and genuine, but they do not make a replica of the wall to take home to use on a regular basis.

Thought for the Day: *The mourning that Jesus blesses with words of comfort moves us to God's strong arms of love and comfort.*

Christ's Call to Counter-Cultural Living (4)

Scripture Reading: Matthew 5:3

Key Verse: *Blessed are the poor in Spirit, for theirs is the kingdom of heaven (Matthew 5: 3).*

Meditation: Most sermons preached on the beatitudes come across as strong exhortations to produce this list of eight virtues. Since most of us fall short, we generally leave church feeling guilty or spiritually inferior. But Jesus did not address His disciples in terms of super expectations.

The people Jesus called "blessed" in verses 1-4 were the small, the weak and the defenseless people of His day. These were people who could do very little, humanly speaking, to change their status. He actually declared those who were humble minded, who mourn and who are meek as blessed without demanding anything from them. Jesus was not affirming their social status in life, but by calling them blessed, He was actually saying, "I am on your side," "I am with you." This word "blessed" in Hebrew suggests a person who is loved, chosen and who is inseparably linked to God. It is both a word of affirmation and exclamation from God himself.

Jesus' radical teaching ran counter-culture to the thinking of His day as well as to ours today. The social upper class of Jesus' day, and even the priestly autocracy, had been invaded and conquered by Greek pagan culture. Much like our present western culture, they taught that the rich and successful were truly blessed of God. Jesus corrects this distorted teaching about blessedness by informing us that the "poor in spirit," the humble-minded people who readily admit their need for God, are the truly blessed. People who quickly admit they are completely helpless without God's help are the very ones who will inherit it all at the end.

Thought for the Day: *The truly blessed people are those who feel their spiritual poverty deep enough to make them cry out to God.*

Christ's Call to Counter-Cultural Living (5)

Scripture Reading: Matthew 5:1-6

Key Verse: *Blessed are those who hunger and thirst after righteousness, for they shall be filled (Matthew 5:6).*

Meditation: The first four beatitudes were spoken to people who were too weak to respond to the demands of Jesus. They themselves were in great distress for they lacked joy, happiness, power and righteousness. So Jesus affirmed the fact that often God meets the needs of people before the people themselves have met all His conditions because they desperately need help, the working of **grace** rather than **law.** Since Jesus pronounced these four different groups as blessed, we, too, must be careful not to put on them conditions, lest we lose the message of grace to those whom Jesus himself did not turn away.

The fourth group is the people who are deeply aware that a right relationship with God and man is painfully absent in their lives. People who feel spiritually empty and starved lack completely those virtues that might approve them before God and man. Yet because of their very honesty and transparency, Jesus calls them blessed, assuring them that they will "be filled."

The Bible speaks of several difference kinds of "righteousness." One is Pharisaic, an external conformity to rules, but Christian righteousness is an inner rightness of heart, mind, and motive, for which Jesus exhorts us to hunger and thirst. Moral righteousness is that quality of character and conduct that pleases God. Paul also speaks of imputed righteousness, that profound revelation that Christ Jesus is made unto us righteousness. It is that distinct impartation of the very life Jesus gives to us so that God sees only the perfection of His Son in us.

Thought for the Day: *All our human acts of righteousness are as filthy rags unless they spring out of our relationship with Jesus "who was made sin for us in order that we might become the righteousness of God through Him" (II Corinthians 5:21).*

Christ's Call to Counter-Cultural Living (6)

Scripture Reading: Matthew 5:1-7

Key Verse: *Blessed are the merciful for they will be shown mercy (Matthew 5:7).*

Meditation: In beatitudes one through four we have observed that the listener is pronounced blessed without making any special pre-conditions. That, however, is not true of the next four beatitudes: The disciples would now be held accountable for the "working out" of God's gifts to them. The call to be merciful is really a response to a call to become a more tender and sensitive person. Mercy is best illustrated for us in the example of the Good Samaritan who not only volunteered to meet the immediate needs of the wounded man, but also then volunteered to provide for the follow-up care as well.

Christ himself modeled mercy from the beginning of His public ministry to His death on the cross. He touched the lepers to show them compassion. He healed the multitudes, most of whom He did not know personally, not because strong faith was present or for some deep theological reason, but simply because He felt compassion for them. The mercy He freely showed to others was rarely reciprocated. As His last gesture of mercy on the cross He assured the penitent thief that "Today you shall be with me in paradise."

While Christ personally demonstrated mercy and commands His followers to be merciful, He also strongly condemns the merciless people. In His kingdom parable, recorded in Matthew 25:41-44, He severely upbraids those who neglected to lift a helping hand to those who were needy. This is also a parable of God's judgment on the church for her lack of being socially involved with the hurting people in her immediate community. God is not impressed by what we do for the significant people, the "big" people around us, if we overlook the "little people."

Thought for the Day: *While being a merciful person may not be a pre-condition for salvation, it is, however, a necessary consequence.*

Christ's Call to Counter-Cultural Living

Scripture Reading: Matthew 5:1-11

Key Verse: *Blessed are the pure in heart, for they shall see God (Matthew 5:8).*

Meditation: God gave us five senses, sight being the most dominant. However, we cannot see the kingdom of God unless we are born again. Without this spiritual sight our human understanding limits us to this world.

Paul says in I Corinthians 2:14, "The man without the Spirit does not accept the things that come from the Spirit of God...and he cannot because they are spiritually discerned." Paul further divides mankind into three classes: The natural man, unrenewed by the Holy Spirit; the carnal man, who has not surrendered completely to Christ and thus is able only to comprehend elementary scriptural truths; and the Spirit-filled man who produces the fruit of the dedicated life (Ephesians 5:18, Galatians 5:22,23).

John Moffatt, gifted teacher and Bible translator, said that those who are not double-minded are blessed and will be admitted into the presence of God. The double-minded would be those first two classes of people mentioned in the paragraph above, the natural man and the carnal man. The double-minded man suggests instability, unsettledness, and lack of personal integrity. The spiritual man, on the other hand, depicts single-mindedness towards God and pure motives.

Thought for the Day: *Practicing the presence of God means focusing the center of our lives on God.*

Christ's Call to Counter-Cultural Living

Scripture Reading: Matthew 5:1-11

Key Verse: *Blessed are the peacemakers, for they will be called sons of God (Matthew 5:8).*

Meditation: The Bible calls God the God of Peace. The members of the Trinity each have a distinct identity yet act in perfect harmony. God also displays positive, good intentions toward all his children. Jeremiah (29:11) reveals God's will to Israel, "For I know the plans I have for you," declares the Lord, "Plans to prosper you and not to harm you, plans to give you hope and a future." Other translations suggest God is actively thinking about our peace.

Jesus, God's sinless Son, coming into our world makes peace possible. Christ made peace with God for us by His sacrificial death reconciling us to God. He also bridged the distance between Jews and Gentiles by creating a new body, the Church in which we are all equal partners being indwelt by the same Holy Spirit.

Peace making is now part of our new family responsibility as members of Christ and of one another. Christ's last will and testament to His disciples was, "Peace I leave with you; peace I give unto you" (John 14:27). The Hebrew word for peace, "shalom" means more than absence of conflict; it conveys a desire for all the goodness of God.

Thought for the Day: *Telling people about God and their place in His community is the most lasting kind of peace making.*

Christ's Call to Counter-Cultural Living

Scripture Reading: Matthew 5:1-11

Key Verse: *Blessed are those who are persecuted because of righteousness, for theirs in the kingdom of heaven (Matthew 5:10).*

Meditation: Jesus announced early in His ministry, that those who followed Him would be persecuted. Not all persecution is elicited by righteousness. Some carnal Christians get into trouble by trying to force their faith on others. Others do unusual things to get attention. The sincere believer seeking to model Christ's life style will be persecuted. The pattern for the Christian's life enumerated in these beatitudes, so radically different from the "world" philosophy often elicits negative responses. For instance, the world does not believe in mourning over sin, but prefers to rationalize it. Meekness is interpreted as weakness. The world has no desire for righteousness, mercy, and purity of heart or peace making.

Jesus taught His disciples to expect persecution and to respond to it positively. He encouraged them "to rejoice and be glad," for persecution serves as a sign they are being true to the demands of living a converted life, thus their present and future salvation. Persecution identifies the Christian with past prophets and martyrs. The persecuted join those godly people who have laid down their lives for Jesus. Sustained by the present promises, the persecuted looks forward to waiting glory and reward.

Peter (who was martyred later) tells us in I Peter 4:12-19, that we must not consider persecution as something foreign, but receive it as a refining process of the impurities in your life. Do not succumb to the natural response of sorrow or shock, but be glad we are now able to participate in Christ's suffering. That means we have the assurance of sharing in His future glory.

Thought for the Day: *Those who become believers in Christ's cross must also respond to His call to love their enemies, for He died for them.*

Hurrying to Jerusalem

Scripture Reading: Luke 18:31-34

Key Verse: *We are going up to Jerusalem and everything that is written by the prophets about the Son of Man will be fulfilled (Luke 18:31).*

Meditation: Jesus was committed to going to Jerusalem. The time was fulfilled for Jesus to be taken up to heaven. He had already been transfigured on the mountain in the company of Peter and John. He could have been taken to heaven from there and missed the suffering of the cross. But He chose the path to Jerusalem. So He precipitated His crucifixion by hurrying to Jerusalem.

Jesus was not a martyr. A martyr dies to prove or fulfill His own beliefs. Jesus died as a deliberate sacrifice for us. Jesus willingly went to the place where prejudiced people could condemn Him to death. His willingness displayed not a need to be a hero martyr, or a foolhardy act, but a fulfillment of the plan of God to free us from sin and from ultimate death forever.

I met a man in India who had faced threats of death because he was a Christian. He declared his willingness to accept death rather than give up his trust in Christ. In the face of those who consider it to their religious credit to burn down churches and kill Christians, my friend was strong. I want Jesus to give me that kind of courage should I ever need it.

Thought for the Day: *Jesus could have called as many angels as He might have needed, but He chose to die for us.*

Requests on the Way

Scripture Reading: Mark 10:32-52

Key Verse: *What do you want me to do for you? (Mark 10:36,51).*

Meditation: Jesus, walking with His disciples on the way to the ultimate assignment that would end His earthly life, heard requests from two different types of people:

James and John wanted special places of honor and power in Jesus' earthly kingdom that they assumed would be created. Blind Bartimaeus asked for healing of his eyes so he could see.

James and John apparently did not comprehend Jesus' most recent declaration, *The Son of Man will be betrayed to the chief priests and teachers of the law...who will condemn him to death...* (Mark 10:33). They must have selectively heard only, *Three days later he will rise* (v.34). Perhaps they did not comprehend any of the suffering, denying its reality as they expected to be affiliated with the earthly Messiah.

Bartimaeus did not hear that teaching, nor could he see the Messiah, but he knew Jesus had power to change his world. He asked and his eyes were healed. His faith must have pleased Jesus. In contrast to the spiritual blindness of James and John, the faith of Bartimaeus reflected the joy of those whose spiritual eyes would see and experience the total restoration through the coming resurrection.

Thought for the Day: *We who follow Jesus must pray for insight to understand, not what we want Him to do for us, but what He wants us to do for Him.*

Entering Jerusalem

Scripture Reading: Mark 11:1-11

Key Verse: *If anyone asks you, Why are you doing this? Tell him, The Lord needs it and will send it back shortly (Mark 11:3).*

Meditation: The healed Bartimaeus joined John and James and the rest of the crowd as they approached Jerusalem.

In the Old Testament the domestic donkey was an indication of a man's wealth (Judges 5:10) and was used by Abraham to go from Beersheba to Moriah (Genesis 22:3). Jesus was fulfilling Zechariah's prophecy (9:9,10) clearly showing all of those aware of scripture in Jerusalem that He was, indeed, the king, *righteous, having salvation.... Proclaiming peace to the* nations...*His rule will extend from sea to sea and from the river to the ends of the earth.*

Jesus promised important positions to all who followed him: the Johns', the James', the Bartimaeus', the adoring crowds, the fickle followers, the sensitive hearts. The qualifications for all were, *Whoever wants to become great among you must be your servant* (Mark 10:43).

Jesus' entry into Jerusalem marked His immediate steps to the cross and demonstrated clearly the demands of His kingdom.

Thought for the Day: *To follow Jesus we must ask that our eyes be opened to His values and priorities.*

Anointing at Bethany

Scripture Reading: Mark 14:1-10

Key Verse: *She did what she could. She poured perfume on my body beforehand to prepare for my burial (Mark 14:8).*

Meditation: The setting of this touching incident is in Simon the Leper's home. Simon was, no doubt, one of those whom Jesus had healed earlier in his ministry. Lazarus, miraculously raised from the dead, was also there along with the disciples. We would expect the disciples to be spiritually sensitive to the evidence of Christ's work in that room.

When Mary, sister of Martha, poured costly perfume on Jesus, He was so pleased and indicated she would always be remembered for this act of love. She showed insight into the purpose of Jesus' life that the other disciples evidently did not comprehend. In fact, they reacted, not with understanding, but with indirect criticism towards Jesus for accepting this gift. *Why this waste? This perfume could have been sold for a high price and the money given to the poor!*

Jesus' answer reflected his acceptance of Mary's preparation of his body for the ultimate sacrifice for us all: She *has done a beautiful thing. She did it to prepare me for my burial. She will always be remembered for doing what she could.*

The disciples missed the heart of Jesus; their acts of charity would reflect a price tag. Mary's spontaneous gift ministered to Jesus as she identified with Him in His coming death.

Thought for the Day: *Some moments come only once. Let us pray for sensitivity to the Spirit's urge to match our dreams and vision with poured-out extravagant love to Christ.*

At the Passover

Scripture Reading: Luke 22:7-20

Key Verse: *I have eagerly desired to eat this Passover with you before I suffer (Luke 22:15).*

Meditation: Christ left the Church the broken loaf of bread and the cup, the Passover symbols that He used in fellowship with the disciples before He went to the cross. The Passover celebrated the deliverance of the Israelites from Egyptian slavery. The Angel of Death had passed over the houses of the Israelites whose doorposts had been smeared with the blood of the sacrificial lamb. The Passover signified physical deliverance from death, but Jesus brought to the entire human race the deliverance from eternal punishment.

Following the Passover deliverance from Egypt, God ratified the Old Covenant made at Mt. Sinai. Regular sacrifices had to be made for the people by the priests at the tabernacle or the temple. The New Covenant made by Christ at the communion service does not depend on human beings. *While we were yet sinners Christ died for us* (Romans 5:8). The blood of Christ, a final sacrifice that provides for all those who recognize their Savior and Lord, ratified this New Covenant.

Jesus' eagerness to eat the Passover with His disciples showed His acting out His coming sacrifice and provision for them on the cross. He wanted them all to participate symbolically in the act that He would actually experience. When we participate in the communion service we remember with gratitude Christ's suffering and provision for us.

Thought for the Day: *Since we are saved solely by grace through the sacrifice of Jesus, the sacraments are not our work for salvation but our acts of obedience to the commandments of Jesus.*

Grief in Gethsemane

Scripture Reading: Mark 14:32-51

Key Verse: *Take this cup from me. Yet not what I will, but what you will (Mark 14:36b).*

Meditation: The three disciples had failed to hear the pain and plea in Jesus' voice when he said, *My soul is overwhelmed with sorrow to the point of death. Stay here and keep watch.* Like children dependent on their father to take care of them, they slept while Jesus worked in prayer. But a few hours later they would face a huge test of their courage.

When Judas appeared with the armed crowds Peter reacted in human abruptness with a sword to cut off the ear of the high priest's servant, Malchus. Jesus rebuked Peter, *"Put your sword away! Shall I not drink the cup the Father has given me?"* (John 18:10,11).

Jesus purposed to fulfill His assignment to be the complete sacrifice for the human race. He was tempted and even requested God to reconsider: *Take this cup from me* (Mark 14:36). He illustrates the human side of His nature. Both Peter and Mark (14:51,72) deserted Jesus in their fear.

Jesus knows how much we need to pray and commune with God. Only in deliberate, disciplined prayer can we find the strength and courage for the challenges of each day.

Thought for the Day: *Only in communion with God will we find protection from temptation.*

Loneliness like Ours

Scripture Reading: Mark 14:26-42

Key Verse: *Could you not watch with me one hour? (Mark 14.37)*

Meditation: Loneliness is one of our society's greatest problems: The loneliness that comes from being separated from significant people and the loneliness of spirit, with no real interpersonal linkage. We can be surrounded by a chattering crowd of people, but feel all alone. The profound "cosmic loneliness" comes from sensing no significant place in our world. Some philosopher said, "We don't know why we were born; what we are doing here, or where we are going."

Jesus, in His humanity, experienced the loneliness of not being understood by others. As we have seen in the past studies, even those closest to Him, the twelve, only half understood His mission in the world. They certainly did not comprehend the obtuseness of their own hearts.

Jesus also experienced the loneliness of being misunderstood and having His motivations questioned. The Pharisees, because of their cultural prejudice, could not understand how He could eat with publicans and other sinners. Jesus could not have any human linkage with these spiritual athletes of Israel. The crowds, too, were fickle, clamoring to be with Him when they were fed or entertained, but siding with the antagonists when bored.

Thought for the Day: *Jesus demonstrated that identification with Him might be a lonely choice.*

Watch and Pray

Scripture Reading: Matthew 26:36-45

Key Verse: *Watch and pray so that you will not fall into temptation. The spirit is willing, but the body is weak (Matthew 26:41).*

Meditation: Jesus prayed alone in the Garden of Gethsemene even though He had taken three disciples with Him. They went to sleep. The word Lent comes from the word spring, suggesting this six-week period came during the spring of the year. It also suggests to us that we get our spiritual spring-cleaning done; there may be neglected corners. The Lenten period provides a time for serious reflection on the life and ministry of Jesus during His last weeks on earth.

Jesus admonished the three disciples to *Watch and pray, for the spirit is willing, but the body is weak.* We need to discipline ourselves to be alert to do both the physical and spiritual disciplines that keep us healthy. The three disciples were, no doubt, exhausted both emotionally and physically from the events surrounding their going to Jerusalem. But they did not listen to Jesus when He asked them to wait with Him and to keep watch with Him. They did not discipline their bodies to stay awake so that they could pray for Him during His severe testing.

Paul speaks of disciplines needed for the body: But *I discipline my body and bring it into subjection...* (I Corinthians 9:27a). We need to discipline the body so it will respond more readily to the demands of our spiritual lives and protect us from temptation. We need also to discipline our spirits and minds towards growth. Let us determine to walk with Jesus during the following days of study of His last days on earth with mind and spirit open to experience what He felt as we learn what He taught.

Thought for the Day: *Grow in grace and in the knowledge of our Lord and Savior Jesus Christ (II Peter 3:18).*

Were You There?

Scripture Reading: Mark 14:43-72

Key Verse: *They took Jesus to the high priest, and all the chief priests, elders and teachers of the law came together. Peter followed him at a distance... (Mark:53,54).*

Meditation: In the past I thought of the events leading to Christ's crucifixion as preplanned by evil men. However, I now realize that Christ was crucified not so much by the intent of evil men, but by the failure of good people. Were we there when they crucified our Lord? Would our attitudes today nail Jesus to the cross? We may be represented in some of the people present at the events:

The Crowd: Probably not one of them got up that morning thinking they would be yelling, *Crucify Him,* on that Friday. They were swept up in the mob psychology. Are we prone to the herd instinct?

The Temple Businessmen: These men dismissed the injunction, *My house shall be a house of prayer for all nations* (Mark 11:17). They provided sacrifices that could be bought right on the temple grounds. When Jesus objected to their method of making money on sacred property, they joined the group who wanted to get rid of Him.

The Politicians: Pilate knew Roman justice. He knew Jesus was innocent. He wanted to do the right thing, but he followed the will of the majority even though his conscience, his education and his wife told him it was wrong. Caiaphas, the high priest, too, succumbed to the expedient rather than making the just decisions.

Thought for the Day: *How often have we allowed ourselves to turn from the written Word to follow the will of the crowd?*

Were You There?

Scripture Reading: Mark 14:43-72

Key Verse: *Every day I was with you, teaching in the temple courts, and you did not arrest me. But the Scripture must be fulfilled. Then everyone deserted him and fled (Mark 14:49,50).*

Meditation: As we were noticing yesterday, others who were "good people" participated in the betrayal of Jesus:

The Religious People: These religious folks were not bad people. They tried to follow the religious laws very scrupulously. In the process, however, their beliefs hardened them into stiff, formal unbending personalities. On one hand, they endorsed the transcendence of God, but they had trouble with His imminence. They were comfortable with God at a distance, but when He got close to them, they crucified Him.

Judas, one of the Twelve: Judas followed Jesus zealously. He wanted the Messiah to be powerful right now. His disenchantment with Jesus' methods led to his inordinate desire for money that led him to steal from the disciples' purse and to betray Jesus to the soldiers.

Peter, Leader of the Twelve: Assurance for the Christian is a wonderful attribute, but self-confidence can be very dangerous. Peter's actions show us that any vows we make in our own power will certainly be broken. When we push ourselves forward by pushing others backwards, we, too, will go back.

Thought for the Day: *If we find ourselves depending on our own wisdom or power we are in danger of betraying our faith, and ultimately, of betraying our Best Friend, Jesus.*

The Cry of Victory

Scripture Reading: John 19:18-37

Key Verse: *Jesus said, "It is finished." With that he bowed his head and gave up his spirit (John 19:30).*

Meditation: "Finished" used by Jesus meant, "nothing more needed to be done." Jesus had completed His task. The work Christ had set out to do was actually perfected. After uttering that word of triumph, Jesus actually put His head back as one could put His head on a pillow before going to sleep.

Jesus came into this world to reveal a God who gives only good gifts to His children. That God is revealed in the story of the prodigal son where the Father runs to welcome the sinner home. He embraces us with forgiveness and reinstates us into His family.

Jesus demonstrated obedience to the plan of the Father for us. He brought His human emotions into harmony with the pain of the cross. Jesus took the bitter cup of death for our sins and drank it all. Jesus voluntarily became that Sacrificial Lamb on the cross of Calvary for us.

Jesus finished His sacrifice for our salvation. He is the Lamb of God slain from the foundation of the world. God knew before Adam and Eve disobeyed in the garden that the sacrifice would be made on the cross by Jesus.

Thought for the Day: *Jesus, the Innocent One, became the sacrifice for our sin so we can become children of God.*

Unlimited Access

Scripture Reading: Mark 15:33-37, Hebrews 10:19-25

Key Verse: *The curtain of the temple was torn in two from top to bottom. The centurion said, Surely, this man was the Son of God! (Mark 15:38,39)*

Meditation: Today we have unlimited access to God through Jesus our Intercessor. The people in the temple worship had not experienced that openness. In fact, those who came to Passover during the week Jesus was crucified came to a place designated the Court of the Gentiles. So the Gentiles could come only that far. Those who were Jews could enter the next precinct of the temple where they could see the priests actually prepare the sacrificial lambs. But they were not permitted in the Holy Place. Only the ordained priests could go into the area where the special utensils stood for burning of the sacrifices, including the prepared lamb. The priests exercised other activities of worship here, but even they could not enter the Holy of Holies where the visible presence of God dwelt in the days of Moses. There the cherubim above the Ark of the Covenant reminded the high priest that he was in the presence of the Almighty God. Should the designated high priest have come without the complete cleansing ritual, he would have been struck dead. He wore a bell and a rope, by which he would be dragged out, should that happen.

God had a plan to open this place in His presence to all men: At the very moment Jesus breathed His last, the curtain split from top to bottom miraculously. It was too high for anyone to have torn it. God opened, through the death of Jesus Christ, the access to His very presence. Now as Hebrews tells us, we can enter the Holy of Holies with Christ as our high priest. He has the authority to ask and the power to act. Not only do we have unlimited access, but we have unlimited representation in Jesus our Advocate.

Thought for the Day: *Our boldness in coming into the presence of God is provided by the sacrifice of Jesus, more powerful than 15 centuries of sacrifices under the Old Testament law.*

Pre-Easter People

Scripture Reading: Mark 16:1-8

Key Verse: *And they asked each other, Who will roll the stone away from the entrance to the tomb? (Mark 16:3)*

Meditation: Too many people live on the wrong side of Easter. They have never really experienced the resurrection life of Jesus. The two women who trudged wearily towards the tomb of Jesus on Easter morning are typical of all pre-Easter Christians. They were preoccupied with the thoughts of death – not life. They were problem-conscious and not possibility thinkers. *Who will roll the stone away from the entrance to the tomb?* occupied their thinking. They knew the soldiers would certainly not open the Roman seal. What is most surprising is that they even went to the tomb in the first place.

The stone over the entrance of the tomb speaks to us of those formidable obstacles that confront all of us: "Oh, if it weren't for___." Life may be going smoothly, then all of a sudden some "boulder" looms before us and limits us forever, we think. Or the prognosis from the doctor knocks hope right out of us and that leaves us numb. Others limit their horizon to the medicine bottles in the bathroom cabinet.

These women, like some of us, were living on the wrong side of Easter – the Good Friday side. Jesus, their beloved friend and teacher had died. How could they express their sorrow?

Thought for the Day: *A natural human emotion is sorrow at a personal loss. Christ has supernatural resources to reveal to us.*

Post-Easter People

Scripture Reading: Mark 16:1-11

Key Verse: *When they looked up, they saw that the stone, which was very large, had been rolled away (Mark 16:4).*

Meditation: The women looked up – a very symbolic action. They took their eyes off the ground where they thought they had left Jesus in the tomb. They looked up to see the stone had been rolled away, an amazing miracle. The grave clothes were lying as if undisturbed. An angel, God'supernatural messenger spoke, *He is not here; He has risen. See the place where they laid him.*

Then, a little later, Jesus Himself appeared to Mary Magdalene. When she went to tell the disciples, they did not believe her. Could this same thing be happening to us? Could Easter be happening all around us, but we miss the message because we have decided to remain on the wrong side of Easter?

An angel was at the tomb of Jesus announcing the Good News that He is alive. An angel is at every dark, hopeless situation of our lives announcing the good news. Christ's victory covers all of life for us. We face no problem or circumstance that Jesus did not face and solve in the resurrection. Jesus was set above every name that was named and over every power. He transcends them all. We will not run into a problem greater than the rock that was moved when Jesus transcended death. As Christians we are walking in His resurrection, which means that death has been turned into life forever.

Thought for the Day: *To be Easter Christians does not mean that our problems will go away suddenly, but it does mean that Jesus will always remain, and that His victory is ours, also.*

The Importance of the Resurrection

Scripture Reading: I Corinthians 15:12-28

Key Verse: *If Christ has not been raised, our preaching is useless and so is your faith (I Corinthians.15:14).*

Meditation: A skeptic said to a Christian, *It seems it would be rather easy to start a religion like Christianity.*

The Christian answered, *Yes, just get a person to be crucified, then rise from the dead, and then appear and reappear enough times to prove he has a body that goes through walls, yet seems like ours.*

Precisely because of the crucifixion and resurrection of Jesus, Christianity is in the world today. The Church, known as the body of Christ, represents the crucifixion of the sinless Son of God to pay the penalty for sin. Christ's resurrection promises eternal life just as Christ's victory over death demonstrates.

Many martyrs are listed in the histories of other religions, but Christ's death was not martyrdom; Christ chose to die in our place, not for a personal cause. He who knew no sin became sin for us that we might be made the righteousness of God.

Jesus walked out of the tomb, having conquered death saying, "I was dead and behold now I am alive forever and ever and I hold the keys of death and of Hades" (Revelation 1:18).

Thought for the Day: *We are free from sin's curse of death, alive forever in Christ.*

The importance of the Resurrection

Scripture Reading: I Corinthians 15:1-8,12-19

Key Verse: *And if Christ has not been raised, your faith is futile; you are still in your sins (I Corinthians 15:17).*

Meditation: Paul gives us three essential reasons why the resurrection of Jesus was absolutely necessary:

First, if Jesus had not been raised from the dead, then Christianity would not be fundamentally different from other religions. When Paul stood on Mars Hill before the philosophy students of Plato, Socrates and Aristotle, he climaxed his message with the doctrine of Christ's resurrection. The resurrection transformed the tragedy of the cross into the Gospel of Good News.

Second, if Christ had not been raised we would still be in guilt and sin with no one to deliver us. Counselors and therapists may assist us to identify the source of our true guilt, but they are helpless to free us from it. Only one person can free us: "He (Jesus) who knew no sin ... became sin for us that we might be made the righteousness of God in Him." Only a sinless crucified Christ supernaturally raised from the dead to appear in the presence of God for us can release us from our guilt and the tyranny of sin.

Third, if Christ had not been raised from the dead we would not have ultimate hope and the grave would be the end of our existence. We are not exempt from deprivation, hunger and pain in this life. We live in a world of accidents, illnesses and death. We experience these consequences of the fall of man, but the resurrection enables us not only to cope, but also to cope with hope. Jesus has the last word about death. That word is *I am the Resurrection and the Life.*

Thought for the Day: *For as in Adam all die, in Christ all shall be made alive (I Corinthians 15:22).*

The Miracle of the Resurrection

Scripture Reading: I Corinthians 15:12-28

Key Verse: *In Christ all will be made alive (I Corinthians 15:22).*

Meditation: My daughter called me one night. Her closest friend's 12-year-old son had just been diagnosed with Hodgkin's disease. *Do you think she could have a miracle for her son, Dad? She is so desperate.*

We all need a miracle. In times of crisis we cry out to God for deliverance. With life out of control or when we are faced with the unknown, we look to divine intervention.

God has given to us the miracle of the resurrection: Jesus returning from death to appear and reappear to His disciples with a body that went through walls, but that consumed regular food. No scientific explanation supports the experience recorded for us in the scriptures. But we know Jesus told His disciples that the temple (His body) would be destroyed but rebuilt in three days.

We choose to believe the miracle of the resurrection from the many witnesses in the Bible, but also for the assurance for ourselves. Life is out of our control, but the miracle of Christ's resurrection puts us in the eternal hands of God through the power of the Holy Spirit.

Thought for the Day: The greatest miracle is our being alive forever in Christ.

The Miracle of the Resurrection

Scripture Reading: I Corinthians 15:12-28

Key Verse: *For since death came through a man, the resurrection of the dead comes also through a man (I Corinthians 15:21).*

Meditation: The resurrection of Jesus is miraculous because it transformed the tragedy of the cross, making it not martyrdom, but deliverance for all mankind. The resurrection not only gives us assurance beyond this life, but the evidence of hope helps us cope with the trials and pain of our earthly existence.

The resurrection also shows Christ's power to deliver us from guilt and sin. Chuck Colson experienced in prison the forgiveness of Christ for his political crimes. He has shared with thousands of criminals how God can deliver them, too, from the guilt of their past. Sins that gnaw away in our minds and emotions can be cleansed by the power of God through Christ. He justifies us so we are safe now and in the coming days.

The resurrection of Jesus demonstrates the freedom we all have to live in this life with God's forgiveness and to look to the future with hope and trust in the One who triumphed over death.

Thought for the Day: *Thanks be to God for victory through our Lord Jesus Christ.*

The Miracle of the Resurrection

Scripture Reading: I Corinthians 15:12-28

Key Verse: *For as in Adam all die, so in Christ all will be made alive (I Corinthians 15:22).*

Meditation: When our daughter struggled with the diagnosis of aplastic anemia she was being treated in the Tokyo Children's Hospital, the best medical facility for blood diseases. Most of the staff were Buddhist and reflected the despair of the diagnosis, coming to her room shaking their heads, *No hope for this one,* they strongly conveyed.

Only one young nurse radiated hope. She came daily with shining face and cheerful optimism. From her we heard there was another hospital, founded by Christians where an esteemed Christian hematologist worked. Transferring there, we found a medical doctor who finally said, *She will need months of treatment, but I want you to know there is hope for this child.*

Christ brings hope in suffering. His resurrection gives us hope for eternal life, but also enables us to cope with our challenges here. Death now does not have the last word. Jesus is the Resurrection and the Life. He died that we might live forever, freed of the dread of eternal death. Every day He gives us hope.

Thought for the Day: *Let your hope keep you joyful.*

Death and Life

Scripture Reading: Luke 24:13-26

Key Verse: *They stood still, their faces downcast (Luke 24:17).*

Meditation: Death hurts. It separates us from the physical presence of the deceased person. Even Jesus wept as He stood at the tomb of Lazarus. Paul expected us to sorrow in our loss. But he did encourage us that we do not sorrow as those with no hope.

I read about a young missionary mother who died of cancer at age 43. She left her husband and four children ages eight to 18. On the lid of her casket her husband had written, "I am not here. I'm out with Jesus. I'll be back at the last trump."

D. L. Moody once said, "Someday you will read in the newspaper that D. L. Moody is dead. Don't believe it, for at that moment I will be more alive than ever I was alive on earth." Later, when he was close to death, he said, "Earth is receding. Heaven is appearing. God is calling me home."

God *will wipe every tear from their eyes. There will be no more death or mourning or crying or pain. No longer will there be any curse. The throne of God and of the Lamb will be in the city. They will see his face and his name will be on their forehead* (Revelation 21:4,22-25 and 22:3-5).

Thought for the Day: *Since each of us as Christians has the eternal quality of life here, we know death is our transition to a fuller dimension of the eternal life we already hold.*

Open Our Eyes

Scripture Reading: Luke 24:12:13-32

Key Verse: *Then their eyes were opened and they recognized him…(Luke 24:31).*

Meditation: Two disciples who referred to Peter and John as "our companions" walked from Jerusalem to Emmaus, about seven miles. They had already heard that Jesus was not in the tomb. They also had heard from the women that Jesus had appeared to Mary Magdalene. Even with such witness evidence they did not yet understand the divine nature of Jesus' mission. The suffering of the cross did not tally with the kingdom they expected Jesus to set up on earth as the Messiah.

They believed that Jesus was a prophet sent from God and that His works showed Him to be supreme over nature and disease. They had heard some of His teachings, perhaps not as much as the twelve, but they believed that He "was the one who was going to redeem Israel." Much like the 12, these two could not comprehend the events that seemed to contradict their dreams built around their prophet-teacher-potential Messiah. Jesus graciously took the time they walked to explain the prophetic scriptures from the beginning. In the process their minds were enlightened and their hearts opened to the miracle of fulfillment of prophecy in Jesus. The final revelation came as Christ broke the bread and shared it with them: "Their eyes were opened and they recognized Him" (verse 31).

Here was the fulfilled prophecy, the crucified and risen Christ, now identifying with them in their present needs, but with a promised future. No wonder they said, "Were not our hearts burning within us while He talked with us on the road and opened the Scriptures to us?" (verse 32).

Thought for the Day: *The Lord Jesus will open our eyes to eternal values with day-to-day power as we walk and talk with Him.*

Between Resurrection and Ascension

Scripture Reading: Luke 24:36-53

Key Verse: *You are witnesses of these things (Luke 24:48).*

Meditation: Why did Jesus come back from death and stay on earth for 40 days before ascending to the Father?

Jesus tarried for 40 days to convince the disciples that He was really alive. His followers last glimpsed Jesus on the cross. They had heard He was put into a tomb. They were skeptical of the two women's reports that the stone was rolled away and the tomb empty. Each disciple had to be certain Jesus was alive.

He appeared specifically to Thomas. As they each and all saw Jesus, these dispirited followers became determined witnesses. The certainty of the resurrection transformed the tragedy of the cross into a triumphant gospel.

He prepared the disciples for the withdrawal of His physical visible presence. When Mary recognized Him, He said, "Don't cling to me." He kept moving in and out of the visible and invisible worlds. He did not need the physical rest and food that His human body used before. The disciples gradually understood that He was with them constantly even though they could not see Him.

Thought for the Day: *Once we believe that Jesus lives in our lives we can witness with great joy.*

Peter and Jesus

Scripture Reading: John 15:15-23

Key Verse: *Simon, son of John, do you truly love me more than these? (John 21:15)*

Meditation: Peter describes all of us so well. He came to Jesus through the influence of Andrew. He had a vocation as a skilled fisherman. He responded to the call of Jesus and left his daily duties to listen to Jesus' teachings.

Peter wanted to learn; he asked questions such as, "How many times must I forgive my brother?" He knew Jesus was the Christ, but in the pressure of the opposition he denied knowing Christ. Strong in resolve, but weak in danger, Peter betrayed His Master.

Now he would learn of grace. When the resurrected Christ appears in Galilee to those disciples who had returned to their fishing, He offers Peter the opportunity to choose to love Him fully and unconditionally.

Jesus explores with Peter the differences between the love of a friend and the divine total sacrificial love. Peter knows he cannot respond in divine love, but Jesus knows he will be equipped later with the power of the Holy Spirit. Peter will then be able to care for and feed the people who want to follow Christ. Peter, empowered by the Spirit whom Jesus sends into the world, will demonstrate the Christian witness in our world.

Thought for the Day: *Even though we stumble in our walk with Christ, He has power to give us, restoring and equipping us for His work.*

Witnesses for Jesus

Scripture Reading: Acts 1:6-14

Key Verse: *But you will receive power when the Holy Spirit comes upon you and you will be my witnesses (Acts 1:8).*

Meditation: As Jesus appeared to the disciples after His resurrection they began to understand that His kingdom was not just for Jerusalem. He was now King of the whole earth and human race. They, as His most trained followers, could proclaim this great news to everyone, starting in Jerusalem, then Judea and then to the whole earth.

The witnessing would only be possible by the power of the Holy Spirit whom Jesus would send to them as they waited in the Upper Room. Peter, empowered by the Spirit, delivers such an eloquent discourse that 3,000 were added to the church.

The disciples anticipated the promises of the Risen Christ. They knew Jesus would come as promised. Now they had solid evidence of God's power through the Holy Spirit in human hearts. They would be witnesses to all. The Messiah would bring deliverance to captives of sin and His kingdom would have no end.

Thought for the Day: *No frontiers exist for Jesus; He is already there. He waits for us to join Him.*

Ascension and Representation

Scripture Reading: Acts 1:7-14, Luke 24:50-53

Key Verse: *I see heaven open and the Son of Man standing at the right hand of God (Acts 7:56).*

Meditation: Christ had shown the disciples He could be with them anywhere, any place in His post-resurrection state. The disciples understood that Jesus was now going away from their physical vision. Now He would be all over the earth at the same time. He would not be confined to any one place.

Christ showed us that the spiritual world is very close to us. The disciples understood and went back to the upper room to celebrate and praise God. Stephen knew heaven was very close to earth. In his last minutes he looked up to heaven and saw the glory of God and Jesus standing at the right hand of God (Acts 7:54-56). The spiritual world with Jesus at the right hand of God presents a completely different existence from earth.

Christ at God's side shows us the ultimate victory of the cross followed by the resurrection: The universe already belongs to Jesus Christ. We have that confidence conveyed to us in Romans 8:37, "We are more than conquerors through him who loved us."

Thought for the Day: *For I am convinced that neither death nor life, neither angels nor demons, neither the present nor the future, nor any power, neither height nor depth, nor anything else in all creation, will be able to separate us from the love of God that is in Christ Jesus our Lord (Romans 8:38,39).*

The Witness of Stephen

Scripture Reading: Acts 6:8-15

Key Verse: *Now Stephen, a man full of God's grace and power, did great wonders and miraculous signs among the people (Acts 6:8).*

Meditation: Stephen exemplifies the man "full of faith and of the Holy Spirit." He was anointed with wisdom and power from the Holy Spirit. The religious authorities became alarmed particularly because the believers in Christ's teaching were increasing and "large number of priests became obedient to the faith" (Acts 6:7).

Stephen was seized and brought before the Sanhedrin. "They looked at him and saw that his face was like the face of an angel" (Acts 6:15).

Not only did his face reflect the glory of God, but also his words covered the history of God's salvation of Israel, which the Sanhedrin should have appreciated. But Stephen brings the final condemnation, telling them they are always resisting the Holy Spirit. They stood condemned by the person they had on trial. They were guilty of murdering Jesus and now they would put Stephen to death.

But Stephen was already in the presence of Jesus, "full of the Holy Spirit, looked up to heaven and saw the glory of God, and Jesus standing at the right hand of God."

Finally, he demonstrated his greatest reflection of Jesus, "Lord, do not hold this sin against them" (Acts 7:60).

Thought for the Day: *When we are anointed with the Holy Spirit we are safe in the arms of Jesus.*

Portrait of Jesus

Scripture Reading: Revelation 1:1-8

Key Verse: *....Jesus Christ, who is the faithful witness, the firstborn from the dead, and the ruler of the kings of the earth (Revelation 1:5).*

Meditation: Jesus witnessed to us of His Father's nature and plan for our world. Jesus said to Thomas, "He that has seen me has seen the Father." He not only tells us verbally about God; He also obeys God's plan and fulfills it in His willing death sacrifice for the human race, for all of us.

Jesus rose from death to give us hope. God pledged Him as the first of a great company who will follow Him. All of us who trust in Christ have potentially conquered the last and grimmest foe, death.

He loves us, frees us from our sins and makes us royalty (kings) and intercessors (priests) before God. Now, by His marvelous act of redemption He equips us to serve dual offices in His work on earth. We have the authority of His power (as King) and the efficacy of His complete sacrifice for us (Priest).

Thought for the Day: *And in addition to all this, He promises to come back to our earth and everyone will recognize Him as the Almighty, who was and is and is to come (Revelation 1:8).*

A Significant Event

Scripture Reading: Acts 2:32,33

Key Verse: *...he has received from the Father the Promised Holy Spirit and has poured out what you now see and hear (Acts 2:33b).*

Meditation: During May we will study the Biblical meaning of the Day of Pentecost, and the Holy Spirit. Pentecost happened 50 days after the resurrection and ten days after the ascension of Jesus. The glorified Jesus received the promised Holy Spirit from the Father and poured Him out upon the 120 waiting in the Upper Room. By the end of the first day, through the Spirit anointed witness of the 120 and the preaching of Peter, 3,000 new converts were added to the church.

Many, many people in the church today seem unaware of this inauguration of the era of the Spirit. Compared with other important dates on the church calendar, Pentecost seems vague. In a church I once pastored a couple said to me, "What in the world is the meaning of Pentecost Sunday?" They prided themselves on having been members of an evangelical Bible believing church, yet had no understanding of such a significant event, both historically and ongoing.

Pentecost fits into the sequence of God's redemptive acts: At Christmas Christ assumed human form to serve as our bridge back to God. On Good Friday Christ died in our place, the sinless for the sinful. Easter assures us Christ broke the power of death, sin and Satan and opened the way for us to return to God. The ascension and subsequent exaltation of Christ at God's right hand provides the certainty of His triumph over every power. Pentecost, the sending of the Spirit, verified the fulfillment of His promises, "I will not leave you orphans; I will come to you" (John 14:18).

Thought for the Day: *All that Christ did for the Church became an inward reality on the Day of Pentecost.*

The History of Pentecost

Scripture Reading: Leviticus 23:15-22

Key Verse: *From wherever you live, bring two loaves...as a wave offering of first fruits to the Lord (Leviticus 23:17).*

Meditation: Beginning with Moses, the Jewish nation celebrated seven annual sacred feasts "of the Lord" climaxed with deep religious joy. They praised God for being their ultimate defender and provider. Rooted in historical happenings of divine interventions, most of them also carried future or messianic meaning.

Three of the feasts demanded compulsory attendance of all males. On the day of the **Passover** they commemorated the deliverance from the angel of death on the eve of the exodus from Egypt. That night blood of an unblemished animal was applied to the doorposts of their homes to spare the firstborn of that home from being slain by the death angel. Today the festival would have its fulfillment when Christ the sinless Lamb was slain for our sins.

The **Feast of Tabernacles** recalled the entrance into the Promised Land of Canaan. First they lived in booths made of branches and boughs of trees. The feast reenacted the initial joy and recalled the lessons of the 40-year detour through the wilderness of unbelief.

Pentecost took place 50 days after the Passover. The Holy Spirit came on the disciples during this commemorative celebration. Significantly, this took place 50 days after Christ's crucifixion and resurrection.

Thought for the Day: *Fifty days after the sinless Lamb was slain, the Spirit was poured out.*

The Symbolic Meaning of the Two Loaves

Scripture Reading: Acts 2:1-5

Key Verse: *... and when the day of Pentecost came... (Acts 2:1a).*

Meditation: On the final day of the Feast of Pentecost the priest took two loaves made of the newly harvested grain and presented them to God. Why just two and not some other number? Biblical scholars have concluded the two loaves symbolized the Jewish and Gentile peoples. God did not desire bread but people.

God's concern for people has been evident since His covenant with Abraham, but not just for Jewish people, *...all peoples on the earth will be blessed through you.* The actualization of that promise to Abraham would wait 2,000+ years, yet God's intention for the world was expressed from the beginning. God used the scattered Jewish people to convert many Gentiles from paganism. Exiled Jewish Christians evangelized the Ethiopian eunuch. He studied the scriptures and was ready to receive the gospel. One of the most outstanding converts recorded in the book of Acts, his subsequent zeal to evangelize his own people is a part of the reason for the history of Christianity in his country today.

The Old Testament Feast of Pentecost (Harvest) was strategically fulfilled in Acts 2 when people gathered from all over the then known world. Peter presented not two loaves to the Lord, but 3,000 converts who were asking for baptism. These 3,000 became the firstfruit of the larger world harvest that was yet to come.

Thought for the Day: *God orchestrated the timing of the Day of Pentecost for the purpose of world evangelism.*

The Missing Person of the Trinity

Scripture Reading: Acts 19:1-17

Key Verse...did *you receive the Spirit when you believed? (Acts 19:2)*

Meditation: After being a missionary over a period of 45 years, I discovered on visiting churches again in the United States that the word, "Pentecost" evoked mixed reactions. Many people misread or misunderstood the meaning of this important day. Dr. Louis Evans said, "A few people have blurred the meaning of Pentecost for many in the church."

Some people view Pentecost as a historical event of the days of the apostles, thus we do not need the spiritual gifts that were in the early church. They emphasize the Father and the Son more than the Holy Spirit, although they recognize the Trinity. In other churches people were excited about the Spirit, and the other two members of the Godhead were almost forgotten. Generally these folks were very evangelistic with a strong emphasis on the Second Coming of Jesus. Some taught a great Pentecost resulting in the completion of world evangelism before the return of Christ. This "future Pentecost" filled them with hope and expectancy.

Other categories include those afraid of the Spirit, those who think of Him as mysterious, and those who sincerely want to understand the biblical Holy Spirit and experience His filling and indwelling.

Thought for the Day: *Which of the five views of the Holy Spirit describes me?*

Acts, the Primer of the Church

Scripture Reading: Acts 1:7,8

Key Verse: *But you will receive power...(Acts 1:8a).*

Meditation: Some Bible scholars view the book of Acts as a historical document with the primitive church in stage one. They believe the church in Acts to be in a transitional stage and the normal church model is found later in the epistles. I agree the book of Acts introduces a new dispensation of the Spirit at work through the church in our world. I also believe we need not try to reproduce all that happened in Acts, but I am convinced the book contains much more than history. Truths and principles are hidden in these inspired pages that must continue to guide the church in the 21st century.

Almost every chapter of Acts records a divine intervention in our space/time world that cannot be explained as a coincidence. Even when God appears to be anonymous, those with "eyes to see" can discern God's unmistakable working. God can come from "outside" our world to accomplish His preordained purpose. God continues to orchestrate His purpose through His church as He moves it from the frontier to the uttermost part of the earth, reversing all that happened at the Tower of Babel.

The Spirit initially was poured out at Jerusalem, the Jewish Pentecost. Later at Samaria, the Samaritan Pentecost. Then at Caesarea, the Roman Pentecost, and finally at Ephesus for the Greek-speaking people. God thus assures us that the outpouring of God's Spirit is the birthright of every believer.

Thought for the Day: *The historical Pentecost can become personal history for every person.*

The Ongoing Significance of Pentecost

Scripture Reading: Joel 2:28-32

Key Verse: *I will pour out my Spirit on all people (Joel 2:28a).*

Meditation: Joel foretold the Day of Pentecost 800 years before fulfillment. Peter then declares in Acts, "This is that spoken before." Never before had there been such an outpouring on so many people. Individuals like Moses, Malachi, David, Daniel, Deborah, and Hannah had been touched before, but never anything like the crowds of people filled as Joel had predicted, even to the God-fearing Gentiles.

The Word of God accompanied this unparalleled outpouring of the Spirit. Visions and dreams and, above all, prophecy, would be extended not just to Israel but to all peoples. This gift would extend through the church age, not as a new revelation, but as a speaking of the truth that had already been revealed, applying the principles of the Word to local and international situations.

During the Old Testament time the Spirit's activity focused on individuals for a specific task. We can better understand the sub-Christian performances of Samson, King Saul and others. In the New Testament the Holy Spirit's work is character transformation. The ultimate purpose of the Spirit's coming on the 120 at Pentecost and on us is to enable all believers to live and speak as Christ's witnesses.

Thought for the Day: *Pentecost, the fulfillment of Joel's prophecy, was a clear signal that God is moving history to His preordained goal and on His schedule.*

The Holy Spirit in the Creation

Scripture Reading: Genesis 1:1,2

Key Verse: *...and the Spirit of God hovered over the waters (Genesis 1:1b).*

Meditation: Throughout the history of the Christian church there has been an unbalanced emphasis on the person and ministry of the Holy Spirit. One extreme neglects or ignores the person of the Spirit. The other disproportionately magnifies the Spirit and thereby eclipses the other persons of the Trinity. The common expression, "This is the dispensation of the Spirit" suggests to the hearer that there is now a discontinuity of the work of the other two persons of the Trinity. Nothing could be further from the truth of Scripture.

In the following several devotional readings we will search the scriptures to find the balanced emphasis on the Holy Spirit and hope to avoid any extremes. From both the Old and New Testaments the work of the Holy Spirit unfolds, and we will be awed by the wonder of God's plan of redemption.

The Holy Spirit is first mentioned in Genesis 1. First, He is referred to as the Spirit of God, suggesting He is side-by-side or close together with God the Father. He is also depicted as overseeing the unordered earth, protecting it before God made it habitable for man. He also appears as powerfully ready to implement God's words, "Let there be..." These three functions of the Spirit in creation of the natural world suggest His future work of redemption of sinful fallen mankind. He is either "hovering over us" or "following after us" as the divine *Hound of Heaven.*

Thought for the Day: *Confident of the Spirit's presence, we can obediently go into all the world.*

The Holy Spirit in the Creation of Man

Scripture Reading: Genesis 1:26,27

Key Verse: *...and breathed into his nostrils the breath of life and he became a living soul (Genesis 2:7b).*

Meditation: The Holy Spirit's work did not stop with His part in the creation of the earth. He would also participate in the crowning work of creation, the creation of man in God's own image. God's image suggests such characteristics as righteousness, holiness, and knowledge. Man alone, of all the creatures, is made in the image of God. Man alone is made a spiritual living being capable of fellowship with God and service for God. The phrase, "breathed into his nostrils the breath of life" points to the unique work of the Holy Spirit in the creation of man. The Holy Spirit was and still is the true spiritual *life-giver.*

The unique spiritual capacities of man were seriously tarnished and warped by the sin and fall of man, yet the ministry of the Spirit continues. Chapter after chapter of the Old Testament reminds us of the continued imminence and omnipresence of the Holy Spirit with mankind. In Psalm 139:7-12 King David records the Holy Spirit mediating God's presence to him even when he tried to run from God. All spatial reality, heights, depths, distances are indwelt by the omnipresence of the Holy Spirit. Even if one could descend to the depths of the earth, hell itself, the Spirit would be there. To David, the question was not, "Where is God?" but rather "Where is He not?"

Thought for the Day: *If we allow the Holy Spirit to breathe on our lives today we can be fully restored to fellowship with and service to God.*

The Holy Spirit in Restoration of Sinners

Scripture Reading: Genesis 6:1-4

Key Verse: *Then the Lord said, My Spirit will not contend with man forever...(Genesis 6:3a).*

Meditation: When Adam disobeyed God, he lost the image of God and forfeited his intimate fellowship and relationship with God. However, the Holy Spirit did not leave mankind in this desperate situation. He continued His ministry of contending and striving with people. While this Old Testament ministry of the Spirit lacked the mediatorial dynamic work of Jesus, yet He was continually moving upon people to help them reclaim what they had lost in the Garden of Eden. There were, however, also warnings of judgment on those who persisted in disobedience. Noah's generation, to which these words are addressed, ignored the Spirit's warning and all but Noah and his families were swept away by the flood in judgment.

This "contending" of the Spirit on a personal level in the Old Testament is best illustrated in King David's sin and cover-up in Psalm 51. The Spirit gave the prophet Nathan the spiritual discernment and courage to say, "David, you are the man." Suddenly, the conviction of the Spirit falls on David as he remembers the danger of the Spirit leaving him as in King Saul's case. He cries out in repentance, "Do not cast me out (like you did Saul), or take your Holy Spirit from me." He repents of his sins, and receives divine forgiveness and acceptance before God. Assured of God's answer, he then writes with confidence, "The sacrifices of God are a broken spirit and a contrite heart."

Thought for the Day: *The marks of biblical repentance are manifested when we stop rationalizing our failures and sincerely cry out with David, "Create in me a clean heart, O God."*

The Holy Spirit in Creativity

Scripture Reading: Exodus 31:1-11

Key Verse: *And I have filled him with the Spirit of God, with skill, ability and knowledge in all kinds of crafts (Exodus 31:3).*

Meditation: In the Old Testament a number of instances are recorded where the Holy Spirit bestows a supernatural enabling which enhances natural giftedness. Several of those persons are mentioned in Exodus 31. The tabernacle must be built as suitable for the awesome dwelling place of God on earth. No simple makeshift design conceived by man, this dwelling design by God was given to Moses on Mt. Sinai by divine revelation. The reproduction of the divine design could only be accomplished by the creative supernatural assistance of the Holy Spirit.

It may be inferred from the test that even before God called Bezalel and Oholiab to this task they had a natural propensity for the work. For the making of the tabernacle furniture and the intricate weaving for Aaron's garments, the Holy Spirit filled them and lifted them to a new creative level that glorified God.

I believe that this chapter can be applied to our lives today. Whenever God has an important work to do in His larger kingdom, He will both call and equip people to accomplish the task. Usually He will call someone who has been faithful in training and the use of his natural gifts. Bezalel and Oholiab's training in Egypt was God's preparation for their work to facilitate worship of all the Israelite nation in a suitable place for God in their midst.

Thought for the Day: *If we dedicate our natural giftedness to God, then in His own timing, He will elevate those gifts to a higher level and be glorified in them.*

The Holy Spirit in Old Testament Man

Scripture Reading: Isaiah 59:21

Key Verse: *My Spirit which is on you...(Isaiah 59:21a).*

Meditation: While we refer to the Holy Spirit as "coming" to the church on the Day of Pentecost, we should not assume that this event marked His first coming to mankind. He was not absent during the Old Testament period. Pentecost certainly marked some new and distinctive differences since Christ's atoning work was completed, but the Holy Spirit has always been present, even before the world was created, according to Genesis 1:2b.

The Spirit's relationship to people in the Old Testament is indicated by the words, *in people, upon people,* and *filling people.* The words, *in people*, however, have the limitation of only certain, selected people having the Spirit in them. However, pagans could somehow intuitively recognize the Spirit's presence in people. Pharaoh, for instance, sensed that the Spirit was in Joseph. All three pagan kings, Nebuchanezzar, Belshazzar and Darius recognized that the Spirit resided in Daniel.

The Spirit is also recorded as "coming upon people" and "filling them." However, unlike the post-Pentecostal period, the Spirit had not yet come to stay in the Old Testament. This limited "coming of the Spirit" was primarily related to doing a certain task for God, and once that task was completed, the dynamic sense of the Spirit's presence was not apparent. This "coming" and "going" of the Spirit helps us to better understand why some people like Samson did not experience a radical character transformation.

Thought for the Day: *The Holy Spirit in His fullness has been poured out on the Church today. All that is needed on our part is to be obedient to walk in all of God's light*

The Holy Spirit in Writing the Old Testament

Scripture Reading: II Peter 1:12-21

Key Verse: *...but men spoke from God as they were carried along by the Holy Spirit (II Peter 1:21b).*

Meditation: Neither the Old Testament nor the New Testament were produced by the mere heightening of man's intellectual or spiritual powers. Nor were they written by the direct dictation of God into the ears of the writers. The first method would reduce the Bible only to the best that man can produce and strip it of its unique supernatural character. The "dictation theory" would completely eliminate the differences in style we find, for example, between the writings of Paul and Peter or between Mark and John.

We believe that the writing of the Scriptures indicates both a passive and active side. As for the content of Scripture itself, we are convinced that the will of the Holy Spirit, not the will of man, determined what was to be written. We are confident that nothing of essential importance was omitted. In other words, all that the church needs to know has already been recorded for us. Peter uses the expression regarding prophecy "they were actively carried by the Holy Spirit as they spoke." The Holy Spirit was the divine source for what was spoken. Paul uses the expression "All Scripture is God-breathed..."

As God spoke to and through human authors, yet He did not bypass or violate their personalities. They each responded to the content of revelation and recorded it in their own vocabulary and through the uniqueness of their own personalities. This makes the Scriptures "the Word of God," but expressed in the words of individual writers.

Thought for the Day: *The clearest evidence of a Spirit-filled Christian is that person's submission to the authority of Scripture as God's revealed Word and will.*

The Holy Spirit in the Old Testament Covenant

Scripture Reading: Jeremiah 31:31-34

Key Verse: *...I will put my law in their minds and write it on their hearts (Jeremiah 31:33b).*

Meditation: In order to understand the Bible better, we must understand both the Old and the New Testament covenants. In the Old Testament God established His covenant through Moses by promising to be Israel's God. This covenant was based on the law, but with the onus of keeping the law placed on the shoulders of the people themselves with repeated "thou shalt" admonitions. The New Testament covenant was based on Christ and ratified by His shed blood on the cross. This new covenant was based on God's promises, in which He himself accepts full responsibility by saying repeatedly, "I will."

I have already mentioned that under the Old Testament covenant the Holy Spirit did not, as a rule, come upon a community of believers, but only upon a selected leader. It seems that the Spirit was most active in times of crisis. When that crucial time passed, the dynamic sense of the Spirit's working seemed to wane. In the Old Testament we have numerous references of the Spirit's presence being removed, whether by the disobedience or the death of their selected leader. The book of Judges suggests a connection between this recurring cycle of death and the immediate spiritual decline of the nation. It appears that the promise of God putting His law in their minds and writing it on their hearts was futuristic and would not be fulfilled until Pentecost had fully come.

Also, under the Old Testament dispensation there remained only a tribal sense of Israel and totally lacking the larger "one body" consciousness that is so apparent after Acts 2. Neither was there any sense of an overflow of the Spirit even in those divinely chosen by God to be recipients of the Spirit. This abundant fellowship of the Spirit would have to wait for the glorification of Jesus.

Thought for the Day: *The Holy Ghost was not yet given (in His fullness) because Jesus was not yet glorified.*

The Holy Spirit in Ezekiel's Prophecy

Scripture Reading: Ezekiel 36:22-27

Key Verse: *...And I will put my Spirit in you and move you to follow my decrees...(Ezekiel 36:27a).*

Meditation: In the Old Testament prophetic writings of Ezekiel we are given a glimpse of what Israel could anticipate under the New Covenant. The prophet was preparing them for the new way God would relate to them under the New Covenant. Seeing Israel's long history of unfaithfulness, God would now take the major initiative in relating to his people.

The future direct action of God and subsequent transformation of His people will be so radical, resulting in the "sanctification of God's name" among the people. Israel's backsliding had profaned God's name among the nations. Even God's judgment of putting Israel in exile was misread by the pagans as revealing the weakness and impotence of God to act in Israel's behalf. Psalm 137 records the pagan nations taunting Israel to sing one of the Songs of Zion as they sat in a foreign land. But a day was coming when God would unilaterally act and redeem His great name in the eyes of the nations of the world. We believe that the day of Pentecost ushered in this new period of history.

This inner change is further described as "God sprinkling clean water over them" resulting in cleansing from all impurities and from all idols. This symbolizes the washing of regeneration from the guilt of sin as well as the deeper cleansing of their sinful nature. Israel's besetting sin was idolatry, and even provision for being set free from this taproot of sin was promised. To insure this process God promised to give them a heart to know Him by putting His Spirit in them.

Thought for the Day: *What Ezekiel anticipated was fully realized and experienced on the day of Pentecost.*

The Holy Spirit in Joel's Prophecy

Scripture Reading: Joel 2:28,29

Key Verse: *And afterwards I will pour out my Spirit on all flesh…(Joel 2:28a).*

Meditation: We are impressed as we read Joel's prophecy at the awesome liberality with which God bestows His Holy Spirit. He is no longer given to a select few for certain duration or task, but He is poured out on all people. The original Hebrew text suggests not mere drops or sprinkling, but the "pouring out" in great abundance. Unlike the Old Testament dispensation, the Holy Spirit would no longer be restricted in the number of recipients or in the quantity of His working.

The promised effusion and diffusion of the Spirit would reach all mankind. Sons and daughters, without regard to gender, would equally experience the abundant fullness of the Spirit. Old men and young men, without reference to age, would experience the boundlessness of the Holy Spirit. Servants, both men and women, without regard to social station, would be equal heirs of the bountifulness of the Holy Spirit. The blessing of the Holy Spirit would be as wide as the world and offered to the entire world without any national or ethnic distinctions.

Another important distinctive mark of the New Covenant would be the continuity of the Spirit's power and working. Since the Spirit was given to inaugurate the last days, we can count on His ministry right up to the very last of the last days. So from Pentecost onwards to the final consummation of human history when Christ returns for the church, we can rely on the Holy Spirit's sovereign work both in the world and in the church.

Thought for the Day: *The sparse individual "drops" of the Spirit in the Old Testament have given way to the "outpouring" of the Spirit in the New Testament.*

The Holy Spirit During Inter-Testament Time

Scripture Reading: Mark 1:1-8

Key Verse: *The whole Judean countryside...went out to him... (Mark 1:5a).*

Meditation: At least 400 years transpired after the last Old Testament writers recorded the words of God. Until recently little was known about the Spirit's working during this inter-testament time. Many Bible scholars assumed that, due to the sins of the people, God had withdrawn His presence from the temples and the people of Israel until such a time that the Messiah would appear.

However, the recent discovery of the literature of the Qumran community near the Dead Sea seems to contradict the supposed absence of the Holy Spirit during this time. Both in the hymns and in their manual of discipline the Holy Spirit is frequently mentioned as the divine purifier of man's mind and heart. We can be assured there has never been a time since creation that God has not been at work in our world. Even when the Shekinah presence of God lifted from the temple, the Holy Spirit's ministry continued in individual lives.

How else can we explain, apart from the Spirit's working, the growing sense of expectancy regarding the coming of the Messiah? The promises of the prophets concerning the Messiah had not been forgotten, at least not by a large number of people. That hope crystallized into eager questioning when someone like John the Baptist appeared. People flocked to hear John, expecting him to be the Messiah. We attribute this atmosphere of intense expectation to the direct ministry of the Holy Spirit.

Thought for the Day: *There has not been a day since the Creation when the Holy Spirit has been absent in our world.*

The Holy Spirit in the Gospels

Scripture Reading: Luke 1:11-17

Key Verse: *...and he will be filled with the Holy Spirit even from birth (Luke 1:15b).*

Meditation: We have observed the general superintending of the Holy Spirit over mankind from creation onward, even through that long period of 400 years between the Old and New Testaments. We noted selected individuals empowered by the Holy Spirit to carry out God's redemptive task. Both before and during the inter-testament period, the Shekinah glory of God was never experienced in the second temple, and the people were generally in a state of apostasy. Yet as the time for the incarnation of Christ drew closer, the Holy Spirit stirred up a remnant of Israelites who responded to His initiatives.

Out of that remnant of godly Israelites came the outstanding family of John the Baptist. Luke describes the angel of the Lord appearing to Zechariah who had been praying for a son. The angel assured him that his prayers had been answered and that his son "...will be filled with the Spirit even from birth." The power of the Spirit would be needed for the double task of bringing wayward Israel back to God and to empower John to serve as the forerunner of Jesus.

John would be expected to do what no pastor could ever do in his own strength: John would have to sacrifice all of his popularity with the masses and transfer all of his followers to Jesus. He would have to fight against all the negative attitudes of his most devout followers who felt threatened by this large-scale defection to Jesus. But John freely relinquished his popularity to Jesus for three important reasons: Jesus was the Lamb of God, He spoke the Word of God, and He would baptize with the Holy Spirit and with fire.

Thought for the Day: *Only those with cleansed human egos can spontaneously say, He must become greater; I must become less.*

The Holy Spirit in the Incarnation

Scripture Reading: Matthew 1:18-24

Key Verse: *...what is conceived in her is from the Holy Spirit (Matthew 1:20b).*

Meditation: The supreme redemptive function of the Holy Spirit, the third person in the Trinity, comes into clear focus as God's time for the birth of Jesus approaches. As we all know, the word "incarnation" includes the totality of Christ's redemptive work: His birth, life, death, resurrection, and ascension. However, the incarnation of Christ actually began in the womb of the divinely chosen Virgin Mary through the miraculous moving and intervention of the Holy Spirit.

Two awesome miracles happened at the conception: Jesus was conceived without the participation of a human father. Then, even greater, because it contains the secret of our redemption, is the fact that Jesus received his human body from Mary, yet He did not inherit the sinful nature common to all who were born since Adam's fall. The Holy Spirit somehow supernaturally intervened to make Christ's future sinless death possible. Christ's humanity was both real humanity, but simultaneously, sinless humanity, and therein lies the hope of our redemption.

Jesus is the only baby in all of human history who had a prehistory. Bethlehem, the place of His birth, was not His beginning. His real beginning dates back to the bosom of God the Father in the agelessness of eternity. John confirms this by the words, "He was with the Father from the beginning." Bethlehem was his "advent," His coming into our space-time world. Christ literally came down from heaven to our world to lift us up to become like Him.

Thought for the Day: *Jesus did not come to earth for a fleeting visit; He was supernaturally birthed here by the direct intervention of the Holy Spirit.*

The Holy Spirit as Prophesied
by John the Baptist

Scripture Reading: Matthew 3:1-12

Key Verse: *...He will baptize you with the Holy Spirit and fire...(Matthew 3:16).*

Meditation: John the Baptist burst upon the scene in Israel with a powerful prophetic voice and message. He broke what appeared to many as the "long silence" of God to announce his message of repentance. Water baptism had been practiced commonly in John's day, especially when Gentiles became proselytes to the Jewish faith. Both to the Jews and Gentiles, water baptism symbolized the washing away of ceremonial uncleanness. John's message of repentance was more distinct in that it called for national repentance and a genuine returning to God that would be reflected in a transformed life style.

John, however, sought to draw a clear line of demarcation between his baptism and the baptism of Jesus. At the best, John's baptism was preparatory for the coming of Jesus and for the deeper work of the Holy Spirit that would follow. Christ's baptism would be superior to John's: While John called for repentance and a profound change in lifestyle, he could not by external rite of water baptism bring about the life changes that would be effected by Jesus.

The baptism of Jesus involved the giving of the gift of the Holy Spirit and the baptism with fire, suggesting both judgment on sin plus cleansing from the pollution of sin. This work of the Holy Spirit is not by the initiative of the Spirit on His own, but rather it is the gift of Jesus to the believer. Paul teaches us in Romans that at conversion every believer is baptized into the Body of Christ and made a part of Christ's body under the Lordship of Jesus. But both baptisms, into the body of Christ and in the Holy Spirit, are gifts of Jesus that would be fully realized after Christ's death, resurrection, and ascension.

Thought for the Day: *The gift of the Holy Spirit that Jesus promised is the real change-agent in the Church.*

The Holy Spirit in Christ's Baptism

Scripture Reading: Matthew 3:13-17

Key Verse: *...and he (John) saw the Spirit of God descending on Jesus like a dove... (Matthew 3:16b).*

Meditation: Bible scholars agree that while each of the three supernatural happenings coincided with the water baptism of Jesus: the open heaven, the voice of the Father and the dove-Spirit descent, that the most important is the Spirit, symbolized by the dove and the Spirit remaining on Jesus. In fact, it was the remaining of the Spirit on Jesus that fulfilled Old Testament prophecy that Jesus was indeed the long awaited Messiah. However, the other two supernatural events were also of great significance to Jesus and to the Church.

The fact that the heavens, shut for 400 years, literally were torn open over Jesus assured the believers of unhindered access to the Father. Jesus can now pray directly to the Father. This is also our assurance that when we put our faith in Jesus, the heavens are open to us as well. Prayer is one of the unique new gifts given to us at conversion. The sign of a truly converted person is that he can pray and say *Our Father.*

The baptism of Jesus also teaches us that, like Jesus, when we surrender our lives to God, the dove-like Holy Spirit will come down on us and remain with us. His is not just a temporary flash of inspiration, but He takes up permanent indwelling in us.

Today we associate the dove with the Spirit, but in the Old Testament and inter-testament period the dove was also associated with the idea of sacrifice. The dove was the sacrifice of the very poor, reminding us of the downward movement of our redemption. Jesus came down from heaven and the Holy Spirit also comes down from heaven. Here Jesus does not come to us as a Lion, but as a humble, gentle peace-loving Dove.

Thought for the Day: *Christ in his baptism models access to God in prayer, the abiding presence of the Spirit and the assurance of sonship.*

The Holy Spirit and Christ in Ministry

Scripture Reading: Mark 1:9-11, Luke 4:1-15

Key Verse: *Jesus returned to Galilee in the power of the Spirit (Luke 4:14).*

Meditation: The Holy Spirit, who came down upon Jesus at His water baptism in Jordan, did not allow Jesus to bask in the open heaven experience or in the place where He heard the reassuring words of His Father's delight in Him. Rather, as Mark tells us, that Spirit drove Jesus deep into the wilderness. The wilderness/desert experience for the Jewish people recalled a host of powerful memories. The wilderness was the place through which Israel had to pass from their journey out of Egypt into the Promised Land. It was God's proving ground, especially for the testing and the preparation of leaders, and Jesus would be no exception.

Biblical scholars have generally agreed that while the Scriptures do not explicitly state that the Spirit led Jesus directly into Satan's presence, at least He was located indirectly where Satan resided: The place of desolation and danger surrounded by wild beasts that roamed at leisure, especially at night. In these dire human circumstances after 40 days of fasting, Jesus would be tempted with Satan's three-pronged attack: To sidetrack Him from God's purpose, to separate Him from doing the Father's will, and to tempt Him to seek His independence form the Father.

Jesus got His victory and, at least, temporary relief, using the same resources accessible to each of us: The divinely inspired Word of God, the fullness of the powerful dove-like Holy Spirit resting on us. Luke assures us that after the 40 days in the wilderness Jesus returned to Galilee in the power of the Spirit.

Thought for the Day: *Our confidence in the divine inspiration of the Scriptures and our recognition of our deep need of the Spirit is the secret of spiritual victory today.*

The Holy Spirit in Our Lives
What is Growing in Your Garden? (1)

Scripture Reading: Galatians 5:16-24

Key Verse: *For the sinful nature desires what is contrary to the Spirit (Galatians 5:17a).*

Meditation: Paul tells the people in the Galatian church that their lives are like a garden in which something is growing. The unregenerate persons and the carnal Christians produce weeds of human nature, but those who are walking in the Spirit are growing the nine-fold fruit of the Spirit. Paul affirms that we are living either in the magnetic field of flesh or in the magnetic field of the Holy Spirit, each contesting with the other. The decision as to which field we live is really up to our making the choice.

We are naturally born into the "flesh-field" by our association with Adam. If we allow the weeds of human nature to grow unchecked, we become more and more covered with that characteristic. We will be focused on ourselves and oblivious to the needs of others. The "flesh" person uses others as tools to enhance his position of superiority.

The fruit of the self-centered person will be (1) the sins of human sensuality that will go progressively from adultery to unrestrained violence, and (2) deliberate sin against the knowledge of God. The boundaries between God and man become blurred and the ethical and moral basis of decision-making is left to the individual, and (3) sins against interpersonal relationships. Whenever God is dethroned from His absolute position, man's sins against man accelerate, breaking down the sense of civility and community.

Thought for the Day: *We rarely, if ever, find any moral restraints in idol worship, for most idols are human projections on inanimate objects of the kind of god man wants.*

The Holy Spirit in Our Lives
What is Growing in Your Garden? (2)

Scripture Reading: Galatians 5:19-21

Key Verse: *The acts of the sinful nature are obvious (Galatians 5:19a).*

Meditation: From the long list of characteristics of the "flesh" or carnal people, the two dominants are self-centeredness and self-gratification. Our present generation, characterized as the "instant" generation, must be immediately satisfied, even if the way of fulfillment is morally or ethically questionable.

Paul does not promise some quick religious experience that would transform the carnal person into a Spirit-person. This church in Galatia was on the verge of slipping away from a good start and Paul was concerned lest his hard work there had been wasted in the sense of eroding results (Galatians 4:11).

Here Paul emphasizes that the nine-fold fruit of the Holy Spirit is generated out of our intentional daily abiding in Christ. To display the fruit of the Spirit we must daily decide to be led by Christ rather than our own erratic voice of conscience. We must daily allow the Spirit to free us, animate and motivate us. None of the fruit is generated out of our own humanity. They come directly from the Holy Spirit who evidences His presence and power in the life of the believer. Whereas, most spiritual gifts may be copied or counterfeited by man, these nine "fruit of the Spirit" cannot be imitated.

Thought for the Day: *Ultimately, spiritual maturity is measured, not by spiritual gifts, but by the nine-fold fruit of the Holy Spirit.*

The Fruit of the Spirit

Scripture Reading: Galatians 5:22,23

Key Verse: *But the fruit of the Spirit is love (Galatians 5: 22a).*

Meditation: The evidence of the fruit of the Spirit is just as supernatural and spiritual as the evidence of a spiritual gift. The fruit of the Holy Spirit is just as needed to live out the Christian life as spiritual gifts are needed to minister effectively. Emphasis only on spiritual gifts can become a divisive force in the church. Whereas each believer has only one main spiritual gift, we are all expected to possess and demonstrate all nine gifts of the Spirit.

Ruth Paxton, a writer in the early 1900's, maintained that the ultimate purpose of the ministry of the Holy Spirit was to produce Christ-likeness in each believer. Some of the nine-fold characteristics of the Spirit-filled person might be generated in a certain disposition, but it is the power of God that makes all nine to be manifested daily in a dynamic relationship to the Holy Spirit Himself.

Romans 5:8 reminds us that "…the love of God is shed abroad in our hearts by the Holy Spirit which is given unto us." It was God's intention from the beginning of the church that love was to be the dynamic by which Christianity would be sustained. Since the word used here is "agape," meaning divine love, we must think of love as a God-like quality, not limited and conditional like human love. We cannot, by our own power, generate this kind of agape love. Agape love will act even when the emotion of affection is not present. This love is not about feeling, but about doing.

Thought for the Day: *The nine-fold fruit of the Spirit motivates us to act for the good of the other person without compensating our own desires.*

The Fruit of the Spirit

Scripture Reading: Galatians 5:22,23

Key Verse: *But the fruit of the Spirit is love, joy, peace... (Galatians 5:22).*

Meditation: Joy has a prominent place in the nine-fold fruit of the Spirit. But we must embrace the other eight fruits as well, if we are to have joy. In other words, I cannot say I desire joy, but prefer to hold on to my impatience and lack of self-control. The Holy Spirit develops all of these fruits in me. If we choose to block Him in one area, we may grieve and block Him from developing the other areas also. We must let go of our self-efforts and allow Him the freedom to work in us on His own time schedule. Like every other area in our lives, a certain amount of time is required before maturity can be expected.

A person exhibiting biblical joy has a refreshing spirit, perceives his suffering as temporary, and as sharing in the suffering of Christ. He knows that God will not abandon him. With this assurance of joy, peace follows.

Jesus greeted His disciples after His resurrection with the words, "Peace be to you." In spite of the human failures of the disciples on the night of His betrayal, Jesus gave to them the gift of peace. Christ's greeting suggests "everything is working harmoniously the way it should for your well-being." Jesus showed them His hands and side, signifying that His death had radically changed into a triumph what had first appeared to be a disaster. Now Jesus extends that promise of peace through the Holy Spirit whom He poured out on His followers on the Day of Pentecost.

Thought for the Day: *Joy and peace demonstrate in the Spirit-filled life that Jesus is in control.*

The Fruit of the Spirit

Scripture Reading: Galatians 5:22,23

Key Verse: *But the fruit of the Spirit is love, joy, peace, patience...*
(Galatians 5:22).

Meditation: The essence of patience or long-suffering lies in our confidence that the Holy Spirit is dynamically at work simultaneously both in our lives and in our circumstances to accomplish God's larger purposes. However, faith must be exercised during this process, for we seldom understand except in retrospect what God's long-term purpose is. However, if we respond negatively with impatience or by demanding an explanation, we will destroy this vital fruit of the Holy Spirit.

Patience is one of the fruits of the Holy Spirit generally lived out in relation to people. An old Eastern proverb, "Patience is power," suggests that the person who waits patiently will be the most influential person in the end. Patience is one of those unique God-like characteristics. God defers judgment on the ungodly in the strong hope that this intentional delay will ultimately lead to their repentance and faith. The Holy Spirit seeks to develop this grace in us so that we do not lose hope in people.

Patience is one of the most essential fruits of the Spirit in the believer's life. Patience will keep us doing God's work regardless of human difficulties and discouragement. Even the unsaved are impressed by this God-like virtue. Fellowship in the church is sustained and deepened by the quality of patience. On the other hand, impatience tempts persons to abuse their power by pushing people rather than by affirming them. Impatience blinds us to what the Holy Spirit desires to do in individual lives.

Thought for the Day: *The divine fruit of patience can always wait a little longer; human pride cannot wait.*

The Fruit of the Spirit

Scripture Reading: Galatians 5:22,23

Key Verse: *The fruit of the Spirit is…kindness (Galatians 5:22).*

Meditation: The quality that most impresses people about Jesus is His kindness to others who are both morally and ethically bad. Jesus demonstrated this gentleness to the woman who was publicly caught in the act of adultery. Instead of engaging her in a public confession and humiliation, He simply bent down and wrote something in the sand. Whatever He wrote apparently brought conviction in those who accused her, resulting in their walking away, one after the other, without any further accusations. Then Jesus was free to restore her battered pride and human dignity. The fact that Jesus attracted sinful people right to the last moment on the cross speaks loudly of the attractiveness of the holiness of Jesus. His holiness was evangelistic and not the separatist life of the Pharisees.

The Scriptures generally refer to kindness as being the preliminary step to forgiveness. Kindness always seeks to understand not just the act, but the real motivation behind the act. A person demonstrating Christian kindness does not insist on the law to be strictly applied, but takes time to look redemptively at the facts of the situation. The overriding concern is to protect the integrity of the person so he/she can spiritually recover.

In Matthew 25:40 Jesus makes an amazing claim for a very simple act of human kindness, "...whatever you did for one of the least of these brothers of mine, you did it for me." In the same paragraph He also speaks of the "eternal damage" that awaits those who have the opportunity to do acts of kindness but who refuse.

Thought for the Day: *A timely, spontaneous act of kindness can have powerful consequences for evangelism with individuals, and significant healing in the body of believers.*

The Fruit of the Spirit

Scripture Reading: Galatians 5:22,23

Key Verse: *But the fruit of the Spirit is...goodness... (Galatians 5:22).*

Meditation: Bible scholars tell us that "goodness" was not a word commonly used in Paul's day. The Holy Spirit would implement it into the lifestyle of people. Goodness might be translated as "generosity," a person who is graced with liberality in spirit and magnanimous in actions to others. "Benevolence" reflects a quality in a person who desires the best for everyone.

The ultimate desire of the Holy Spirit is to make of each believer a good, generous, benevolent person. So the character trait is made possible as we allow the Holy Spirit to cleanse our human motives. Only with the cleansing will the divine fruit of goodness emerge. So God and goodness are intimately linked, as we possess one, we will reflect the others.

Jesus "went about doing good." That "doing good" should be the distinguishing mark of every genuine Christian. Jesus was always ready to help, to be inconvenienced, and to be generous to those in need. Years ago I met three persons at Asbury Theological Seminary: Dr. McPheeters, president emeritus, Dr. E. Stanley Jones, retired missionary apostle to India, and Dr. Frank Laubach, the builder of literary work in the world. Age had not dimmed their understanding of God's vision for them in the world. They reflected the Holy Spirit's fruit of goodness in their love for people, and their spirituality was expressed not in esoteric religious language, but in practical concrete deeds. All three demonstrated their love by promoting the well being of others.

Thought for the Day: *Spirit-filled goodness is often expressed to people who have no way to repay us.*

The Fruit of the Spirit

Scripture Reading: Galatians 5:22,23

Key Verse: *But the fruit of the Spirit is…faithfulness (Galatians 5:22).*

Meditation: Without the deeper ministry of the Holy Spirit in our lives, none of these graces can ever be expressed. Only the Holy Spirit's divine presence in the subconscious part of our being can possibly bring about this radical transformation that is counter-cultural and confronts the works of the carnal nature. The Spirit-fruit test is the only valid measurement of spiritual maturity. When all nine fruits of the Spirit are manifested simultaneously and continuously, then a full Christian character will be demonstrated.

Faithfulness is also known as the loyalty of love. A person exhibiting biblical faithfulness will act and react even to troublesome people in the following ways: He will remain steadfast in carrying through on promises and commitments. He will be supportive of members in the body regardless whether his role is visible or hidden. His faithfulness will be especially directed to members of his own family, including his parents. A faithful person is motivated by a sincere desire to be of service to God regardless of the channel. A faithful person will use his influence and authority with integrity and purity. Like Moses, it was said by God "…he is faithful in all my house" (Numbers 12:7b). A faithful person's whole life will be marked by trustworthiness, leaving no room for compartmentalization or private agenda.

Jesus demonstrated faithfulness from childhood. When the doctors of the law acclaimed Him as a child prodigy, He obediently returned to His parents to work and provide for them. He went to the synagogue each Sabbath before His public ministry. His example was consistent faithfulness.

Thought for the Day: *The most significant achievements of our lives will remain largely hidden until much later. Therefore, we must be faithful to death.*

The Fruit of the Spirit

Scripture Reading: Galatians: 5:22,23

Key Verse: *The fruit of the Spirit is...gentleness... (Galatians 5:23).*

Meditation: A gentle person esteems others as being more important than they are. That person will gladly relinquish his own power and authority in order to have a redemptive influence in the life of a non-Christian. Someone once asked Dr. Albert Sweitzer, holder of three earned doctorates, who was the greatest person he had ever met. He hesitated a moment and then answered, "No human being is capable of determining the greatest person he has ever met. In reality it may be that unknown person who at this very moment has gone out in love and mercy to help some needy person."

Most of us have met people with great natural talent who seemed poised and capable of doing much good in the world. But, sadly, they flashed so brightly before us like a meteor illuminating the path across the sky, only to burn out and disintegrate almost as suddenly. The gifted people have great strengths, but if they are not controlled by the Spirit of gentleness and humility, little lasting good will result from their lives.

Tragically, in this century gentleness is not a highly coveted quality. Even as we call pastors and select leaders for our Christian organizations, we are prone to look for the strong who appear successful. Success is usually measured by materialistic and not spiritual standards. True Biblical gentleness will always be manifested in two directions – toward God in total submission, and toward man in a gentle helping spirit. True biblical gentleness is born out of a deep felt humility before God. John the Baptist was a first cousin of Jesus, but referred humbly to himself as a mere "voice in the wilderness" emphasizing the message and not the messenger. He was able to announce to his loyal followers, "Behold the Lamb of God who takes away the sin of the world."

Thought for the Day: *Only those who manifest the fruit of gentleness can be used to restore those caught in sin.*

The Fruit of the Spirit

Scripture Reading: Galatians 5:22,23

Key Verse: *But the fruit of the Spirit is... self-control (Galatians 5:23).*

Meditation: When Paul says "self-control" he is not referring to rigid inflexibility aimed at extinguishing laughter and joy from our lives. The very opposite is true. The self-control of the Spirit actually liberates us from inordinate self-preoccupation and frees us to become the creative and spontaneous people God created us to be.

The whole purpose of self-control is to enable us to concentrate on our strengths, rather than despising ourselves because of our failures or in comparing ourselves with other people. Self-control enables us to say "no" to the lesser things in life so we can say "yes" to the best. At least three major areas in our lives can get out of control. In the physical area, it is usually manifested by inordinate appetites for food or pleasure. In the mental area, being out control usually comes as a result of suppressed anger or guilt that is then projected on those around us or even back upon ourselves. Anger and guilt are the twin emotions that appear right after each other. Spiritually being out of control usually comes by our taking life in our own hands and making rash decisions without committing it to God and seeking His perspective. Failure in any of these areas often causes deep self-loathing and a sense of failure.

Self-control is the crowning fruit of the Holy Spirit fruit cluster that holds all the other fruit together. It enables us to hear and respond to the guidance of the Holy Spirit. The control of the Holy Spirit will keep us from being driven by our own feelings or by some sudden impulse of the human personality.

Thought for the Day: *God wants us to manifest the nine-fold fruit of the Spirit so we will nourish all the body of Christ.*

Spiritual Gifts

Scripture Reading: I Corinthians 12:1-11

Key Verse: *There are different kinds of gifts, but the same Spirit (I Corinthians 12:4).*

Meditation: Not only does the Holy Spirit work in us to produce the fruit studied in the past month, He also wants to develop in us the gifts designated for specific work in Christ's kingdom.

Gifts of the Spirit listed in Romans 12 are gifts of service, prophecy, teaching, exhortation, giving and acts of mercy. God wants to equip His people for ministry by giving them the capacity through the Holy Spirit to help other people in specific ways.

Ephesians 2 describes gifts for leadership like apostles, prophets, evangelists, pastors and teachers.

I Corinthians 12-14 describes motivational gifts like words of wisdom, knowledge, acts of faith, healing working of miracles, the prophesying of specific events, the ability to distinguish spirits, various kinds of tongues, and the interpretation of tongues. I Corinthians 13 describes the loving atmosphere in which all of these gifts should be exercised.

I Peter 4 highlights gifts for stewardship like hospitality, speaking and serving.

The greatest gift to us from God is the gift of the Holy Spirit. He, the Holy Spirit, has the authority to then give to each of us that spiritual gift that can be best used to minister to the body of Christ. The goal is for us all to come to full development for the good of the kingdom of God.

Thought for the Day: *Gifts are given for the common good, to be used to serve each other so that we all work together in unity.*

Spiritual Gifts

Scripture Reading: Romans 12:9-21

Key Verse: *Live in harmony with one another (Romans 12:16).*

Meditation: As we study the gifts of the Spirit we must remember that not everyone has all the gifts. Jesus equips us with the gifts that in us will best serve His kingdom. He gives us gifts that will be enhanced by our personalities. He will also give us great joy and courage as we use the abilities inherent in those gifts.

Just because a Christian friend has a gift of teaching does not mean I have that gift. Neither should I covet that gift or feel deprived. Rather, I must look to God for His direction so I can discern the gift I do have and how I should use it for Him.

With these cautions in mind we will realize that the way God has gifted us will give us direction for our lives. I could not relax until I preached the Word of God. That does not mean I was never scared, tired, or disappointed. But there is that urgency: Woe *is me if I preach not the gospel of Christ.* One aspect of my personality is encouragement, and that led me to want to pastor where I can nurture and strengthen people in their faith and service to God.

To be satisfied in the work you do, you must sense God's specific call for you to do that work. With that call will come an understanding of the gifts God has given you. You will recognize God's pleasure as He blesses you and reaches others through you.

Thought for the Day: *In a harmonious orchestra some play the major instruments and others play secondary ones, but they are all necessary to produce beautiful music.*

Spiritual Gifts

Scripture Reading: Romans 12:3-8

Key Verse: *We have different gifts according to the grace given us (Romans 12:6).*

Meditation: Those who have accepted Christ as their Savior and who have recognized Jesus as their Lord are baptized by the Holy Spirit and given specific gifts for service. Service to Him signifies the dedicated use of the gifts of the Spirit. The power is for the advancement of the understanding of the gospel of Christ in the world. Jesus must be the emphasis of the work done for Him.

Prophecy: This sharing of the truths of God should bring conviction to people so they understand that God wants them to turn from their sinful ways and follow Him. To recognize this gift, it helps if others see it in you and encourage you to use it in church or other groups.

Service: God links the servant gift close to prophecy because Christ symbolized and modeled the servant role and spirit. Even as He preached, He cared for the followers, feeding and nurturing them in every way.

Teaching: Those awakened by the prophetic proclamation need to be taught the Bible so they will understand their new faith. They may not even recognize that their previously learned behavior needs to be changed unless they learn from the teachings of Jesus.

Exhortation seems to include a passionate and oratorical style of persuasion to drive the hearers to accountability before God.

Giving and Acts of Mercy: The power of the Spirit augments these abilities with a witness for Christ that gives eternal meaning to the good deeds. Mother Teresa blessed every act of mercy with Christ's words so the recipients knew that Jesus was touching them through the dedicated sisters.

Thought for the Day: *People can be selected by their giftedness for positions and responsibilities. They will be happy and the church and society will benefit greatly.*

Spiritual Gifts

Scripture Reading: Ephesians 4:1-13

Key Verse: *But to each one of us grace has been given as Christ apportioned it (Ephesians 4:7).*

Meditation: Paul tells us in Ephesians 3:7,8 that grace was given to him, including the directive to preach to the Gentiles the riches of Christ and to make known the plan of God to everyone. In Ephesians 4 he urges unity of the body of Christ, the church. He then ties the great plan of God to the work that is to be done by those He gifts for various responsibilities:

Apostles: The "sent ones" were first the circle of Twelve in Jerusalem, then Paul, Barnabas and Silas in Antioch and later others with special assignments. Today persons sense God's special empowerment to make the gospel known where no one else will go.

Prophets: Those who speak forth to others for God will bring inspiration and understanding of the scriptures as they are already given to us, all that we need for godliness.

Evangelism: Tied closely to "the sounding forth in prophecy" is the ability to so present the "good news" of the gospel that persons respond in repentance, and obedience to the call to follow Christ. Others recognize when a person manifests this gift.

Pastors: Called to shepherd those who have chosen to follow Christ, the pastor cares and nurtures, listens and prays, using the Word of God to help the believer develop into a strong disciple.

Teacher: This person can explain the scriptures and make them relevant so that the hearer knows better what the Lord is trying to say and how that life should reflect Jesus. The teacher helps the hearer to make personal applications of the Bible to his life.

Thought for the Day: *When we accept, recognize and use the gift God has given us, we reflect the kingdom of God to the world.*

Spiritual Gifts

Scripture Reading: I Corinthians 12:1-30

Key Verse: *There are different kinds of gifts, but the same Spirit (I Corinthians 12:4).*

Meditation: Paul says the believers are a "body" made up of Christians. The healthy church or "body" recognizes Christ as Lord and the source of their salvation. They recognize the Holy Spirit as the energizing power of their existence.

The second mark of a healthy church is diversity. The Holy Spirit distributes a variety of gifts and energizes many ministries among the members. This diversity frees each person to contribute that special gift or ability to the total activity of the group. No one person has to be able to do everything. The third feature is unity: There *should be no division in the body, but that its parts should have equal concern for each other (12:25).*

Unfortunately, in the Corinthian church a rift had arisen between those who manifested different gifts. Rather than thinking of a church being dominated by one particular gift, it should be characterized as an orchestra with many different kinds of instruments, all playing to create a beautiful melody to the Lord. Each person is essential to the body (verses 21-26); each person needs the other. Members should care for each other. Chapter 12 is followed by the chapter on love (13). With these directions all can work together to demonstrate to the world the ideal of the body of Christ.

Thought for the Day: *Prophecies cease, tongues are stilled, knowledge will pass away, but love never fails.*

Spiritual Gifts

Scripture Reading: I Corinthians 12:4-13

Key Verse: *All these are the work of the same Spirit, and he gives them to each one, just as he determines (I Corinthians 12:11).*

Meditation: Paul lists gifts of the Spirit evidently being manifest in the Corinthian Church:

Wisdom, the words spoken to instruct the hearers with God's message for them personally (Acts 4:8-12) spoken through Peter by the Holy Spirit.

Knowledge: Similar to a prophetic utterance, but deals with the present instead of the future. Peter spoke with the gift of knowledge when he understood Ananias and Sapphira had held back some of the price of the sold land and were deceiving the church (Acts 5:1-3).

Faith: The ability to believe God would supply needs and to pray with that assurance. I know a missionary with this great faith.

Gifts of Healing and the working of **Miracles:** I have not seen these personally, but friends who work in countries like India and Indonesia have described such gifts and the astounding results for the glory of God. God chooses to use these gifts and results where there is the need and the people will give the credit to God.

Prophecy: the ability to speak about something that would happen in the future, very similar to discernment. I have met people with **Discernment** and a kind of prophetic ability. This gift can be easily misused, and gives a heavy responsibility to those who are so gifted.

Tongues and the Interpretation of Tongues: These are to be used as partners so that those who hear the unknown language will understand what is being said and will be inspired, educated or directed by the Spirit. This gift seems to be different from the gift of languages described in Acts when the gospel was being given to many different language groups and they all understood the message.

Thought for the Day: *We are all members of the body of Christ, each with the gift or gifts the Holy Spirit has given us to bring health and energy to everyone in the fellowship and to reflect the love of God.*

Prayer and Healing

Scripture Reading: James 5:13-20

Key Verse: *He should call the elders of the church to pray over him (James 5:14).*

Meditation: Regardless of whether the source of our sickness is physical, emotional or spiritual, James gives both the sick person and the church valuable advice. These healing principles have been employed by the church throughout history and are relevant for us today.

The sick person should not be passive about the illness. While the sick person, for many reasons, may not be able to pray with strong faith for his own healing, yet he must exercise some faith and some initiative. He must have enough faith to ask the spiritual leaders of the church to pray for his healing.

James did not direct the sick person to seek out a faith healer, but rather the elders of the church. This sound advice recognizes that spiritual gifts should be exercised primarily within the context of the body of Christ. In that way, there is always mutual accountability, for it protects the person with the gift of healing from the temptation of abusing the gift.

Another reason for going to the church elders rather than to an individual is that most healing does not take place instantaneously, but gradually. We do not understand, but healing is sometimes postponed indefinitely. These kinds of varied circumstances require ongoing emotional and spiritual support that a traveling faith healer cannot provide. The directive to *call the elders* as opposed to calling one elder suggests that the gift of healing needs to be exercised by the church as the whole rather than by an individual.

Thought for the Day: *Any sickness in the church should alert the whole church to prayer.*

Healing Step Two

Scripture Reading: James 5:13-20

Key Verse: *...and anoint him with oil in the name of the Lord (James 5:14b).*

Meditation: The second step in the healing process: The spiritual leaders of the church anoint the sick person with oil. Oil in the Bible was used for a variety of purposes, which sheds additional light about the usage here.

In Bible times oil symbolized natural medicine. It was commonly accepted that whenever it was applied to the skin it would assist in the release of the God-given healing power resident in the body. In Luke 11 the Good Samaritan poured oil and wine into the wound of the seriously hurt man by the roadside.

At other times oil was used in consecrating priests or kings when they took office. It signified that the person anointed with oil was being set apart for God's special purpose. This use of oil suggests that the person is not to seek healing only, but also to use the restored health to serve God better.

Oil most often symbolized the Holy Spirit. Those anointing the sick person are to look beyond the oil directly to the Holy Spirit Himself for His supernatural touch. Since the Holy Spirit already indwells the believer, He will, as Paul teaches us in Romans 8:11b, *give life to your bodies through his Spirit who lives in you.* In this same context, Paul affirms that He, the Holy Spirit, is the One who raised Jesus from the dead.

Thought for the Day: *The power for healing is the same power that raised Jesus from the dead.*

Prayer Believes a Higher Law

Scripture Reading: Matthew 17:14-22

Key Verse: *Nothing will be impossible for you (Matthew 17:20b).*

Meditation: Dr. Taguchi, hematologist at Tokyo's Children's Hospital, outlined for us the predictable course of aplastic anemia in our five-year-old daughter.   His prognosis was guarded, but his personal direction was "Don't waste money on treatment."

Weighed down with his human evaluation, we left his office on feet of lead.   The doctor's scientific analysis left no room for intermediary causes.   But at our home shortly afterwards, a Japanese believer came with flowers and a card.   Without saying anything, she bowed deeply with tears in her eyes and left us quietly, as she had come.   Inside the card she had penned this Scripture, *With man this is impossible but with God all things are possible* (Matthew 19:26).

The words were her testimony.   Only a few years earlier she herself had the diagnosis of fatal tuberculosis.   She had come to our Christian tent meeting as a last resort.   When she believed in Christ as her Savior, she suddenly began to experience His healing.   She knew by her own experience that faith and prayer had put her in touch with a power greater than any medical evaluation could explain.

We learned through our daughter's gradual recovery that God can, if He chooses, overrule one law with another to effect a miracle.   A miracle is not the breaking or suspending of a law, but the operation of another law that we finite beings know nothing about.   God is the Creator and Sovereign over every law, so prayer to Him offers possibilities as unlimited as His dominion over our world.

Thought for the Day: *What may seem supernatural to me is very natural to the One who is Almighty.*

Misconceptions of Prayer

Scripture Reading: Matthew 6:5-8

Key Verse: *But when you pray, go into your room, close the door and pray to your Father who is unseen (Matthew 6:6a).*

Meditation: Whenever Jesus, the Incarnate Son, says anything about prayer I determine to listen and become a practitioner. First, He tells us how not to pray. While there is nothing wrong with praying in public, yet Jesus warns us lest we pray horizontally to men rather than vertically to God. Public prayer should not be used for public display. Piety directed towards men will be unnoticed by God. Evangelical believers, too, must be on guard lest they use public prayer for witnessing evangelism and become ostentatious.

The common mistake people were making was thinking that repetitive prayer would be more efficacious. This quantitative preoccupation was really pagan in origin, for they tried through their much asking to fatigue the gods into answering them. This whole idea would make God into a grudging giver. No wonder Martin Luther advised, "Prayers should be brief, frequent and intense."

Jesus also corrects our view as to the place of prayer: For the Jewish person, the ultimate place was in the temple. For us, that sacred place may be our church altar. Jesus, however, insists that any room will do, even a supply room, provided the door can be locked to shut out distractions. Besides, it is our private, not our public prayer, that best tests our motives as to whether it is for human praise or divine approval.

Thought for the Day: *A secular room can be made sacred if our motive is to be seen of God and not of men.*

The Wrong Way to Pray

Scripture Reading: Luke 18:8-14

Key Verse: *The Pharisee stood up and prayed about himself (Luke 18:11a).*

Meditation: A young boy asked his father, "Daddy, we read in the Bible that Moses, Isaiah and others saw God and heard Him speak to them. Why, then, doesn't anyone see or hear God today?" The father hesitated and then answered wisely, "Perhaps, son, we are not bowing low enough to see him." This really was at the heart of the Pharisee's problem. He stood unbowed before God and missed seeing Him.

When Moses saw God in the desert, he immediately hid his face and was afraid to look up. Isaiah the prophet immediately fell prostrate in the temple doorway, crying out, "Alas, for me. I am going to die." A person having a genuine encounter with God displays humility, a sense of God's holiness, discernment of hidden sin and a desire to live ethically with obedience to the vision. Sadly, not one of these evidences of a genuine encounter with God can be detected in the Pharisee.

The Pharisee's prayers were not actually addressed to God. We do believe God will listen to every sincere prayer directed to Him, but the Pharisee was not talking to God, but with himself about himself. It appears he was hoping that others in the temple would be as impressed with him as he was.

Thought for the Day: *Help us, Lord, to bow our hearts before you so that we will hear you speak to us.*

The Wrong Way to Pray

Scripture Reading: Luke 18:8-14

Key Verse: *The Pharisee stood up and prayed (Luke 18:11a).*

Meditation: The two men went to the temple for the same purpose, to pray. But the intent to pray is where the similarity ends. The way they prayed and the outcome of their prayers was radically different. The Pharisee went home as he came; the publican went home justified before God by divine grace.

Thankfully, this particular organized religious sect of the Pharisee no longer exists. Interestingly, however, the spirit of the Pharisees is still very much alive and well even in the best Bible-believing churches. Churches who boast of "what we don't do" are particularly vulnerable. The Pharisees wrongly interpreted holiness as withdrawal from the world, a sign of mere negative goodness. Jesus, on the other hand, modeled positive goodness by going into the world and changing people through the Gospel.

The Pharisee's body language tells us his attitude before God. He was so focused on himself that he could not perceive where he was standing and what was happening around him. Close to his entrance to the temple he could have seen where the priest had placed the sin offering on the altar. Within a few yards there was that large curtain behind which dwelt the awesome holy presence of God. But in the midst of this sacred atmosphere the Pharisee's heart is tilted upward in pride. Instead of focusing on the altar or the sacred curtain, his roving eyes fixate on the publican. No wonder he left the temple as he came, full of himself.

Thought for the Day: *If we look at those around us rather than looking to God, we will surely miss experiencing the gift of God's grace.*

Overcoming Barriers to Prayer

Scripture Reading: Luke 11:1-13,18:1-8

Key Verse: *And will not God bring about justice for his chosen ones who cry out to him day and night? (Luke 18:7)*

Meditation: These twin parables on prayer are often mistakenly understood as parables of comparison rather than parables of contrast. But God is not like the reluctant neighbor or the insensitive judge whose unwillingness we must somehow overcome by our prayers. These unbiblical images of God are a serious barrier to a growing prayer life for many Christians.

Prayer is not overcoming God's reluctance. Rather prayer is the means by which we access God's willingness to work. We, by prayer, open ourselves to serve as channels and workers together with God. Prayer is not man's invention, but God's plan. God appointed two other members of the Trinity to assist us. Jesus is at God's right hand and the Holy Spirit is within us.

Another barrier we must overcome is the adoption of certain role models for valid prayer. We tend to think we must emulate people like Paul, Martin Luther or John Wesley, who prayed non-stop for hours. This imposed standard discourages many from attempting to grow in prayer. While we thank God for the marathon prayers, we know God also uses "sprinter" prayers, short but intense. God does not measure our prayers by the length, but by our heartfelt desire to please Him and do His will.

Thought for the Day: *My prayer goal: Seek to saturate in prayer everything I attempt for God so that my service for God does not exceed my devotion to Him.*

God's Power in Prayer

Scripture Reading: Matthew 16:13-20

Key Verse: *...whatever you bind on earth will be bound in heaven and whatever you loose on earth will be loosed in heaven (Matthew 16:19b).*

Meditation: Most of us have heard people say rather dejectedly, "Well, I can't do much for God anymore, but I guess I can still pray." The clear inference is that prayer is about one notch higher than complete inactivity. Oswald Chambers would disagree; he said that prayer is not just preparation for work; it is the real work.

Jesus teaches us in this chapter that ordinary people have the potential of exercising extraordinary power through prayer. The keys that Jesus promised to Peter were not limited to him, but for all who confess "You are the Christ, the son of the Living God." The prayer of even the youngest Christian who seeks to live in the Spirit has the potential of actually paralyzing the power of darkness.

As we bind Satan on earth in the name of Jesus, we discover in the course of time that it has already been done in heaven. So the act of binding Satan's power, or loosing God's power is never lost or wasted. Our human waiting is only that period of time during which God is clearing up other matters to make room for the answer.

Since the power of Hades could not prevail against Jesus, we can also be confident that no strongholds or fortifications of Satan will restrain Christ's mandate to evangelize the world. The outcome of the Church's mission has already been predicated in victory: "And the gospel of the kingdom will be preached in all the world as a testimony to all nations, and then the end will come" (Matthew 24: 14).

Thought for the Day: *We go against Satan's power not in order to win the victory, but to announce the victory Christ has already won for us.*

When the Church Prays

Scripture Reading: Acts 12:1-25

Key Verse: *But the church was earnestly praying for him (Acts 12:5b).*

Meditation: If someone invited you to pray, saying, "It is really a matter of life and death," would you take him seriously? Some Bible scholars believe that the difference between what happened to James (who died by Herod's word) and Peter (who was miraculously released) can be attributed to this specially called prayer meeting. There is no record in Acts of a similar all-church prayer meeting for James. If King Herod were alive, he, too, would have to confess, albeit reluctantly, that even for him that prayer meeting was a matter of life and death.

With the imprisonment of Peter, that leader of the twelve, the church was plunged into its second deep crisis, but they did not panic. They prayed. They did not know when or where the next blow from Herod would fall. In desperation, they fell on their knees before God. Even though their faith in God was not perfect, yet some remarkable things began to happen.

While they prayed, a literal transfer of power took place. Suddenly pompous Herod does not hold the authority, but the praying church comes in control. Three events follow: First, the angels come to rescue Peter. Next, God's special delivery messengers open locks and awaken Peter. Then, not long afterward, Herod, the vainglorious king is struck and eaten by worms. *But the word of God continued to increase and spread.*

Thought for the Day: *Prayer is that mysterious connecting link between our human situation and God's sovereign power, a life and death matter of importance.*

Two's and Three's of Prayer

Scripture Reading: Matthew 18:19,20

Key Verse: *Again I tell you that if two of you on earth agree about anything you ask for, it will be done for you by my Father in heaven (Matthew 18:19).*

Meditation: Earlier Jesus taught the importance of individual praying. Here, the complementary truth of fellowship in prayer is stressed. The Christian needs both in order to develop fully the potential in prayer.

The immediate context of this sweeping promise was given in relation to dealing with the *brother who sins against you.* However, there is no indication it should be limited to that concern alone. Admittedly this "agreeing on anything and getting everything" sounds like a dangerous doctrine. We are tempted to edit this statement and make it more restricted. But it is dangerous to limit what Jesus promises. An equally perilous thing would be to overlook the obvious constraints that Jesus himself stated.

Two or three people who happen to show up at prayer meeting cannot decide to tell God what they need. The stated condition, **"gathering in His name,"** implies the real gatherer is Jesus. In other words, the two or three are the ones who are obedient to Christ's initiative to pray.

Praying in Christ's name indicates that our requests must have His sanction and that our ultimate motive in asking is to please Him. To meet this condition we must make a radical surrender to Christ's lordship and be sensitized in our asking by the indwelling Holy Spirit.

The *anything we ask* suggests the final condition as *being definite in prayer.* Too many prayers are so generalized that they become vaporized before they reach God.

Thought for the Day: *Together we pray specifically in obedience to Christ to receive the answers He promised.*

Prayer and Perseverance

Scripture Reading: Luke 18:1-6

Key Verse: *Then Jesus told his disciples a parable to show them that they should always pray and not give up (Luke 18:1).*

Meditation: If I were to ask you, "Since you became a Christian, what has been the most difficult discipline for you to maintain?" I can almost guess your answer. Even Billy Graham, when asked that question by interviewer, Larry King, replied, "The greatest struggle in my Christian life has been to maintain a constant prayer life." If this is true of Billy Graham, it is probably true for most of us as well.

An anonymous survey of ministers' prayer time revealed that the average prayer time was one to two minutes a day. Prayer is not just a struggle for laity, but for the clergy, as well. In fact, this need for help in prayer dates all the way back to the disciples themselves who after observing Jesus in prayer, asked, "Lord, teach us to pray." I am encouraged by the response of Jesus. He did not scold his disciples for asking for help. Neither did he relegate prayer to some mystical realm, but he immediately set out to teach them to pray. Prayer is not just caught; it is also taught.

In this teaching of Jesus, He elevates prayer to a new level of fighting against all that would cause us to collapse spiritually. Prayer, then, is not just some catharsis by which we exorcise negative struggles. Jesus implies that prayer is our primary source of spiritual power and energy. When Paul describes the Christian's armor, he sets prayer by itself, inferring that prayer is the means by which each part of the armor is more effectively used.

Thought for the Day: *Let us be open to Christ's admonishment to us to follow Him in prayer that brings the power to keep us going for Him.*

Following Christ's Example in Prayer (1)

Scripture Reading: John 17:1-26

Key Verse: *That the world may believe that you have sent me (John 17:22b).*

Meditation: Have you ever thought, "If only I could have heard Jesus pray, how different my prayer life would be?" We can hear Jesus pray in John 17, recorded verbatim, the longest continuing prayer recorded in the gospels.

We believe it was preserved to prefigure Christ's ongoing intercession in heaven for us. It teaches us Christ's primary concerns for the church, and to serve as a model for our praying.

"He who least needs to pray for himself prays most effectively for others." Jesus is certainly the master praying person. Even though He was still in the incarnate body facing the greatest test of His humanity, He made only one request for Himself, "And now, Father, glorify Me in your presence with the glory I had with You before the world began."

We know the path back to that glorification was routed through Calvary. The clock of history for the crucifixion was set back in eternity, for "the Lamb that was slain from the creation of the world." No wonder this high priestly prayer is sometimes referred to as "The Prayer of Consecration," for Jesus was both the priest and the sacrifice, reminding us that intercession is never without cost.

Jesus prays for His disciples and for those who believe, "That they may be one" (17:11), a means to world evangelization. He prayed that the "world would believe that You sent Me" (17:22b). Christian unity and effective Christian witnessing are inseparably connected. Only as the Church manifests the oneness that transcends the diversity of denominations, cultures and races, will the message of Christ be credible.

Thought for the Day: *Help me, Jesus, to remember that today you are still praying for the Church and for me just as You did in this chapter.*

Following Christ's Example in Prayer (2)

Scripture Reading: John 17:6-26

Key Verse: *As You sent Me into the world, I have sent them into the world (John 17:18).*

Meditation: Jesus' first request was for the church to manifest her oneness "that the world might believe." Four other specific requests follow:

1. "...that they may have the full measure of My joy within them" (17:13b). Christ's joy cost His death on the cross. He..."did not consider equality with God something to be grasped...and became obedient to death, even the death on the cross" (Philippians 2:6b, 8b). His joy was providing salvation for the whole world. Jesus prays for the kind of redemptive joy for us found through pain and concern for others.

2. "My prayer is not that you take them out of the world, but that you protect them from the evil one" (17:15). He wanted us to stay in the world and be victorious over the evil one, not just for our safety, but to be a resource to reach others.

3. "Sanctify them...I have sent them into the world" (17a, 18b). Christ does not want His church to pattern her lifestyle after the Pharisee, like the holiness model of withdrawal from the world. Rather, He wants us to follow the evangelistic model of going into the world to transform it.

4. "...and to see my glory..." (17:24). Christ wants His followers to experience the very ultimate of fellowship with Him, not just after death, but now. "Blessed are the pure in heart for they shall see God" (Matthew 5:8).

Thought for the Day: *I will help change my world by letting the radical prayer of Jesus change me.*

Why Pray? (3)

Scripture Reading: Matthew 6:5-8

Key Verse: *...for your heavenly Father knows what you need before you ask him (Matthew 6:8).*

Meditation: I was a very young Christian when I left home and enrolled in Bible college to prepare for the ministry. Along with two other freshmen, I was placed in a room with one upper classman. I noticed immediately that the upper classman had certain prescribed devotional habits that he followed conscientiously. I observed on the first evening that after reading his Bible, he switched off the desk light and knelt by his bed to pray. I decided to imitate him, but he kept praying long after I had gone over my regular prayer routine several times.

Gradually, I began to learn the difference between my idea of prayer and his practice. I had thought of prayer primarily as "informing God of those spiritual needs which I and other people had." So my prayer requests were naturally narrow and restrictive, leaving many of my other personal interests unexpressed because I assumed God was interested only in "spiritual" concerns. In contrast, my roommate's prayer was relational, a means of getting to know God better and becoming His friend. Because of his growing intimacy with God, he felt free to lift his total life before the Lord for review and renewed direction.

It is only natural to ask, since God, because of His omniscience knows all about our needs, why is prayer necessary? While prayer certainly does not exclude asking, it goes beyond that to the act of opening our whole lives before God and inviting Him to respond in His wisdom and love toward us. Prayer is also necessary to free the hand of God to work through us; it gives Him permission to effect what He desires to do with and for us.

Thought for the Day: *I will pray today realizing God desires a growing trust-filled relationship with Him rather than just being informed of our most pressing spiritual needs.*

Following Christ's Direction in Prayer (4)

Scripture Reading: Luke 11:1-4

Key Verse: *When He finished, one of His disciples said to Him, "Lord, teach us to pray, just as John taught his disciples" (Luke 11:6).*

Meditation: The disciples encouraged me by their honesty, "Lord, teach us to pray." I am sure that to express their inability to pray after two years with Jesus must have been a difficult confession to make. But Jesus did not rebuke them for not being farther along in their prayer life. I am also motivated to learn more about prayer since Jesus seems to indicate prayer is not just "caught," but there are things that can be "taught" through listening to the teaching of Christ.

In this model prayer for the disciples, Jesus underlines three revolutionary truths about prayer: First, we are taught we can actually take a "family-like" approach to God and call Him "Father." We are not to be intimidated like the Jews of His day, who mistakenly attached such sacredness to God's name they were afraid to say it aloud. Jesus encourages us to cut through all the sense of God's inaccessibility and remoteness by simply addressing God as "our Father," "our heavenly Father."

Second, while we should develop this warm approach to God, we should not become sentimentally irreverent. We should always keep in mind our Father is also the transcendent God and ruler of the heavens who deserves our worship, reverence and awe.

Third, Jesus portrays God as our Father in heaven, yet we are encouraged to bring Him all of our earthly and human concerns. Things like daily bread, anything we need on a given day; forgiveness, so we can forgive others; deliverance from temptation, and from the evil one.

Thought for the Day: *Since prayer is both "taught" and "caught," I will intentionally seek to incorporate Christ's model prayer for the disciples into my way of praying.*

Praying to the Real God of the Bible (5)

Scripture Reading: Matthew 7:7-12

Key Verse: *If you, then, though you are evil, know how to give good gifts to your children, how much more will your Father in heaven give good gifts to those who ask Him? (Matthew 7:11)*

Meditation: "God is a better God than you think He is" was the way one man experienced his pilgrimage in prayer. For the first 15 years of his Christian life his subconscious image of God was that of a stingy personality who gave just enough to get by.

But one day he was challenged by Matthew 7:11, so he decided to put it to a test. He had to admit as he looked over his prayer list that it reflected none of his personal desires. He had purposely repressed them, thinking they were not sufficiently spiritual in nature to warrant bringing them to God.

Recalling he had three things in life he always wanted to do, he prayed, hesitantly at first, "God, if You are really a better Father than I have given You credit for being, these are the three things I have always wanted to do that I am sharing with You. I do not deserve what I am about to ask, and if You decide not to give them, I will not be upset. But if You choose to demonstrate Your personalized love and interest in me, here are the things I would like to do."

He left on a trip soon after, and when he returned home several weeks later, to his great amazement all three requests had been fulfilled. Someone has said, "When we pray, coincidences happen; when we do not pray, they don't."

Thought for the Day: *Since our prayer requests reflect our image of God, I will re-examine my prayer list to see if they reflect the truths of the key verse for today.*

Praying to the Real God of the Bible (6)

Scripture Reading: Luke 15:1-32

Key Verse: *...his father saw him and was filled with compassion for him; he ran to his son, threw his arms around him and kissed him (Luke 15:20b).*

Meditation: "Unless you see and understand God as Jesus portrays Him in this chapter, you will never really know the God of the Bible," said one of my seminary professors in a class on parables. That unforgettable statement has often prompted me to return to this chapter to rediscover what God is really like. It helps me counter-balance warped images of God that hinder me in prayer.

Chapter 15 of Luke is about lost things and lost people: a lost sheep, a lost coin, a lost younger son in the far country, and a lost older brother at home. But Jesus reminds us that lostness is never impersonal: The sheep is lost to the shepherd; the coin is lost to the woman; the two sons are lost to the father. This image of God reminds us that all lost people are lost to Him.

We are also motivated to pray because Jesus teaches us that lost things and lost people are still valuable. They are so valuable as to deserve around the clock searching until they are found or they return. This is the heart of the God to whom we pray.

Jesus reminds us that regardless how things and people happen to get lost, their being found is a cause for celebration and not for rebuke. The God to whom we pray is waiting, watching and longing for lost people to return to Him. Even if they make a little effort and just turn toward His house, He is the one to run to meet them.

Thought for the Day: *The God to whom we pray is waiting to lavish His love and forgiveness on us even before we complete our confession.*

Praying with a Warped Image of God (7)

Scripture Reading: Luke 11:1-13

Key Verse: *...Don't bother me; the door is already locked and my children are with me in bed (Luke 11:7).*

Meditation: "The actual amount of time the average Christian prays daily is about two minutes." While I want to believe this statistic is not a true sampling, yet it gives a disturbing finding about the actual practice of prayer.

If "we are just too busy to pray," the solution could be to get a time manager to rearrange our schedule. The real reason we do not pray more may be more complex.

In this parable Jesus alludes to the defective unbiblical image of God many people hold. If our dominant image of God is that of the reluctant neighbor who does not want to be inconvenienced, then we probably will not pray very often except in a crisis. Is that not the only time some people pray?

When a pastor responded to a requested appointment, the man startled him by saying, "Pastor, I need a new God. I grew up in a home where God was described like a policeman who only appeared when His law was broken. But since coming to your church I have heard about a God who is a loving Father who wants to give good gifts to His children. He is the kind of God I need."

Could it be that in order to pray more, some of us need to shed our old misconception of God and embrace the real God of the Bible?

Thought for the Day: *God, our heavenly Father, has a 24-hour open door policy, so before we knock, His door is already open.*

Praying with a One Sided Image of God (8)

Scripture Reading: Luke 18:1-8

Key Verse: *Yet because the widow keeps bothering me, I will see that she gets justice, so that she won't eventually wear me out with her coming (Luke 18:5).*

Meditation: I vividly remember the visit and the emotions: We went with a gaily-wrapped gift to the home of parents with a new baby in the parish. But to our astonishment the father asked, "What's in the package, a stone?" I am sure he intended some kind of humor, but it was not funny at the time. I wanted to say, "I am not the kind of pastor who wraps up a stone and gives it to a newborn child."

Remember, Jesus once asked, "Which of you, if a son asks for bread, will you give him a stone? If you, then, though evil, know how to give good gifts to your children, how much more will your Father in heaven give good gifts to those who ask Him" (Matthew 7:9,11).

Jesus chose two negative images in the twin parables on prayer (the insensitive judge and the reluctant neighbor). Apparently, He chose this method of teaching because people, subconsciously, have projected these sub-biblical images on God. Who wants to knock on the door of a reluctant God or beg before an insensitive God? Could it be these warped images of God are some of the greatest barriers to overcome in order to build a growing prayer life?

In strong contrast to these negative images, Jesus teaches us that even if a reluctant neighbor will give in to a persistent request, and even if an insensitive judge will give in to the demands of a helpless widow, then how much more will your Father in heaven give good gifts to His children!

Thought for the Day: *Before you begin praying to God, correct your image of Him until you see Him as so much better than any human father could ever be.*

The Good News about the Holy Spirit and Prayer (9)

Scripture Reading: Luke 11:1-13

Key Verse: *...How much more will your Father in heaven give the Holy Spirit to those who ask Him! (Luke 11:13b)*

Meditation: At the close of a missionary conference in Oregon a lady said, "Before coming to the conference my husband vowed he would never pray in public, but after hearing about the Holy Spirit and prayer, he changed his mind."

Although I personally had been taught the wonderful truth of Jesus being our advocate at God's right hand, I somehow missed the complementary truth of the Holy Spirit being our advocate right inside of us. How encouraging to discover later the two intercessors, one above and one within us.

Actually, the teaching of Jesus is very clear at this point. Remember the disciples had seen Him praying. They asked to be taught to pray. Jesus ended His discourse with, "If you really want to learn to pray, ask the Father for the Holy Spirit, the Spirit of prayer."

The Holy Spirit is the Father's highest gift He can give to His children. Through the Holy Spirit's indwelling we can actually partake of God's friendship. God actually comes inside us both to talk to us and to listen when we pray. The Holy Spirit in us is also God's pledge of His ongoing friendship with us.

I am aware these words about asking the Father for the Holy Spirit were spoken before Pentecost and now, in a sense, that need has already been met. Yet I ask you, have you intentionally received and released the Holy Spirit to be the Spirit of prayer in you?

Thought for the Day: *Since God is the kind of Father who hears our requests, why not ask Him now to release the Spirit of prayer in you?*

More Good News about the Holy Spirit and Prayer

Scripture Reading: Romans 8:26,27

Key Verse: *In the same way, the Spirit helps us in our weaknesses...*
(Romans 8:26a).

Meditation: When I became a Christian at the age of 16, because of my awe and reverence for God, I had a number of fears. I feared unless I grew spiritually very quickly I would grieve the Holy Spirit and lose Him. I still carried that lurking spiritual anxiety inside me, even after leaving for Japan as a young missionary. I am afraid it often kept me from being honest about my weaknesses, which seemed too threatening to deal with at the time.

Because of this inordinate fear of losing the Holy Spirit, I can still vividly remember the moment when the liberating truth of the key verse dawned on my spiritual consciousness. I wanted to shout the good news everywhere that my weaknesses do not cause the Holy Spirit to leave me. On the contrary, it is my very weakness that calls for the Spirit's help. Acknowledged weaknesses are, in fact, the primary qualification for the Spirit's assistance.

When our older daughter was five she had aplastic anemia and she was completely dependent on blood donors for several months. Our second daughter, only 16 months younger, also needed a lot of support during her sister's hospitalization. But I noticed that each time I was away from home, upon returning, I would ask about our older daughter first. Somehow her vulnerability made her especially precious to me.

Essentially Paul is saying here that our weakness endears us to the Holy Spirit. Other translations read, "our present limitations," "our infirmities call for His aid," "He takes hold with us in our weakness" and "He lends a hand with our weaknesses."

Thought for the Day: *Since my weaknesses qualify me for the Holy Spirit's help, I will not be afraid to be transparent before Him and others.*

More "Good News" About
the Holy Spirit and Prayer

Scripture Reading: Romans 8:26, 27

Key Verse: *...we do not know what we ought to pray for... (Romans 8:26).*

Meditation: Most of us can identify with Paul's frustration when he asked God, "Why this infirmity; why don't You remove it?" But as Paul experienced, most of our prayers for the removal of "troublesome infirmities" are not answered as hoped. The answer to our prayers may come in a totally different way than expected. In the process of our trials we find ourselves supernaturally sustained by the Holy Spirit Himself.

The original New Testament word for "help" is much broader than our English usage: It is a composite word indicating the Spirit's help is all embracing. Whatever our need may be at a given moment, we can count on His adequacy and support. At times the Holy Spirit may actually "step into the harness" and help us pull the load. At other times He keeps us from being completely crushed or overwhelmed. The prime secret behind "the perseverance of the saints" is found in this unremitting assistance of the Spirit.

The particular weakness Paul identifies here in Romans 8 relates to all of us: "...we do not know what we ought to pray for..." We could paraphrase that to mean that Paul often found himself in situations where, because of inner pressures or external circumstances, he did not know how to pray. Being an apostle did not give Paul immediate access in understanding the complexities of life, but he was confident of the Spirit's constant and divine undergirding.

For all of us, in addition to how to pray and what to pray for, there is that ongoing struggle of continuing to pray and not knowing how to pray as we ought. The "good news," however, is that our human extremities, when acknowledged, become a divine opportunity for the Holy Spirit to pray in us.

Thought for the Day: *Each time I pray I will acknowledge I cannot pray as I ought without the help of the Holy Spirit.*

More "Good News" About
the Holy Spirit and Prayer

Scripture Reading: Romans 8:26,27

Key Verse: *...but the Spirit Himself intercedes with us with groans that words cannot express (Romans 8:26b).*

Meditation: I can still see the frail, silver-haired former missionary leaning heavily on her cane as she slowly made her way to the place where I was standing. She looked up with shining blue eyes and said, "Because of my age and arthritis I can no longer kneel and pray like I used to do as a younger missionary in China. But, praise God, I know I can still touch God, for the Holy Spirit is praying in me and for me."

Sometimes the Holy Spirit helps our weakness in prayer by directly prompting us to pray. Zachariah referred to the Holy Spirit as the "Spirit of supplication" (Zachariah 12:10), the asking Spirit. The essential nature of the Holy Spirit is to pray. At other times the Holy Spirit helps us to recall an appropriate scripture or promise we need to anchor our prayers so we are not tossed about by subjective feelings. In fact, we should intentionally open our hearts to the Spirit's prompting as we read the Bible devotionally.

Paul not only assures us of divine help in prayer, but he tells us specifically how the Spirit prays: "He intercedes for us with groans that words cannot express." I am simply awed to think the divine Holy Spirit is groaning in prayer in every Christian. Not only does this knowledge give me a whole new appreciation for the Holy Spirit, but it also creates a new expectancy of the potential of prayer. For at the very time I may be struggling most in prayer with poorly phrased sentences and inarticulate feelings, I may actually be praying most eloquently because the Holy Spirit comes to my rescue.

Thought for the Day: *Whenever I pray, the Holy Spirit superimposes His strong intercession over my prayers of weakness and makes them efficacious before God.*

More "Good News" About
the Holy Spirit and Prayer

Scripture Reading: Romans 8:26-28

Key Verse: *...the Spirit intercedes for the saints in accordance with God's will (Romans 8:27b).*

Meditation: A touching story is told of an orphan boy in England: One day an elderly minister stopped by the orphanage to speak to the children. He closed his talk with, "Regardless how desperate you may be in life, if you will stop long enough to pray, God will surely come to your rescue."

Some years later the words of the minister came back to the boy, so he decided to go and pray. He knelt down by a tree and started to repeat the letters of the alphabet. Soon someone from the local church walking nearby heard the recitation. Intrigued, he saw the boy by the trees and said, "What are you doing?" The boy replied, "I'm praying." "No you're not," the man answered, "you are just saying the alphabet." "I don't really know how to pray, sir, but I thought if I just gave God the letters of the alphabet, He would put them together into a prayer for me."

This story actually illustrates the secret behind some of those amazing answers to prayer that were offered with an utter sense of human weakness. The Holy Spirit literally took our "groans and sighs" and translated them into prayers. Since the Holy Spirit knows the will of God in advance, He always intercedes for us "according to the will of God," and that is why those prayers were answered.

While most of us often quote Romans 8:28 we fail to see it in its context. Paul's confidence "that in all things God works for good of those who love Him..." is preceded by the promise of the Holy Spirit's help to all those who do not know how to pray.

Thought for the Day: *I will be confident today that because of the Spirit's intercession for me, all that happens to me God will somehow fit into a pattern for my good.*

My German-Russian Ancestors

Scripture Reading: Judges 6:11-15

Key Verse: *...My clan is the weakest in Manasseh, and I am the least in my family (Judges 6:15b).*

Meditation: Put yourself in Gideon's place and you will understand his negative response to God's call. Israel had just come out of 400 years of oppressive slavery in Egypt, and now they were in bondage again to a nomadic tribe, the Midianites. The tribe of Manasseh, not being noted for any significant past accomplishments, could not boast of any present prominent leaders. Gideon, being the youngest of the family, sensed his inferiority both from family and from his age.

The Schultz/Schoen family clan, my ancestors, were simple, hardworking German farmers in Russia. Catherine II, a German princess, at 16 married Peter II of Russia. After her husband's early death she became Empress of Russia and ruled ironhanded from 1730 to 1796. She invited German farmers to Russia promising land, religious freedom, exemption from military service and taxes, and preservation of the German language and culture. My ancestors joined this migration in the late 1700's. From Germany and Poland they settled in Ukraine, the breadbasket of Russia even today.

Their good life halted, however, in 1914, the beginning of World War I. Russia fought Germany and in order to secure Russia's borders against feared invasion, most immigrants were shipped inland, some as far as Siberia. German males, like my father and his brother, my Uncle Ted, were inducted into the Russian military. This forced military assignment continued after World War I and the beginning of the revolution that pitted the Czar's troops against the Communists.

Thought for the Day: *When Christian immigrants lose their freedom they either succumb to slavery or choose to become refugees. My parents chose to become refugees.*

My Parent's Decision to Leave Russia

Scripture Reading: Exodus 1:6-22

Key Verse: *Then a new king, who did not know about Joseph, came to power in Egypt (Exodus 1:8).*

Meditation: New kings or rulers rarely feel any sense of obligation for the promises their predecessors have made, especially to foreigners living in their land. Less than 100 years after the death of Catherine II the immigrant Germans faced this prevailing mood. Lenin and his Communist party seized control of the government after the abdication and subsequent assassinations of the last Czar and his whole family. New land reforms moved all of the farmers towards communal farming with the government demanding much of the harvest.

My father, Ewald, and my mother, Herta, were married in the middle of all this great political and social upheaval. As depicted in the musical, "Fiddler on the Roof," what happened to the Jewish people in Russia also happened to the Germans living there. On the positive side, this period of social restlessness resulted in a deep moving of the Holy Spirit among the lay people of the Lutheran churches. The "Bruber" were biblically well read and spiritually alive. Protracted prayers and evangelistic services resulted in the conversion of my parents. This was an important factor in their decision to emigrate to North America in 1926.

My parents and my mother's younger sister, Hannah, sold or gave away all their remaining possessions, boarded a ship and sailed for Halifax, Canada. Then they took a train to Edmonton, Alberta where mother's brother, Emil, had immigrated earlier. The farewell to their parents and relatives, except for Ted, my father's brother, was final, and they never saw that part of their families again.

Thought for the Day: *Like Israel's growing uneasiness in the Egyptian land of Goshen, God used the pressures of the Communists to move many German people out of Russia.*

Life on the Alberta Frontier

Scripture Reading: Deuteronomy 7:7-12

Key Verse: *The Lord set his affection on you and chose you not because you were more numerous than other people; you were the fewest of all people (Deuteronomy 7:7).*

Meditation: God told Israel He heard their cry of distress and delivered them, not because they were strong or morally more righteous than their neighbors, but simply because He loved them. That, too, is the only reason I can give for God's rescuing my family from the next 70 years of communistic religious slavery in Russia. In a sense, it cost my parents a lot to leave Russia. They would not see their other family members again or be able to visit the graves of their first four children. They discovered quickly that life in Canada did not match the colorful brochures circulated in Russia. But I never once heard them voice any regret for deciding to come to Canada.

My mother's brother, Emil, who had immigrated earlier met them in Edmonton and helped them find work on a farm. After two years they were paid with a few cows, horses, chickens and hogs and moved to a 160-acre farm close to the village of New Sarepta. They bought the land on a 20-year mortgage from the Canadian Pacific Railroad. Except for a few acres, it was covered with trees that had to be removed by hand tools and hard labor with horses. Tractors did not appear until 20 years later.

I have only positive memories of early austere years in the home of an immigrant family. I cherish the values of the dignity of hard work, the reality of the short life of material possessions, the necessity to trust God daily for all necessities. The warmth of the church community surrounded us, giving us time to visit and care. If we were poor, we were not aware of our poverty.

Thought for the Day: *My parents' faith risk made it possible for all of us to be reared in an evangelical church with three graduating from Bible School.*

My Growing up Years

Scripture Reading: Psalm 68:1-6

Key Verse: *God sets the lonely in families; he leads forth prisoners with singing... (Psalms 68:6a).*

Meditation: Every religious refugee has felt the truths of this favorite psalm of the Israelites. My parents and thousands of others were motivated to leave Russia by this promise. An autocratic government would no longer coerce them, and they would have their own home and be able to enjoy real family life.

Our first home was a renovated granary, built quickly before the winter snows and frigid weather. Twins, Margaret and Norman, were born in June, and thanks to mother's making heavy feather covers, they survived the winter. Then, after I was born, followed by my sister, Gertrude, my folks built the second house, a two-story building 20 x 35 feet. Over a mile from our house the community provided a one-room schoolhouse and a teacher for eight grades. We walked that distance, rain or snow, until my high school days when we were then bussed to Leduc High School 15 miles away.

Next to my family the most significant shaping of my life and spiritual priorities I trace to my home church. Seven pietistic lay preachers who had experienced revival in Russia led our evangelical church people in Bible studies on any subject from Holiness to the Second Coming of Jesus. Whenever I return to my home area I visit the church cemetery to recall the memories of those departed loved ones and those godly saints who modeled for me the holy life.

Thought for the Day: *The most sacred memory of my childhood is that of my family and my church members on their knees in prayer.*

The Interventions of God in my Life

Scripture Reading: John 15:1-17

Key Verse: *You did not choose me, but I chose you… (John 15:16a).*

Meditation: In John 15:16 Jesus reminds the disciples how they became His followers. They did not have self-generated spiritual impulses of their own, but Jesus took the initiative and intentionally invited them one by one. Through the ministry of the Holy Spirit He still invites us individually today. This explains my conversion, one of the most unlikely candidates for the kingdom even 30 minutes before I was converted.

I remember sitting at the wall side of a long pew in church purposefully to avoid anyone inviting me to go forward. I felt safe against the wall with my friend, Herman Hiebner, sitting beside me as a buffer. I had not listened to the evangelist, the Reverend A. E. Stickel. I had blocked him out completely. But when the invitation hymn was being sung something very strange seemed to be happening to my friend beside me.

The hand with which he held the hymnbook started to shake making it difficult for me to follow the lines. Then he surprised me by grabbing my arm saying, "Helmut, let's go forward and get saved." With those words he turned and with me in tow, he walked to the altar. Before I fully realized what was happening I found myself standing at the altar before the whole congregation. Herman then knelt at the altar and began a prayer of repentance. I knelt beside him and found myself praying the same kind of prayer. After some time the Reverend Wurfel, our pastor, came and quoted I John 1:9, assuring us that God had heard our repentance and that we were now children of God.

Thought for the Day: *Most of us, like Saul of Tarsus, were resisting God, but we got saved because of the irresistible grace of God.*

The Interventions of God in My Life (2)

Scripture Reading: Amos 7:10-14

Key Verse: *Amos answered Amaziah, I was neither a prophet nor a prophet's son...but God took me from tending the flock and said to me, Go, prophesy to my people Israel (Amos 7:14).*

Meditation: Many ministers from farm backgrounds tend to identify with the prophet Amos. Amos was not born into a family of prophets nor had he attended the training school for prophets. His only claim to the high office of prophets was that God suddenly took him and commanded him, "Go and prophesy to my people Israel."

On the night that Herman and I were saved, the pastor encouraged us to give our testimony to the congregation. While I was speaking, something indefinable happened inside me. In retrospect, I believe that as I witnessed publicly, the Holy Spirit witnessed inwardly to my human spirit that I was now a child of God. Simultaneously, the Holy Spirit began to pour out God's love in my heart (Romans 5:5). I began to feel a spiritual concern for my unsaved friends and I actually expressed it. Also, hidden in that outpouring of divine love in my heart was the beginning of my call to preach.

Two months later, while attending Moravian Church services in our community, I heard what seemed an audible voice saying, "Helmut, I want you to be a minister." I tried to rationalize the call, thinking, "Oh, God is just testing my willingness to obey Him." But whenever our encouraging youth leader, Sadie Kublick, would ask me to have a part in the evening service, afterwards someone would say to me, "Helmut, isn't the Lord calling you to preach?" Finally, the Lord confronted me, saying, "Helmut, behind your pretended humility, you are not really trusting me to give you supernaturally what you do not have naturally. Rely on me; I will give you everything you need to be a minister."

Thought for the Day: *Effective ministry is ultimately determined not by human talent, but by the Holy Spirit's supernatural gifting.*

The Interventions of God in My Life (3)

Scripture Reading: Genesis 12:1-8

Key Verse: *The Lord had said to Abram, Leave your country, your people, and your father's household and go to the land I will show you (Genesis 12:1).*

Meditation: Genesis 12 tells us about Abraham's faith call to leave the known behind and start for an undisclosed destination without an address. Acts 7:2, however, gives us a clue, "The God of glory appeared to our father Abraham while he was still in Mesopotamia." Hidden in that revelation to Abraham was such an overwhelming display of divine glory that Abraham could never again question the divine authority of God. While he stopped for a while at Haran, perhaps at his father's incentive, God let him know this was not his final destination.

I have found great encouragement from the life of Abraham during the past 55 years. In retrospect, I believe that if we sincerely seek God's will, He will prod us out of our Haran's of indecision and help us get back on track again.

After two years of questioning God's will, I finally told my parents and the church people about my call. I also announced my intention to enroll in Bible school. No one acted surprised, and my parents said they would help me with some of the costs, provided they had good crops. I prayed for a bumper crop. During the first week in August, the crops started turning yellow, assuring us of abundance. But on that first Sunday in August an ominous cloud appeared, with hail suddenly blowing from the west. I could actually hear the rolling of the hail in the clouds as it approached with a powerful wind. Large hailstones driven by a 75 mile per hour wind mowed our crop down within 20 minutes. Humanly speaking, all that remained for me were dashed hopes, and at the best, postponed dreams.

Thought for the Day: *Genuine faith does not always understand what God is up to, but it does mean that He is with us and that we are ultimately not in the hands of fate, but in His hands.*

The Interventions of God in My Life (4)

Scripture Reading: Hebrews 11:1-6

Key Verse: *Now faith is being sure about what we hope for and certain of what we do not see... (Hebrews 11:1).*

Meditation: To me the verse is saying, "Faith is seeing with the eyes of the imagination what is not yet visible to my physical eyes." True faith implies implicit confidence in God's unchanging character and in His faithfulness to do what He has spoken to us personally or through the Scriptures. I am referring specifically to those promises that the Holy Spirit has personalized to our minds.

I will never forget the waves of disappointment rolling over me as I walked out to survey for myself the damage by the hail to the fields of wheat. Not one field was spared. But in the middle of my litany of complaining to God, He answered saying, "Helmut, if I want you to go to Bible College, I will open the way for you; just trust me." At that time, I was unaware of God's distant plans for me in faith missions, but God knew and this was His first step to teach me about faith.

Farmers around us plowed over the fields in which the grain had been too ripe to expect a second growth. Other fields were left, in hope the stubble would sprout and at least produce green feed for the cattle. Three days later a special visitor attended our weekly prayer meeting. Ewald Kadatz was a grain farmer who owned several sections of land. The hail had missed his fields, but he needed additional help to harvest his crops. He was a good friend of my parents and asked them if one of their boys could help him. By working long hours six days a week for the next seven weeks, I earned enough to pay for my first semester and part of the second.

Thought for the Day: *Faith is not so much a feeling of emotion, but a simple trust in the faithfulness of God even when human circumstances seem most perplexing.*

The Interventions of God in My Life (5)

Scripture Reading: Psalm 85:1-13

Key Verse: *Will you not revive us again, that your people may rejoice in you... (Psalm 85:6a).*

Meditation: The psalmist in chapter 85, writing after Israel returns from exile, outlines four truths about revival. Revival comes from God and cannot be generated by man. The human responsibility is to pray to God for revival. A genuine revival restores lost spiritual joy. The ultimate evidence of revival will be a refocused life from self to God.

With a mixture of excitement and anxiety, I arrived at Hillcrest Christian College in Medicine Hat, Alberta to relate to people I did not know. I did not expect to walk into a spiritual revival. The revival started in the girls' dorm after the Sunday evening service. Prayer and singing by the girls seemed to ignore the school's 11:00 p.m. curfew. The men in my dormitory realized they needed to be in prayer, also. After the initial time together, we paired off, a freshman with an upper classman, for heart searching and intercession.

My prayer partner, a senior named Art Brown, asked if I had placed my all on God's altar. He also inquired whether I had experienced deeper cleansing, filling and empowering of the Holy Spirit since my conversion. I admitted that I did not know what he was talking about, but I realized I could not minister without that power. He inquired if I would be willing to even be a missionary for God. I sincerely agreed and God revealed himself to me. I will share that in the next reading.

Thought for the Day: *The secret of continuous personal revival lies in keeping the living sacrifice, which is one's self, on God's altar.*

The Interventions of God in My Life (6)

Scripture Reading: Romans 12:1,2

Key Verse: *Therefore, I urge you...to offer your bodies a living sacrifice... (Romans 12:1a).*

Meditation: At a retreat someone observed, "It takes the average Christian more than ten years to move from conversion to the Romans 12:1,2 call to full consecration. No wonder Paul used the strong words, "I urge you." A decisive surrender is absolutely necessary to become a transformed person and for our worship and service to be pleasing to God.

In my time of prayer with Art at the Hillcrest revival I finally said that big "yes" to God. I acknowledged Christ's lordship over all of my life. I must add that I have had to continually update that commitment on many occasions. Back in 1949 I did not know all that would be included in that initial commitment. But my intentions were irrevocable, eternal yielding of my life to Christ's Lordship and control.

When I made the complete surrender to Christ, I did expect some overpowering emotion. In fact, I felt nothing except a quiet assurance that I was completely in God's hands. I went back to my room and soon fell asleep. However, I was awakened the next morning by a vison of the glorified Jesus who seemed to be looking down at me with love and acceptance. I immediately got out of bed and knelt to worship and pray. I found myself repeating, "Jesus, I worship you; Jesus I love you." I do not know how long that sense of Jesus' presence lasted, but I sense the effects even now, 50 years later.

Thought for the Day: *Oswald Chambers said, "The Holy Spirit desires to do in every believer subjectively what Christ has done objectively for us on the Cross."*

The Interventions of God in My Life (7)

Scripture Reading: Ephesians 1:11-14

Key Verse: *...having believed, you were marked in him with a seal, the promised Holy Spirit... (Ephesians 1:13b).*

Meditation: Paul emphasizes that every Christian at conversion receives the sealing of the Holy Spirit. The Holy Spirit is the Old Testament "promised one" who now serves as our guarantee for the realization of God's future promise. We Christians should warmly respond to the Holy Spirit's initiative in our lives. We should move beyond that stage of having the gift of the Spirit to being filled with the Spirit as in Ephesians 5:18.

In reference to my personal Pentecost experience recorded yesterday, I want to say that the vision /dream is not a normative experience intended for everyone. Given the complexities of my personality and my deeply felt insecurities regarding the call, I see the dream as the assurance to me that God knew I needed. I knew I was now fully accepted by Jesus and was inwardly equipped to serve Him by the sanctifying presence of the Holy Spirit.

I was not transformed into a mature saint. The sanctification of my personality needs and insecurities will continue until I breathe my last breath. But I do know that since that encounter with Christ and the Holy Spirit at Hillcrest Christian College, the following realities continue in my life: I continue to love Jesus. I experience closeness to and the reality of the spiritual world. I have a new power to minister beyond natural giftedness. I want to continue to grow in Christ's likeness. I want to keep obeying any new revelations of God's will for my life. I want to confess any failure or sin, and I aspire to see Jesus, that my worship of Him will finally be perfected.

Thought for the Day: *Acts 1:8 continues as a divine promise and the divine provision for victorious living.*

The Interventions of God in My Life (8)

Scripture Reading: Philippians 1:1-5

Key Verse: *I thank my God every time I remember you (Philippians 1:3).*

Meditation: Paul thanked God for his friends at Philippi. Since he did not use this approach with every church, we know that was not a manipulative strategy, but a sincere exercise. His gratitude was not just for friendship, but for "partnership in the gospel," that they, too, shared with him in the spreading of the good news of Christ.

I am thankful for the people at Hillcrest Christian College. Schools need a visible visionary founder, teachers and administrators who share the leader's vision, and a host of supporters and promoters.

The founder, Reverend F. S. Magsig, projected the vision of a school to produce workers for the kingdom of God and modeled great Bible teaching. For the students his two great passions were that each person would experience the cleansing and empowering of the Holy Spirit and that each would become fruitful Christian workers, whether lay people, pastors or missionaries. Working with Mr. Magsig, dozens of teachers and staff members sacrificed salary in order to see the grace of God at work in the lives of students. Many church people, especially in the Medicine Hat area, gave generously of their time and resources to make education possible at the lowest imaginable tuition.

Thought for the Day: *Let us pause to give thanks intentionally with a joyous memory recalling those who in some significant way have touched our lives in our churches, and at the schools where we studied.*

The Interventions of God in My Life (9)

Scripture Reading: Psalm 37:23-26

Key Verse: *If the Lord delights in a man's ways, he makes his steps firm (Psalm 37:23).*

Meditation: At Hillcrest each student was encouraged to adopt some Bible verse of portion of scripture as a "life verse." These verses would have been personalized to us during a time of crisis or decision-making. In future similar times, we would have additional insights and directions from these scriptures. I continued to practice this discipline and found myself returning to Psalm 37 and its larger context. In the King James Version it reads, "The steps of a good man are ordered by the Lord." God has used this assurance in the daily step-by-step walk with Him to keep me from being worried about the future events of my life.

Until March 1952 I had simply assumed that God's call, "Helmut, I want you to be a minister" meant North America ministry. Now in my senior year at Bible College, I was making plans to meet the ordination requirements of my denomination. I expected to pursue advanced education at an accredited college in Oregon where friends had gone. But two weeks before graduation my plans were changed. At a local Saturday night Youth for Christ Rally near our school, God singled me out from among 300 other young people. He personalized a missionary challenge to me. The concept of a "call to preach" broadened to include Japan.

Thought for the Day: *God has a plan for each person, but He rarely reveals it all at once. He usually allows it to be discovered in the daily steps of obedience.*

The Interventions of God in My Life (10)

Scripture Reading: I Corinthians 16:5-9

Key Verse: *Because a great door for effective work has opened to me, and there are many who oppose me (I Corinthians 16:9).*

Meditation: After World War II General Douglas MacArthur was appointed Allied Administrator of Japan. He skillfully directed the change in government from dictatorship to democracy. He was loved and respected by the Japanese who had expected a much harsher occupation force. The General believed strongly in the need for both missionaries and Bibles for Japan. Perhaps he is the only supreme commander in history to issue a call to the church to send 10,000 missionaries and one million Bibles to an occupied country.

In 1952 seven years after the unconditional surrender of Japan to the Allied Powers, the "window of opportunity" for the gospel was still wide open. The spiritual vacuum resulting from the Emperor's denial of his divinity and the debilitating psychological loss of the war made the Japanese more open to Christianity than at any other time in its 2,000 years of history. It was thought by many that if this door would remain open, Japan could become a Christian nation.

As the elderly evangelist at that youth for Christ rally shared MacArthur's call for missionaries and Bibles for Japan, he paused and looked at his audience. "If I were a young man like some of you, do you know what I would do? I would rededicate my life to God and go as a missionary to Japan," he challenged. He appeared to point his long finger at me and asked, "Why don't you go?"

Thought for the Day: *I believe that whenever God sovereignly opens a door for the gospel He is simultaneously calling the church to enter that open door.*

The Interventions of God in My Life (11)

Scripture Reading: Isaiah 58:11-14

Key Verse: *The Lord will guide you always (Isaiah 58:1a).*

Meditation: As I walked back to my dormitory after the Youth for Christ meeting, the long finger of the evangelist seemed to keep pointing at me. "Why don't you go" could not be easily dismissed. As a young man just starting my ministry and with no debts, my plans were not yet concrete. I had no romantic commitments and I had vowed as a freshman that I would be willing to be a missionary. My only prayer would be, "Lord, if you are in this, please show me that next step."

I did not expect "the next step" to be revealed as quickly as it actually happened. Within a week a large brown envelope arrived in the mail, sent by Dave and Louise Maetche, alumni of Hillcrest. I found inside a copy of the OMS monthly magazine. On the back cover were 25 squares to be filled by pictures of young men to go as missionaries to Japan. Fifteen squares were still blank. The bold print blazed, **"Ten have already responded; where are the other 15? Will you be one of them?"**

Inside the envelope the personal letter read, "Helmut, as we prayed about these 15 needed young men, your face kept coming before us. We do not know your plans for the immediate future, but perhaps you could apply and see what happens."

As these coincidences began to happen, I knew that I had to take the next step. I applied and within the next month I was accepted to go to Japan with OMS for two years.

Thought for the Day: *When we pray surprising coincidences often happen, but when we stop praying coincidences do not happen.*

The Interventions of God in My Life (12)

Scripture Reading: Isaiah 58:11-14

Key Verse: *The Lord will guide you always (Isaiah 58:1).*

Meditation: I will never forget that letter of acceptance by the late president of OMS, Dr. Eugene Erny. After sentences of congratulations, he closed with this paragraph: "OMS is a faith mission. That means we do not help you financially with your required support. If God is in your call it is our confidence that as you share your testimony God will call people to pray for you and support you."

At that time the monthly allowance was $105 plus monies for travel, equipment and deputation travel. The total was $4,000. That, 50 years ago, was a tremendous faith challenge.

My mother, a financial realist, said to me in German, "Helmut where are you going to get all that money?" By the sound of her voice, I could tell the amount was larger than I had first comprehended. So I followed the advice of the past, "Talk with your best friends and listen carefully to their advice." I chose Wilbert Frederick, a home church friend known to be objective and not given to flattery. With no preamble or warning I said to him, "Wilbert, what would you think of my going as a missionary to Japan?" He answered simply, "Helmut, if you go, I promise to give you $150." Fifty years ago that was equivalent to $1,000 today. I knew I had one-fortieth of my support, and that God would call 39 others like Wilbert. What amazed me most: I had not expected a financial response to my question to Wilbert.

Thought for the Day: *God often prepares people in advance to respond to a need in order to strengthen our feeble faith and keep us from becoming dropouts.*

The Interventions of God in My Life (13)

Scripture Reading: Matthew 6:1-8

Key Verse: ...for your Father knows what you need before you ask him (Matthew 6:8b).

Meditation: The length of our prayers does not make them more effective. In contrast to prayer to pagan deities that advocate repetition, Jesus teaches us that God is our loving heavenly Father who knows our needs even before we ask Him. Our asking is not to overcome His reluctance, but to respect His willingness to care for us and to deepen our personal relationship with Him.

God not only knew my needs for the missionary journey, but He also prepared people to help meet those needs. At the Grace Evangelical Church in Rudyard, Montana, I was the first missionary to present the congregation with the opportunity to participate. God touched their hearts and seemed to say things to them that I did not include in my testimony. Their sacrificial giving overwhelmed and humbled me.

One young mother handed me seven carefully rolled $20 bills and with tears in her eyes said, "I have been saving this egg money for something, and I believe the Lord wants me to help you to go to Japan." Knowing she was the sole provider for her family, I suggested she keep some of the money but she responded, "Jesus told me to do it." Fifteen years later her oldest daughter and husband went to Haiti with OMS. I understood why Jesus had prompted her to give so sacrificially.

The treasurer and I counted the offering and faith promises. We were awed to discover a total of $1,400 had been given or pledged.

Thought for the Day: *God delights in choosing the weak of the world so that in the final analysis all credit and praise may be returned to Him.*

The Interventions of God in My Life (14)

Scripture Reading: Luke 18:18-29

Key Verse: *Peter said to him, We have left all we had to follow you! (Luke 18:28)*

Meditation: Before the crucifixion of Jesus, Peter sometimes reflected a rather commercial view of discipleship -- "What's in it for me?" Jesus assured him and His other disciples that the person who gives up everything for the kingdom would be repaid many times over in terms of homes, parents and siblings. David Livingstone lost his wife and his health in Africa, but when someone asked him about his sacrifices he replied, "Sacrifice? I never made a sacrifice in my life." Most missionaries I know would agree with Livingstone. I feel that those who send us, people who become our parents and the promised siblings, make the real sacrifice. During my past 50 years God has given us homes and support through those who keep us encouraged.

After the Rudyard, Montana experience, I contacted churches in western Canada, 15 of which invited me to come, and God supplied an average of one share in each church bringing my total to 30. My home church in New Sarepta, Alberta took the last ten needed shares. They have continued to be part of that enlarged family Jesus promised. Soon I was on my way to California where OMS was headquartered. On the way I met Rolland Rice, an OMS missionary who had started the second Every Creature Crusade in Japan. "Rollie" had memorized the entire book of Revelation along with other scriptures. He helped me understand that his love of the Bible had helped endear him to the Japanese people.

Thought for the Day: *In the light of the cross of Christ, missionaries can only say, "We are unworthy servants; we have only done our duty."*

The Interventions of God in My Life (15)

Scripture Reading: John 6:1-15

Key Verse: *...Here is a boy with five small barley loaves and two small fish, but how far will that go among so many? (John 6:8b)*

Meditation: Jesus had every right to be annoyed with the crowds following him. He had planned a needed rest for himself and the disciples, but instead of being irritated by the intrusion of the crowd, He responded with love and compassion. The recording of the boy's resources feeding the multitudes teaches us as well as it taught the disciples. When Jesus calls us to the humanly impossible task, He himself actually expects to do it. Jesus generally performs His miracles after we give Him what we have. Jesus provides resources beyond the immediate crisis.

At OMS headquarters in Los Angeles, California, I met Dr. Eugene Erny, the president, and a Spirit-filled leader of 25 years. Both the headquarters' staff and other crusaders warmly welcomed me, including Austin Boggan, who would be going to Japan with me. Austin, a graduate of Asbury College, had served in the US Navy, and was not daunted by the prospect of a ten-day ship journey like I was.

The message of Dr. Dick Hillis, president and founder of the postwar mission now called Send International, highlighted our commissioning service. His message was on John 6 and entitled, "Just for Me." Dr. Erny led the service and asked Mrs. Lettie Cowman, a co-founder of OMS with her late husband Charles, to lead in prayer. I remember her strong sense of expectancy as she committed both Austin and me to God's care.

Thought for the Day: *When we commit to Jesus our equivalent of five loaves and two fish, they become enough for the need.*

The Interventions of God in My Life (16)

Scripture Reading: Matthew 6:1-4

Key Verse: *...your Father who sees in secret will reward you (Matthew 6:4b).*

Meditation: Everyone from the OMS office came to see us out of the port in Los Angeles. The OMS family made me feel more special than ever before in my life. During the next ten days Dr. Erny's words came to me, "There is no instant spiritual magic in getting on a ship and crossing the ocean. You will discover you act and react on the mission field just like you did at home. The new culture, language and culture shock may reveal heretofore unknown weaknesses in your life."

The ten days on a freighter with only 12 passengers afforded a great opportunity to be quiet before God and prepare myself for the coming task. Sunday on the ship was Easter Sunday, but also a typhoon Sunday. Austin, my bold ex-navy roommate, always the evangelist on land, decided to ask the captain for permission to have an Easter service. I was appointed to preach. The ship tossed so violently that no one could stand up without holding to something. Holding on to my Bible with one hand and the railing with the other, I preached an up-and-down sermon. One of the crewmembers came to our cabin afterwards for prayer, which made the effort very rewarding.

Arriving in Japan, we found no one to greet us. What a contrast to our sendoff! Due to international time, the OMS people in Japan thought our ship was arriving the next day.

Thought for the Day: *We must not expect human acclaim, but seek rather the approval of God.*

The Interventions of God in My Life (17)

Scripture Reading: I Timothy 4:11-16

Key Verse: *Don't let anyone look down on you because you are young, but set an example... (I Timothy 4:12a).*

Meditation: Paul warns Timothy he would be watched with a critical eye because he was young. He advised Timothy to live so that his behavior would silence the critic. His behavior covered speech, daily life, life style, love, faith, and purity. If a Christian worker's life style exceeds the world standards, his message will be heard in spite of his youth, ethnic origin or cultural difference. This was the challenge for each of us young men in the Every Creature Crusade.

A warm welcome waited for us on the OMS Japan campus. Five men preceded us: Lowell Williamson, Frank Davis, Dale Neff, Charles Kempton and Ray Huey. Ray worked mostly in the office, but visited the rest of us at the evangelistic sites frequently with his accordion. That helped get us back on key after a long time of singing without an instrument. After a month's crash course of Japanese, we joined our teams with seven members each: Two Japanese preachers and one missionary speaker sharing every third service, three lay people for children's work and personal work after each service, plus one interpreter for the missionary.

During the day we systematically distributed gospel portions to each home in the area, usually the gospel of John. In the afternoon we prepared for the evening service which ran six evenings a week for about four weeks in each area. We then tried to organize the new believers and seekers into a church and turned them over to the OMS-related national church body. Those years, 1950-1958, were great years of response to the gospel. Our ability to form new groups exceeded our ability to train pastors to lead them. We had to slow our ministry or remain longer in one place. We did form over 70 new groups in that time.

Thought for the Day: *When God's Spirit sovereignly moves on a nation, more can happen in four weeks than in any previous four years before or since.*

The Interventions of God in My Life (18)

Scripture Reading: Luke 10:1-12

Key Verse: *...the harvest is plentiful, but the laborers are few...* *(Luke 10:2).*

Meditation: Our evangelistic team in Japan participated in the Youth for Christ rallies that were conducted in every city and larger towns. Among the seven evangelists and gifted persons from the English-speaking world was Dr. Fred Jarvis, a well-known missionary evangelist in Japan.

During the forenoons we went house to house distributing invitations. The sound truck went up and down the narrow roads of a town to announce the meetings. However, in the early afternoon we got a telegram from Tokyo saying Dr. Jarvis was ill and could not come. We were only a few hours away from the meeting time and were in quite a state of shock.

Every seat in the city hall filled with a total of about 1,000 people. People happily joined in singing new songs, mostly gospel choruses. Several Christians gave heart-warming testimonies and one of the members of our team gave a short gospel message. He asked people who wanted to believe in Jesus to raise their hands, and 900 were raised. Assuming he may have been misunderstood, he gave the invitation again, but with the same response. How could we do personal work with only 20 people available? We took a group of several at one time and did the best we could.

That night we experienced the bountiful harvest and the shortage of workers.

Thought for the Day: *As Christian workers we are aware that the Great Commission consists of more than proclamation. To be lasting it must be followed with one-on-one discipleship.*

The Benefits and Challenges of the Short-Term Missionary Assignment

Scripture Reading: Acts 14:26-28

Key Verse: *...they gathered the church together and reported all that God had done through them... (Acts 14:26).*

Meditation: When Paul and Barnabas returned from their first missionary journey that lasted about one year, they reported to Antioch, their sending church. To those who had commissioned them they give an account of "all that God had done through them." God in His sovereignty had opened the door of faith to the Gentiles. The first missionary venture finished in triumph with new churches being planted in many of the places they visited.

Many missionary agencies discover that a high percentage of their career missionaries have first served on short-term assignments. My two years of work in Japan would fall into that category. Many benefits come from that experience.

It broadened my call and vision. Although I had felt impressed to be in the ministry at 16, I had assumed it would be in North America. However, after two years in Japan, I returned for a total of over 30 years. With John Wesley, I feel "the world is my parish." In my daily prayers I travel to other parts of the world where I have never been in person, but I understand can be open to the work of the Holy Spirit.

The short-term experience provides direction about future decisions and prevents dropouts. Some people discover they are not equipped emotionally to work in a cross-cultural environment. Others find stimulation and satisfaction working with a new language and a different culture. They sense a special affinity with the people and intentionally return to the field.

Thought for the Day: *Every Christian student should experience a short-term assignment in order to test his or her call and to gain a world vision.*

The Benefits and Challenges of the Short-Term Missionary Assignment

Scripture Reading: Acts 11:1-18

Key Verse: *...So then, God has granted even the Gentiles repentance into life (Acts 11:18b).*

Meditation: Nothing is quite so exhilarating to a spiritually alive sending church than to hear that God has used the missionary they supported to witness to Christ in another country. Often the missionary will be asked by the believer to witness or perform the baptism. The sending church will be energized as they see how the Great Commission can be a reality.

Those who participate from the home church of the short-termer will grow in their dedication to the ministry in the home community. I was one of the first young people in New Sarepta to go overseas. Many people asked to receive my bimonthly prayer letter. Reverend Ginter, our pastor, kept challenging the church to pray for additional workers. His faith took him beyond the congregation of 70 people at that time.

When, after two years overseas, I wrote that I was returning home, one of the members responded, "Helmut, our church has been so blessed and united in prayer for you. I am almost sorry to hear you are coming home." I assured him I would be returning to Japan. That seemed to encourage him. Ten years later a large number of young people from that church had been called to the ministry and mission field. Not only did the church grow numerically, but also in financial giving and dedication to missions. That passion continues to this day.

Thought for the Day: *When the church carries out her task to the full limits of possibility, God often does the "impossible."*

The Benefits and Challenges of the Short-Term Missionary Assignment

Scripture: Acts 8:26-39

Key Verse: *Now an angel of the Lord said to Philip, Go south to the road, the desert road (Acts 8:26a).*

Meditation: God providentially worked out the details of this encounter between Philip and the Ethiopian. The angel of the Lord initiated the action and sustained the activity until the Ethiopian himself requested Christian baptism.   Before Philip could become God's instrument for world missions, he had to be willing to move from his comfort zone, leaving behind a very successful ministry in familiar territory, trusting God implicitly for detailed directions. Each of us experiences a similar reaction when we accept a short-term missionary assignment.

The further benefit of the short-term assignment is that the missionary himself stretches his faith. Part of that growth comes from working cooperatively with pastors and Christians who have made a radical decision to follow Christ. On our team, the Reverend Saito and the Reverend Kobayashi had spent three years in prison for their faith. Their proclamation that Christ would return to judge the world challenged the supremacy of the Emperor. The military government tried to silence these pastors by imprisonment. They prayed daily for the Allies to win the war so they would preach the gospel again.

Then, there is the amazing discovery that God uses us not in spite of our being foreigners, but because of it. People come to see and hear us out of curiosity. Years later a Japanese pastor told me he had come to the meetings because he wanted to practice his English. He was saved, called to the ministry and had bi-lingual services in his church near the Japan International Airport.

Thought for the Day: *Even when the missionary leaves, the witness of the Holy Spirit continues.*

The Benefits and Challenges of the Short-Term Missionary Assignment

Scripture Reading: Isaiah *6:1-8*

Key Verse: *Then I heard the voice of the Lord saying, Whom shall I send? And who will go for us? (Isaiah 6:8a)*

Meditation: Someone has said, "A high view of God results in a clear view of sin and human depravity.   Only those who have been made holy will be capable of hearing and responding to God's call, 'Who will go for us?'" If we cannot hear God's call because of uncleanness, we will also miss God's deeper missionary concern for the world and fail in taking the gospel to the nations.

The short-term missionary is a sign of the universal fellowship of the Christian church.   In a sense the missionary will always remain a foreigner.   Because of his very foreign-ness, he is a constant reminder to the national church that genuine Christianity embraces the world. The God who calls us to be missionaries is a God who wants everyone to hear his plan of salvation.   To the question, "Who is a missionary?" we answer, "Anyone who hears God's call, 'Who will go for us?' is a missionary."

A Japanese pastor observed, "We cannot refuse the missionary or his message for we would be refusing God.   Our churches need missionaries." Every missionary is astonished that God uses his/her testimony to call others into His service in other countries or to serve in their own nation.

Thought for the Day: *The missionary reminds churches everywhere that we are called to the entire world.*

The Benefits and Challenges of the Short-Term Missionary Assignment

Scripture Reading: Acts 20:36-38

Key Verse: *They all wept as they embraced him and kissed him (Acts 20:37).*

Meditation: Paul was saying a very sorrowful good-bye to the believers at Ephesus. Paul tore himself away from them in order to board the ship to Jerusalem. I witnessed many such partings during my time in Japan, underlining the value of their ministry.

The spiritual fruit of a short-term missionary will continue even if he does not become a career missionary. Numbers of people are baptized each year that have been touched by short-termers. The short-termers may assume support in others, and continue to carry a world concern back to the local church.

A short-term experience will assist those who have not finished their academic preparation to concentrate on an appropriate study program that will best equip them for the role they anticipate on the field. Some students change their majors after working for a short time on the mission field.

Observations of family life among the missionaries will aid the short-termers in his/her choice of a spouse. Being aware of necessary spiritual and character qualities enables a couple to serve better as a team. They will consider academic preparation, flexibility, personal sense of call, culture sensitivity, spiritual maturity and physical and emotional wholeness.

Thought for the Day: *Missionaries must leave new converts behind, but God and His grace will remain to build them up in the faith.*

The Benefits and Challenges of the Short-Term Missionary Assignment

Scripture Reading: II Corinthians 11:16-33

Key Verse: *...I bear in my body the marks of Jesus... (Galatians 6:17b).*

Meditation: As Paul reluctantly lists his credentials in II Corinthians 11, he mentions not his successes, but his sufferings. The 23 items touch almost every possible suffering for a human being. Paul was marked with real scars.

I have never heard a missionary message on the above text. Perhaps that is why missionaries have an unrealistic view of the mission field. Even those who have studied missions arrive without an understanding of the demands to be faced. How we deal with these challenges without becoming hypercritical or cynical will determine whether we will return as career missionaries.

A short-term experience provides a wonderful opportunity to work through inherent illusions. One illusion is "easy identification" with the people of the adopted country. Just eating with chopsticks or paging through a "Learn Japanese in a Hurry" book will not erase our foreign-ness. Even two years of living mostly in tents with the men did not make me an "insider." Everywhere I went for the two years, children followed me like the Pied Piper, calling out, "Gaijin-da, gaijin-da," meaning, "You are a foreigner; you are an outsider." I had to accept that my blond hair and height marked me as different from the Japanese homogeneous society. Gradually I learned that God can use me in spite of my being an outsider, perhaps because of it.

Thought for the Day: *The missionary's primary identification is not in externals, but in the spirit with an attitude of humility.*

The Benefits and Challenges of a Short-Term Missionary Assignment

Scripture Reading: Romans 1:18-32

Key Verse: *And exchanged the glory of the immortal God for images made to look like mortal man and birds and reptiles (Romans 1:23).*

Meditation: The next illusion is that of thinking the people from the non-Christian world are earnestly searching after God. Pastors would say to me as I spoke in deputation meetings, "I envy your going to places where people are really seeking God." With that context I was shocked to discover all those magnificent temples, earnest praying, and burning of incense did not reflect a true, but a misguided search for God. I discovered no genuine sorrow for sin, but rather a means to manipulate the gods to give good luck, protection, and prosperity.

I faced my sentimental idealization and replaced it with biblical anthropology. Romans 1-3 traces man's downward steps from lofty monotheism to the worship of idols. Paul summarizes man's predicament in I Corinthians 2:14, "The man without the Spirit (natural man) does not accept the things that come from the Spirit of God, for they are foolishness to him, and he cannot understand them, because they are spiritually discerned." No matter where a man is born, until he encounters the ministry of the Holy Spirit, he is moving naturally -- not to God, but away from God.

God is searching after man. Since Pentecost the Holy Spirit "poured out on all flesh" assures us that there is no place where we go alone, and that there are no hopeless persons in the world.

Thought for the Day: *The hope for worldwide evangelism and revival has its true origin in the "poured out Holy Spirit' on the world.*

The Benefits and Challenges of a Short-Term Missionary Assignment

Scripture Reading: II Corinthians 4:1-12

Key Verse: *But we have this treasure in jars of clay to show that this all-surpassing power is from God and not from us (II Corinthians 4:7).*

Meditation: Next, we naively think the new converts will be instantly transformed. From stories of converts standing up boldly in the face of persecution, I assumed all converts would be that brave. Awed by the first idol burning I witnessed by a widow and her daughters, I was disappointed when three months later they lapsed in their faith and dropped out of church. After illness and a series of "bad luck," her neighbors told her that her husband's spirit and her other ancestors were offended at her Christian actions. She purchased a new and more expensive idol shelf to appease their anger. From this painful experience we learned no convert is automatically safe; all Christians are in intense spiritual warfare. Our only hope for new believers to persevere in the faith is the assurance of the indwelling Holy Spirit who is the only Almighty Spirit in the world.

We are also prone to think missionaries are special saints. No, we are simply like the people who mentor us. We are all saints in calling, but far from being perfected. People say such nice things about the short-term missionary at home that we lose sight of our shortcomings and weaknesses once we arrive on the field. We reflect the blindness of our own perceptions. A missionary remembers when the words of an older career missionary hurt her. The older missionary said, "Since I was sanctified I do not feel the need to apologize to anyone." Her response did nothing to heal the broken fellowship that would last a long time for both of them.

Thought for the Day: *The genuine missionary admits to hurting people and seeks to change his/her behavior so as not to be offensive.*

The Benefits and Challenges of a Short-Term Missionary Assignment

Scripture Reading: Acts 11:22-24

Key Verse: *He was a good man, full of the Holy Spirit and of faith (Acts 11:24b).*

Meditation: The early church looked for workers with the following spiritual qualities: A person of integrity and trustworthy character; a person full of the Holy Spirit; one with the gift of wisdom, being able to apply the scriptures to life situations. In every age people with these same qualities will continue to be effective in the advance of the church.

A short-term missionary provides an opportunity to test cross-cultural relational abilities and spiritual giftedness. Most people recognize that national pastors and church leaders are in charge. A partner relationship recognizes each person's unique giftedness. OMS seeks the approval of the national church for each new missionary application. If the missionary has served before as a short-termer, the church already knows and trusts him/her.

At my farewell as a short-termer, one of the Japanese seminary teachers asked me, "Schultz Sensei, why did you come to Japan?" I replied that I had come because God had called me. Everyone was quiet for a time and then one senior teacher said, "I am glad that God called him; now we know he will come again." Then our field leader, Dr. Roy Adams, said, 'The Japanese church and the OMS want you to go home and get additional preparation, find the right wife and come back to Japan." This twin affirmation and direction sealed my call to return to Japan for another five terms.

Thought for the Day: *Christ sees past the externals of our lives and knows our true motivations in ministry.*

Furlough and Divine Guidance

Scripture Reading: Proverbs 3:1-8

Key Verse: *In all your ways acknowledge him and he will make your paths straight (Proverbs 3:6).*

Meditation: The Holy Spirit endued Solomon with extraordinary wisdom before Solomon's accession to the throne. Proverbs gives us divine guidelines for making wise choices in life. Most of us have made decisions one day that we have regretted the next day. However, if we humbly stop and tap into God's omniscience, we will experience God's personal direction and His removal of barriers to His chosen goal for us.

As I left Yokohama to return home after my two-year assignment, the words of the Reverend Nobechi and of Dr. Roy Adams kept ringing in my ears: Get additional training; find a good wife; return as soon as possible to Japan. I had thought I would just pick up my life's plans where I had left them two years ago. I would go to seminary in Oregon for my preparation where a possible scholarship awaited me. That offer sounded very attractive since my assets amounted to less than $200. But I had no inward peace about that plan.

I left the Canadian West Coast and traveled to Winona Lake, Indiana for the OMS annual conference.   There I joined three other Japan crusaders, Lowell Williamson, Charles Dupree and Austin Boggan. Lowell was taking summer school at Asbury College in Kentucky. Charles and Austin were starting Asbury Theological Seminary there. I visited Asbury with Lowell and liked the warm spiritual atmosphere present in the chapel and classes. The dean promised he would transfer my Hillcrest credits as allowed for the liberal arts curriculum.

Thought for the Day: *Since God knows the present and future, it is best to submit our plans to Him for editing and redirection, if necessary.*

Furlough and Divine Provision

Scripture Reading: Philippians 4:10-19

Key Verse: *And my God will meet all your needs... (Philippians 4:19).*

Meditation: Paul assures his benefactors at Philippi that his God will do for them what he himself is incapable of doing, supplying their needs. This assurance of divine supply indicates the church had given so generously that they themselves were now in need. God's giving is always commensurate with His divine wealth, assuring us that our needs will be met.

On my arrival at Asbury College I was told the dorms were full. God provided a room off campus that was better for me than a dorm. I had a quiet place to study and I developed a deep friendship with John Underwood that would last a lifetime. John and his wife, Helen, made a room in their basement called "The Schultz Room" where we could store our essential belongings while in Japan. These things were readily available each furlough.

Even though the studies were demanding I joined two campus organizations, Student Volunteers (a missionary challenge group) and the Ministerial Association that coordinated student outreach to jails, the Salvation Army and other activities. Charles Dupree, with his wife, Jo Ann, gave me a car since they were returning to Japan. I took the preaching responsibility for a small church that was under the direction of the Ministerial Association. The car also took me to the close city of Lexington, Kentucky to the Good Samaritan Hospital where a very special person was in the nursing education program. Norma Jean will tell you her story in the following pages.

Thought for the Day: *The past providential care of God should be rehearsed regularly. The review gives us confidence for the next venture of faith.*

God's Providence

Scripture Reading: Matthew 4:18-22

Key Verse: *Follow me and I will make you fishers of men (Matthew 4:18).*

Meditation: My life began on a little farm in Kentucky as the second child and first girl born to Ollie Fant and Lida Ruth Tulley Hickerson. I cannot remember any details of my early childhood before four years old. Then my mother was burned severely in a kerosene stove explosion accident while preparing a Memorial Day dinner for the extended family. The whole community mourned the death of the young woman who left three children, the youngest nine months. I was told my mother was a wonderful praying Christian.

No doubt God heard her prayers for me and answered by giving me a heart to hear the voice of the Holy Spirit. One day, at the age of nine, listening to a religious broadcast in my room, I heard the challenge to win other people to Christ. Kneeling by my bed I responded to the verse, "Follow me and I will make you fishers of men."

I was always interested in local church "revival" meetings and sometimes my father would advise me not to get "too religious." At elementary school and at church my best friend was the pastor's daughter, Jeannette Baldwin. One day she told me she would be going to a private Christian boarding school where her father used to teach. I told her I would go with her. My father, who had married again, agreed.

Thought for the Day: *God's Holy Spirit is always looking for the person who will listen to His voice.*

Good News for Everyone

Scripture Reading: Romans 10:8-13

Key Verse: *The same Lord is Lord of all and blesses all who call upon him (Romans 10:12).*

Meditation: At Mt. Carmel High School we attended daily chapels and weekend church meetings. Jeannette invited me to go to the altar and pray with her for us to become Christians like the people at the school. I invited Jesus into my heart and testified to God's change in my life to the people at home. We also understood clearly the exhortation in Romans 12:1 to offer our total selves to God for His service. I experienced the cleansing of the heart and empowering of the Holy Spirit for God's service. Jesus became my Savior, Sanctifier and Guide.

Missionaries spoke regularly at Mt. Carmel and we prayed for them and the people they represented at our weekly prayer meetings. In the late 1940's two missionary women from China spoke to us about God's work in Asia. I felt compelled to be an overseas missionary. From age 15 on I prepared for that calling. My studies were college preparatory and I knew I also needed biblical studies. After high school graduation in 1951 I applied to Kentucky Mountain Bible College, on another campus, but under the same organization as the high school.

During high school I had traveled with the school president, Dr. Lela McConnell, in musical groups to represent the school. Usually I spent my summers in this ministry and very little time at home. One summer I stayed on the campus, working to prepare the place for the next school term. My father also helped me with the tuition and was most supportive.

Thought for the Day: *The family of God encompasses all that follow Christ and provides a haven of protection and provision for all who confess Him as Lord.*

God Provides

Scripture Reading: Psalm 27:4-14

Key Verse: *In the day of trouble he will keep me safe in his dwelling; he will hide me in the shelter of his tabernacle...(Psalm 27:5a).*

Meditation: My father did not want me to think of working overseas. He could not conceive of his daughter appearing to prepare for some kind of fantasy dream. When I entered Bible college he would not communicate with me. He could not make any sense of such studies. But God gave me a dear aunt, Julia McFeena, my father's sister, who, with her husband, Charles, always welcomed me into her home. They had also reared my sister, Nina, after my mother's early death. God touched many individuals at the school who knew of my situation. They helped to provide many of the necessities that girls need. I still have the Bible given to me by one of the high school staff and many devotional books to encourage me.

I spent my summers working in Indiana, first at a Girl Scout Camp and then in the Lutheran Hospital in the nursery where the head nurse, Mrs. Hornberger, encouraged me in my studies and modeled for me a caring proficient nurse. The parents of Nancy Amspaugh, a classmate, provided a place for some of us working students to live.

After graduation from Bible college in 1954, I still expected to go to China, even though the political climate was grim and missionaries were moving to other countries. Knowing I needed practical skills, I entered nursing education at Good Samaritan Hospital in Lexington, Kentucky. My father was delighted, thinking I had regained my common sense once more and would have a profession for life. He spoke to me again and I was welcomed to go back home.

Thought for the Day: *The way of obedience to God is full of surprises and rewards.*

The Transition Adjustment

Scripture Reading: Isaiah 58:11-14

Key Verse: *Then you will find your joy in the Lord (Isaiah 58:14a).*

Meditation: I entered the school of nursing with a scholarship requiring only that I work for the hospital for a year after I graduated. My friend, Jeanette, had gone straight to nursing from high school and was a senior when I entered the program.

Going from seven years of total Christian environment and a very strict regime to the freedom of the nursing environment was a major transition and adjustment for me. Many Christian student nurses were there and we joined the Intervarsity Nurses Christian Fellowship where the chaplain, Dr. T. O. Harrison, encouraged and helped direct us spiritually. Teachers took time to show me how to analyze my reactions and helped me to give my best to the program and to my studies. I later returned to the school of nursing on my first furlough to teach Growth and Development of Children and Diseases of Children.

Our class helped to staff the hospital during our second and third years of study with so many hours of practical work that my transcript is almost unbelievable in the hours we "practiced." We also experienced assignments in Psychiatric Nursing in Washington, D.C. at St. Elizabeth's Hospital and at the Tuberculosis Sanitarium at Cincinnati, Ohio. No doubt the total program at Good Samaritan prepared me for the adjustments to be made cross-culturally and academically in the future that awaited me in Asia.

Thought for the Day: *God prepares us for the future by giving us challenges in the present.*

Meeting Helmut

Scripture Reading: Genesis 24:1-7

Key Verse: *Will you go with this man?   I will go, she answered (Genesis 24:58).*

Meditation: Among my class at Good Samaritan was Phyllis Erny, wife of Robert Erny, son of the president of OMS. She, Bob and I would often go together to events at Asbury College and Seminary. Bob's car was very unreliable and we would laugh as we made our way often slowly over the 20 miles to the town of Wilmore.

Dr. Erny was the missionary speaker at the seminary conference. Afterwards we stood on the sidewalk together while Bob fixed a not unusual flat tire. Helmut Schultz joined us and I was introduced. The whole group enjoyed ice cream sundaes afterwards at the local drug store.

The next week Helmut called me at the nurses' dorm asking about a possible date on Sunday night. I told him I was interested, but I was scheduled to speak at a church in Paris, Kentucky about 15 miles north of Lexington. He indicated he would come to the service. I heard later that when he entered the church as a guest (I was already on the platform) the ushers apologized that the pastor was absent and had a substitute speaker. I was very nervous, but Helmut says he remembers the outline.

So I preached to him on our first date and he has done most of the preaching since. I discovered he was looking for a girl called to the mission field before meeting him. The other requirement was that she be a nurse. I met the criteria. We dated for over a year that included a missionary conference at Winona Lake, Indiana. We were engaged in February 1957 and married on August 17, 1957.

Thought for the Day: *God puts us in the right place to meet the right person at the right time when we are in the right relationship with Him.*

Our Wedding Day

Scripture Reading: Proverbs 18:22

Key Verse: *He who finds a wife finds what is good...(Proverbs 18:22a).*

Meditation: Norma Jean and I were married on August 17, 1957 in the same church where we had our first "date." The president of OMS, the late Dr. Eugene Erny, performed the moving ceremony on a beautiful hot summer day. Relatives, classmates and friends honored us with their presence.

Like most students in those days, we had little money, so for our first three days we stayed at the OMS Center in Wilmore while the missionary residents, Paul and Jean Pappas were away. My next part of the plan I would not recommend: On Tuesday morning we left for Michigan where I had been asked to speak at some evangelistic meetings Wednesday through Sunday. We did not tell the people at the church that we were newlyweds until the last service. Needless to say, they were greatly surprised.

Since the church had not had evangelistic meetings often and did not know about "altar calls" we had prayer rooms. One farmer had me come to his home and pray with him during the noon lunch hour. On the last night an elderly lady said, "I remember as a young girl 60 years ago having meetings like this; this was really wonderful."

We finally got around to having a honeymoon location by going to Niagara Falls on this trip, since we were close anyway! Pictures show Norma Jean in the beautiful gardens by the Falls, and also we walked through the Shakespearean Park in Ontario. An English bone china cup reminds us of our revival honeymoon trip in Wilmore, Michigan, and Ontario.

Thought for the Day: *God includes extras for us as we follow His leading and timing.*

Unexpected Provisions

Scripture Reading: Philippians 4:4-14-20

Key Verse: *And my God will meet all your needs... (Philippians 4:19a).*

Meditation: Our first home was a small trailer not equipped with bathing facilities. I was in my senior year at Asbury College. Norma Jean took classes at Asbury as well as working 3:00-11:00 p.m. at the Good Samaritan Hospital as her scholarship obligation. After she returned home at midnight we would go to the seminary trailer facility for showers.

My family had not met Norma Jean so we took our long Christmas vacation to go to Alberta. Grace EUB Church in Vancouver, BC invited us for pre-Christmas services. The board voted to underwrite our missionary personal support shares at $300 per month. This amounted to half of our total requirements that included field shares, equipment and transportation costs. Even though Grace was starting a new church plant in an adjoining city and anticipated pastoral changes, they were faithful to their commitment for the next five years. We cherish this dedicated friendship and participation in the missionary work we represented to them.

In order to start language school in September, we wanted to be in Japan by August. Amazingly, most of the people who had supported me formerly renewed or doubled their shares. When we were down to needing just $75 a month, we had exhausted all of our contacts. Just at that time OMS Canada invited us to a missionary conference at Oetzel EUB Church pastored then by The Reverend and Mrs. Ted Losch. That church took the rest of the support, and we were cleared by OMS to go to Japan. As the freighter left Everett, Washington, total strangers who had heard this was our first wedding anniversary presented us with a beautiful flower bouquet. We learned they were part of the Navigator group who also was seeing friends off on the ship.

Thought for the Day: *The confidence of faith missions is that if God is in your call He will also call supporters and prayer warriors to send you.*

Language School in Tokyo

Scripture Reading: I Corinthians 14:6-12

Key Verse: *...Unless you speak intelligible words with your tongue, how will anyone know what you are saying? (I Corinthians 14:9)*

Meditation: Someone has observed that when the missionary is in language school he/she seems to disappear. For some countries one year of study is sufficient, but Japanese language demands at least two years. We attended three hours of classes a day at school and were expected to study two hours for every hour of class, totaling nine hours a day. Struggling to persevere, we wanted to keep the vision and enthusiasm for ministry that brought us to the country. Some missionaries were tempted to give up and use a translator. Our encouragement came from the Word of God, and our missionary leader, Dr. Roy Adams, and our fellow missionaries. We also had a Bible study group with college students who remained our friends through the ensuing years.

Knowing the language not only provides communication in necessities like shopping, personal care and business, but also is essential to developing interpersonal relationships. Even those Japanese who speak English revert to their mother tongue to express matters of the heart and spirit. People know that you are trying to understand their hearts when you speak in their language. They are disarmed and more responsive than when an interpreter is used.

We learned how important it is to pray for the missionaries in language school, knowing that they will be better prepared to interact in a positive way when they have learned the thoughts and reactions of the people.

Thought for the Day: *I will never forget the words of a senior pastor to me, "Schultz Sensei, my people seem to listen harder to you, a missionary, than to me."*

Our First Assignment: Northern Japan

Scripture Reading: I Corinthians 9:19-27

Key Verse: *...I have become all things to all men so that by all possible means I might save some... (I Corinthians 9: 22).*

Meditation: Upon graduation from language school Norma Jean and I were appointed to the northern district of Japan and lived in Sendai, the leading city of the northern part of the main island of Honshu. Fortunately, Charles and Jo Ann Dupree, sensing Sendai a strategic future center of OMS, had supervised the building of a missionary residence there. At that time our OMS-related church organization did not have a church building in this city of 500,000 people.

In order to be effective, the church in Japan must give some promise of permanence with a building, land and a cemetery, the essentials for effective evangelism. Together with the Dupree family, our first task was to purchase land in a strategic part of the city both visible and served by public transportation. We found a plot close to our residence. People responded to the appeal letters from both the Dupree and Schultz supporters, so we were able to build a parsonage with a meeting room that could accommodate about 30 people.

By the time we returned from an extended study leave, the national church had appointed The Reverend and Mrs. Yamaguchi as pastors. Norma Jean used a small room for Sunday school for Malita and Juli, our two daughters who were born in Kentucky. The worship group kept growing to a need for a larger facility primarily funded by gifts of the local believers.

In addition to ministering to 12 other churches in the northern area, I preached in Sendai Church once a month. We expanded the contacts for the church through neighborhood English classes and Norma jean hosted cooking classes with a Bible Study that became an extremely effective means of evangelism to be used by others in OMS and other mission organizations.

Thought for the Day: *The missionary who is open to the creative ideas of the Holy Spirit will find a meaningful way to share the gospel.*

A New Church is Dedicated

Scripture Reading: Matthew 8:5-13

Key Verse: *Then Jesus said to the centurion, Go! It will be done just as you believed it would (Matthew 8:13).*

Meditation: We found the northern district extremely challenging as we returned for our second term of five years. In addition to Sendai, twelve other churches requested weekend meetings. Returning home on Mondays, I started work on another sermon in Japanese requiring up to 40 hours of preparation. I could use the same sermon many times. As the churches heard I was using Japanese, invitations started to come from other districts where there were no resident missionaries.

The Sendai church continued to grow under the Yamaguchi's leadership. Phase II blueprints and funding created great excitement in the local church and in the denomination. The church was there to stay.

Norma Jean and I had the privilege of hosting Dr. Kazuo Kobayashi, the academic dean of the Tokyo Biblical Seminary, for the dedication day. His powerful message on the dynamic faith of the centurion commended by Christ inspired us all. Back at the house during refreshments, Kobayashi Sensei said, "Your ministry here is much appreciated. I feel the Lord is preparing you to teach at the seminary. Please pray about it and begin to disengage here. I was stunned, but promised to pray as he had suggested.

Thought for the Day: *When we sincerely pray for guidance we are sometimes amazed at the way God works.*

A New Door Opened in Tokyo

Scripture Reading: Revelation 3:7-13

Key Verse: *See, I have placed before you an open door that no one can shut ... (Revelation 3:8a).*

Meditation: During the next few months we wondered how we should respond to Dr. Kobayashi's request. We could not discuss it with the northern pastors or the other missionaries. I was reminded that during our study furlough I had felt led to take an extra year beyond the Master of Divinity degree. The Master of Theology degree in the area of pastoral care was exactly what they wanted in the seminary. Could it be that God was preparing us for the position even before we were invited? Norma Jean, too, had finished a degree in teaching English that could also be used in the seminary.

At that time we learned that our field director, the Reverend Wesley Wildermuth was called to another field and would not be returning to Japan. I was appointed to serve as the "acting field leader" for the next year. I commuted to Tokyo three or four days each month for committee meetings, and joint-national church and mission boards. While far from ideal, everyone cooperated and senior missionaries worked hard to keep everything going in Tokyo while I was in Sendai.

After those 12 months I was elected field leader, which meant our whole family would move to Tokyo. In retrospect, I am grateful to all our field missionaries who made it possible for me to lead the field for a total of ten years.

Thought for the Day: *When it is God's will that our place of ministry change, we need not force the change, but wait for Him to open the right door according to His schedule.*

The New Challenges of Tokyo

Scripture Reading: Philippians 1:1-8

Key Verse: *...I have you in my heart...all of you share in God's grace with me (Philippians 1:7b).*

Meditation: I soon learned that there were many traditional expectations of the field leader both by the Japanese and the missionaries. Since 1951 the custom was that Japanese be the president of the seminary and the OMS field leader be the vice-president. So I was vice-president! The field leader automatically became the OMS representative on four joint church/mission committees. I found myself trying to speed the agenda of pushing for a quick execution of plans and goals. One day a church leader said to me, "Schultz Sensei, what is the big hurry? Remember that though you go on furloughs, all of us are staying right here and we promise to finish the job." That was a good lesson for me to learn early in the appointment.

In addition to caring for Malita and Juli, and the teaching of English at the seminary, Norma Jean's "job description" included the traditional expectations: coordinating hospitality for overseas guests, parties for TBS students at Christmas and graduation, welcomes for new missionaries and visitors, and open house for everyone anytime. In addition, she always tried to make friends with women outside the campus or the church, by teaching neighborhood English and cooking classes.

Over the next ten years I never tired of being the OMS representative at every church dedication, welcoming new students to Tokyo Biblical Seminary and challenging those graduating, congratulating the wedding couples, preaching at TBS retreats and at chapel, ministering at annual conferences and deeper life conventions in most of the districts.

Thought for the Day: *Being a missionary is a reciprocal experience in which we receive more than we give.*

The Inner Circle of Friends

Scripture Reading: Matthew 26:36-46

Key Verse: *He (Jesus) took Peter and the other two sons of Zebedee (James and John) and he began to be sorrowful and troubled (Matthew 26:37).*

Meditation: Jesus personally called twelve disciples to follow Him, and we assume He loved them all equally. However, on three different occasions he seems to indicate a preference for Peter, James and John. These three are sometimes referred to by Biblical scholars as "Christ's inner circle" or "Christ's inner trio." We do not know who really initiated the forming of this circle, but it seemed beneficial to all, including Jesus.

I observed this same dynamic at work between pastors and missionaries in Japan. Some pastors seemed to adopt a certain missionary as a friend forever. At times it may be the missionary who takes the initiative and starts the bonding process. My experience is a mixture of both. My first inner-circle friend in Japan was Hideo Takahashi Sensei.

When we first met he was single, a recent graduate of Tokyo Biblical Seminary. I knew a little Japanese and he knew only a little English, but my interpreter, Kunio Kubo, was with me. Takahashi Sensei insisted I speak at their New Year's Eve service. He closed the service with short comments and prayer for the whole church. We bonded at that time, and for the next 49 years he remained my warm personal caring friend. We exchanged pulpits several times and his ultimate gift of trust was asking me to baptize some of the converts he had led to Christ. Since 1953 God has added many to my inner circle of friends.

Thought for the Day: *Each inner-circle friend is a special gift of God to teach us the deeper meaning of love.*

A Missionary Survey Trip

Scripture Reading: Acts 1:6-11

Key Verse: *...and you will be my witnesses...unto the ends of the earth (Acts 1:8b).*

Meditation: A number of years ago I joined a group of field missionaries in a very lively discussion with Dr. Donald McGavran, considered the father of the Church Growth Movement. He answered our questions as to when a country should be considered fully evangelized. He said, "Whenever everyone in that country can either walk or use normal transportation available to get to a church." To the question as to when a national church should be considered fully indigenous he answered, "when it can reproduce itself in a culture different from its own."

During my last year in Japan one of the most meaningful experiences of my missionary life took place. I accompanied Dr. Yuzo Matsuki, the general superintendent of the Japan Holiness Church, in a missionary survey trip to the Philippines and to Taiwan, where Japanese missionaries were already serving. In Davao City on Mindanao Island, we worshiped with Philippine believers that Etsuko and Petro had won to Christ. In Manila we visited the OMS-related Faith Bible College and a number of church planting teams. Each of the team captains asked Dr. Matsuki to send missionaries from Japan to help them. One said, "If you do not have missionaries ready to send, why not send us some of your seminary students? We will train them and inspire them to return as career missionaries."

On our return flight Dr. Matsuki said, "The time is ripe for the Japanese Church to begin sending out more missionaries; we will begin with short-term summer seminary students." When I heard him make this commitment I saw by faith the full circle of the Great Commission in Japan.

Thought for the Day: *The most strategic time for the missionary to leave the field is when national pastors are leaving to become missionaries.*

Pastor to Missionaries

Scripture Reading: I Thessalonians 5:1-11

Key Verse: *Therefore, encourage one another and build each other up, just as in fact, you are doing (I Thessalonians 5:11).*

Meditation: Along with many other mission organizations, OMS became concerned in the 1980's about retaining their personnel. Even some who had anticipated a life career in missions left the field before finishing the first term. Many served in isolated places having little contact with those who spoke their language, and they had no pastoral counselor. The field leader tried to fill this role, but it is difficult to be open with those in administrative authority.

The OMS leadership asked us to consider utilizing our past missionary and pastoral experience to help them develop this ministry. Encouraging the people in their fields of work and counseling the younger recruits was a very challenging and rewarding work. In the five years we spent in this assignment, we witnessed God's working in the larger OMS world. In addition to counseling with missionaries personally, we spoke in the national churches and pastors' meetings. Our travels took us to the South American fields as well as the European and Far East. Going north to south was not nearly so demanding as the great east to west time differences. We continued the travel ministries schedule until on one of the trips the Japanese church leaders and missionaries invited us to serve as interim field leader for another period of three years.

Thought for the Day: *Mission leadership must continue to be sensitive to the needs of their missionaries by providing unbiased and prepared member care persons on a regular basis.*

A Centennial Celebration

Scripture Reading: Matthew 24:3-14

Key Verse: *And this gospel of the kingdom will be preached in all the world… (Matthew 24:14a).*

Meditation: In May 2001 OMS and the Japan Holiness Church held the first centennial celebration in Japan, the place where OMS was born. The Japanese pastor-evangelist, Juji Nakada, invited the Cowmans and the Kilbournes to join him in Japan. These three families had met earlier in Chicago when Mr. Nakada studied at Moody Bible Institute. Both the Cowmans and Kilbournes had been so impressed with Nakada's zeal to start a school like Moody in Japan, that they had been supporting him in his studies in USA. Nakada, a strong evangelistic speaker, saw the many young people who responded to his message of Christ and realized the need to provide a training institute to educate these converts in the scriptures and to prepare them to be church planters.

One hundred years later we returned to the city where it all started. A historic visual presentation of the beginning days led to the World War II era when all evangelism was stopped by the military government. Tears filled our eyes as we saw the record of those imprisoned for the duration of the war, some even dying in prison for their faith. Some of us who went to Japan in the early 1950's knew the surviving pastors personally. We relived how they sacrificed to restore their churches and begin their ministry again after the war.

A most moving service included the testimonies of Japanese missionaries serving now in Taiwan, Brazil, Malaysia and the Philippines. As an indication of their vision, they designated their main offering to build a centennial church, not in Japan, but in the Philippines.

Thought for the Day: *Since the God of the Bible is a sending God, so must His body become sending churches.*

A Centennial Celebration Challenge

Scripture Reading: II Chronicles 16:7-9

Key Verse: *For the eyes of the Lord range throughout the earth to strengthen those hearts fully committed to Him... (II Chronicles 16:9a).*

Meditation: I was invited to speak at one of the morning sessions at the Japan Centennial celebration. That invitation seemed to be God's seal on our decision to attend this gathering where we would see pastors and former seminary students now living all over Japan, but meeting in one hotel in Tokyo.

My message based on the reading from II Chronicles covered three areas:

1. The amazing fact is that men are not searching after God, but God is searching after us. In all things spiritual the pattern shows that God takes the initiative.

2. God's searching is universal; no country is exempt. Wherever we go in the world we can be sure that God has preceded us. Looking at the text from the New Testament perspective, we can go forth into the world confident that God's Holy Spirit has been poured out on all people.

3. God is very selective; He is not looking for minimally interested multitudes, but for individuals whose hearts are set on righteousness and holiness. God's priorities have not changed. He is still looking, not for natural talents, charisma or even academic excellence. He looks for single hearts focused on Him. Wherever such a person goes he will find, through the power of the Holy Spirit, Jesus Christ there with him.

Thought for the Day: *The only way we can account for the early growth and impact of the OMS-JHC is that the founders Nakada, Cowman, and Kilbourne each had a single heart towards God.*

A Great Mentor

Scripture Reading: II Kings 2:1-18

Key Verse: *Let me inherit a double portion of your spirit, Elisha replied (II Kings 2:9b).*

Meditation: A tribute to the late Dr. Roy P. Adams, my field leader and spiritual mentor, would make this series complete. I was told when arriving as a young missionary in Japan, "Uncle Roy has a lot to teach anyone who asks and remains to listen." I became one of those who stayed to listen to his reflections over 30 years of experience in Japan and China. His extraordinary influence in mission affairs took place out of public notice. He tried to be sensitive to the needs of the missionaries and national leaders, but sometimes had to make difficult decisions based on his knowledge and long experience.

He identified potential leadership in students and younger pastors and helped them in graduate studies overseas. They returned to pastor the larger churches and teach at the seminary. The most outstanding leaders in the past 30 years were directed, trained and encouraged by Dr. Adams.

Someone observed that it is difficult to become a leader in the Japanese church unless you are also an effective preacher of the Word of God. Uncle Roy demonstrated this ability with his rare expository preaching gift. Effectively wielding "the sword of the Spirit" under the anointing of the Holy Spirit, he preached the victorious life message and demonstrated it in his own personal life. He buried his first wife in China and returned to the USA with three small children. After his second wife died, he returned for a preaching mission to Japan. He ministered to others while working through his own grief.

Thought for the Day: *Being affirmed by a significant leader enables a person to believe in his/her God-given potential for ministry.*

A Faithful Friend

Scripture Reading: I Corinthians 9:13-23

Key Verse: *Though I am free and belong to no man, I made myself a slave to everyone... (I Corinthians 9:19).*

Meditation: My Japanese co-worker, Kanji Komi, spent most of his early life through middle school in Japanese–occupied Manchuria, where his father worked as an employee of the Japanese Railroad from 1937-45. Repatriated after World War II with only the clothes they were wearing, Mr. Kanji Komi found a job and determined to learn English. He found an English class taught by Laura Mock, a missionary from the Evangelical United Brethren Church, USA, who led him to the Lord. Soon he discovered OMS, where he worked from the late 1950's to 2001.

Mr. Komi, behind the scenes, multiplied the ministry of each OMS missionary. Particularly during the years I served as field leader, he was my right-hand person. His wisdom and counsel enabled us to work through many sensitive issues in national church/missionary relationships. I credit the many years of harmonious partnership that we still enjoy in Japan with his humble servant role.

Mr. Komi's desk reflected the main passions of his life: The calculator and computer show his careful management of the OMS-related bookstore and his annual financial reporting to the Ministry of Education, saving OMS and the seminary thousands of yen by meeting the tax-exempt requirements. His desk also had four Bibles: Japanese, English, Greek and Hebrew, all of which he used for the most accurate translations and interpretations in all of OMS 100 years of history. He made all of us missionaries look better than we were, but he would not take credit, even when I entered his name in the manuscript of some of my Japanese sermons. He did not talk of servanthood; he practiced being a servant.

Thought for the Day: *Servanthood is most eloquently expressed, not in sermons, but in living deeds to our fellow Christians.*

Lessons From Churches We Served

Scripture Reading: II Timothy 1: 3-7

Key Verse: *...fan into flame the gift of God... (II Timothy 1:6).*

Meditation: In the 1920's at Asbury College Dr. H. C. Morrison carried a special concern for the "preacher boys." A very distinguished evangelist, he carried the same aspirations for those called to preach. In addition to classroom studies, Dr. Morrison organized a number of independent "Ministerial Chapels." These small gatherings started under provided tents where summer teams from Asbury could evangelize and even start new churches.

During my second year at Asbury I took over one of these, Lane's Chapel named for the donor of the land and help with the building. A classmate, John Merwin, helped with the adult Sunday School and some of the preaching. On the first Sunday six adults and four children attended. John and I encouraged fellow college students to attend to boost the number to 20. Gradually others came from the community.

I learned that life-long friendships come from shared ministry: John and his wife, Peggy, later served as fellow missionaries in Japan and other parts of the world. Robert Bickert served in the Philippines as leader and seminary teacher. Other encouragers, like Philip Falk and Ethel Mayer continued to stand with us in ministry through 45 years.

At Lane's Chapel I also learned the Bible is an inexhaustible source for preaching, so I did not need to be anxious about the next sermon. Parishioners who endured constantly changing young ministers developed amazing patience and hope, making us confident of God's affirmation for the future.

Thought for the Day: *Surely God must have a special reward for all those people who listened to my elementary sermons with affirmation.*

Lessons From Churches We Served

Scripture Reading: John 15:1-16

Key Verse: *...fruit that will last... (John 15:16).*

Meditation: Midway United Methodist Church asked me to serve them after their pastor had completed his seminary work in the middle of the church year. The people knew me from my having evangelistic services there previously. We would be going to Japan in a few months, but the people chose us to be their short-term pastor.

The active congregation of 60 persons attended both Sunday morning and evening services. They provided a spiritual atmosphere of expectation that called for the best preaching I could offer. Being lovingly affirmed by them and working together, we saw the church begin to grow. Even though we had to go to Japan after only six months there, good things happened in the congregation.

I learned that a missionary concern can be born through faithful preaching of the Word and by personal obedience to the Great Commission. As we left, the congregation provided a sewing machine and vacuum cleaner for our home in Japan. For me their gift of a briefcase became my traveling library and small suitcase in Japan. Charles Leigh, a faithful layman, shared, "God ministered to me while you were here and that is part of the reason I have gone overseas on over 20 witness and work crusades." In addition, God raised up many in the congregation who have prayed for us through 45 years.

Thought for the Day: *Whatever the duration of our ministry, all work done while abiding in Christ will last.*

Lessons From Churches We Served

Scripture Reading: Philippians 1:3

Key Verse: *I thank my God every time I remember you (Philippians 1:3).*

Meditation: We returned to Wilmore after our first five years in Japan. I took additional studies at Asbury Theological Seminary and Norma Jean completed an English major AB at the college. After being in class for three months, Norma Jean sensed restlessness in me and began praying for an opening where I would preach regularly. She "happened" to visit the college alumni office and heard a district superintendent inquiring about possible students who could pastor a church left vacant in the middle of the church year. That door opened to me to serve the next four years at Graefenburg, Kentucky United Methodist Church.

This period is best defined as our miracle home leave: Norma Jean completed her degree requirements at the college while teaching at her nursing alma mater. I completed a Bachelor of Divinity and Master of Theology at the seminary while pastoring the church.   Together we welcomed two daughters, Malita Kei and Juli Anne, into our home parsonage and church family.   Sixteen months apart, they enjoyed much attention and we accepted the help from the loving parishioners to rear our daughters. Many, including Alice Gibbs and Ina Stucker often cared for the children while we carried out our day duties. The church people have followed all of us with their prayers, but especially the girls, back to Japan and now in their separate careers.

Graefenburg Church reflected the Philippian church model: Caring for the pastor, finding funds, giving personally like Johnnie Slucher often did as church treasurer, and praying for all of us regularly.   Their mission emphasis continued to reach us in Japan and wherever we went.

Thought for the Day: *Positive affirmation gives strength for ministry, while needless criticism drains strength needed to minister.*

Lessons From Churches We Served

Scripture Reading: Acts 20:25-38

Key Verse: *Now I commit you to God and the word of His grace (Acts 20:32).*

Meditation: We responded to our OMS president's request to be vice-president of homeland ministries. Toward the end of that three-year commitment, I found my blood pressure was too high to donate blood. Lloyd John Ogilvie had observed that we must listen to our bodies, for the body will tell you something. I listened to my body and to the Holy Spirit who showed me that the cause of my stress came from my not working in the realm of my spiritual giftedness, which was preaching and teaching. Most of my energy was being consumed in administrative tasks that left little time for ministry.

In the midst of the perplexity, World Gospel Church in Terre Haute, Indiana asked me to consider the position of senior pastor. The church had supported us for ten years and I was knowledgeable about its history and commitment. The founding pastor, The Reverend Carl Froderman, had insisted on the mission statement, *We are raised by God to help carry out the Great Commission to the world.* The goal of the church was to give at least 50 percent of its budget to world missions.

With a favorable vote, we spent the next eight years in a great stretching experience of our lives. God blessed our united effort as a congregation and the mission budget doubled. This congregation reinforced the importance of teaching and preaching the word of God, the challenge of integration of diversity while keeping unity, the sincere humility of academically prepared people, the generosity of those with means who did not manipulate, and that home missions and overseas missions are both very important outreaches for a church.

Thought for the Day: *Only a truly mission-minded church can really sing all the verses of All Hail the Power of Jesus Name.*

Learning From the Japanese Church

Scripture: Ephesians 3:14-21

Key Verse: *...he may strengthen you with power through his Spirit in your inner being (Ephesians 3:14:17).*

Meditation: In our mission's policy the missionary does not become a pastor of the national church, except perhaps in the pioneer stage and then ideally in conjunction with a mother church or national pastor. We did, however, regularly visit the churches for fellowship and mutual encouragement. The OMS-related national church conference numbered over 200 pastorates and preaching points. I could not visit them all, but I did visit over 100 at least once, and fellowshipped with most of the Christians at Spiritual Life Conferences. God taught me three main lessons:

1. They were eager to hear and responsive to the teaching about the Holy Spirit. Invariably I was asked to speak specifically about the Holy Spirit's ministry to Christians. I realized the preciousness and power of the Holy Spirit's ministry in my own life. We all need to be strengthened with power by His Spirit in our inner being.

2. I was always spiritually challenged and awed by the expectation expressed in their invitations. Seekers became believers, believers became Spirit-filled; and young people heard God's call to the ministry or missionary work.

3. I was deeply touched by the generosity of the churches as they insisted on paying travel expenses and giving honorariums. During our last years there, the national church helped to support other missionaries and us.

Thought for the Day: *God has equipped each of us uniquely for what is needed for the edification of the body of Christ where He has placed us.*

Lessons From Churches We Served

Scripture Reading: II Corinthians 11:16-33

Key Verse: *Besides everything else, I face daily the pressure of my concern for all the churches (II Corinthians 11:28).*

Meditation: After serving as "pastors-to-missionaries" for five years, Norma Jean and I were invited by the Japan church and the OMS missionaries to return to Tokyo in 1993. There we helped in the transition from older to younger leadership. Returning to the USA, we had no plans to retire from ministry. In Wilmore, Kentucky, the Community Missionary Church offered a "part-time" pastorate with opportunities to accept invitations to speak at other supporting churches.

The academic institutions of Asbury College and Asbury Theological Seminary in Wilmore with a combined student body of 3,000 has been a source of about one-third of the missionaries in OMS. Pastoring a small church in this unique setting had challenges to the future teachers, pastors and missionaries who made up the congregation. Those students who chose our church wanted to participate actively in the outreach and program of the church in order to learn and grow in their chosen field. We watched them develop as they led, taught and preached. We followed them after graduation and rejoiced to see how God used them as that church's "extended family."

I carry these observations from that rewarding experience: We are never too old to take additional training. Some of the seminary students were in their second career. One spent five years in studies and then died in her second year of church ministry, but her life was so meaningful that neither our church nor her pastorate would ever be the same again. I gained a new empathy for pastors of small churches, struggling to meet multiple needs with little staff. Finally, I learned the great spiritual and emotional demands made on every pastor who seeks to win persons not reared with biblical ethics or models.

Thought for the Day: *In each ministry opportunity God is preparing us for our next assignment.*

Lessons From Churches We Served

Scripture Reading: Romans 8:28,29

Key Verse: *...in all things God works for the good of those who love him... (Romans 8:28).*

Meditation: Most of the time we do not understand God's guidance except in retrospect. We did not realize when we took the pastorate in Wilmore with one-third of the members being college and seminary students that God was preparing us for our next assignment that would be a campus ministry. After being out of the North American pastoral setting for 20 years, we really needed the close one-on-one relationship to help us catch up with the thinking and aspirations of students before we embarked on our campus assignment.

Another positive result from our work in Wilmore was my experience of giving sermons from a Bible book, a topic or from a biography in the scriptures. Each series covered five to 15 sermons. In the same way for the campus ministry I continued the discipline of preparing series of sermons. I re-lived my 30 years of missionary experiences and incorporated them into the messages.

Being diagnosed with colon cancer resulted in my taking a less demanding assignment to 12 college and seminary campuses, representing OMS, challenging students to go overseas witnessing to Christ's salvation. All of the events in my life have directed me to write the material that is presented in this book. God is giving me the strength I need to fulfill my campus obligations as well as continue to be creative as I trust Him for each day of my life.

Thought for the Day: *Trust in God's guidance for the future even though you cannot comprehend His purpose today.*

Lessons From Hezekiah's Illness

Scripture Reading: II Kings 20:1-11

Key Verse: *This is what the Lord says, Put your house in order for you are going to die; you will not recover (II Kings 20:2).*

Meditation: Hezekiah, the good king of Judah, had just witnessed the Lord's powerful intervention against King Sennacherib with Assyria losing 185,000 soldiers. But before he could celebrate this triumph, a strange terminal disease attacked Hezekiah. Instead of accepting this sentence of death delivered to him by the prophet, Isaiah, Hezekiah turns to God in prayer.

We can be guided from this context in times of serious illness or other crises. Let us remember it is never too late to pray, regardless of the circumstances. Hezekiah did not ask or demand specifically to be healed, but asked God to remember him. He believed that prayers could reverse the sentence of death. He sincerely prayed with weeping, probably not only wanting to live longer for his own sake, but to carry out the spiritual reforms he had started. He believed that prayer and divine sovereignty worked together. He did not believe that divine healing necessarily excluded the use of known remedies, so he applied lumps of figs to the boils that apparently helped to extract the poison in his body.

Note that a miraculous healing does not transform a person into a mature saint. Within days of his healing, Hezekiah is tricked by a Babylonian ambassador and falls victim to pride by displaying all the treasures that would later be taken by the enemies. Hezekiah failed to consult Isaiah, who would have warned him against the trickery of the spying nation.

Thought for the Day: *We dare not let down our guard, especially after a great answer to prayer.*

When Life Seems Out of Control

Scripture Reading: Ecclesiastes 3:1-8

Key Verse: *There is a time for everything...a time to be born and a time to die... (Ecclesiastes 3:1,2).*

Meditation: Solomon lists 14 opposite events that happen in time. He reminds us that there are two particular events over which we human beings have little or no control -- the miracle of birth and the reality of the time of death. My oncologist told me, "There is nothing more we can do." Apparently both the two surgeries and two protocols of chemotherapy did nothing to stop the pernicious spread of colon cancer to the liver and lungs.

Hospice care includes a chaplain, a social worker and a registered nurse. Placed under their care a person can anticipate a life expectancy of six months or less, according to the guidelines of their licensure. My negative reaction to this prospect was disappointment that there is not yet a cure for the malicious colon cancer. I had to face the fact of my mortality and that I was now, like Hezekiah, considered a terminal patient.

Norma Jean and I agreed we would not cancel any of our scheduled meetings at the colleges and seminaries. We would continue to carry out our ministry as long as we had the physical ability provided by the grace of the Lord Jesus. While we realized the cancer in the body was real, we knew that I was in God's hands and that He, not the prognosis, would have the last word.

Thought for the Day: *While all people are subject to the limitations of time, yet we simultaneously carry within us the potential that transcends time.*

The Positive Value of Affliction

Scripture Reading: Psalm 119:65-72

Key Verse: *It was good for me to be afflicted so I might learn your decrees (Psalm 119:71).*

Meditation: The psalmist makes several personal observations of the value of affliction: It can serve as a correction to the human propensity of going astray, a great temptation especially during the last lap of our human journey. It can enhance our appreciation of God's Word and deepen our relationship to God. To the psalmist's list I would add the following:

1. To be able to talk objectively and plan for the coming months without being preoccupied with each day.
2. To intentionally and personally thank each person who has encouraged and affirmed us.
3. To appreciate each passing season and note the personal significance of the religious holidays.
4. To relive with your spouse the experience of the past years, 45 in our case. To review the rearing of our children, Malita and Juli Anne, and to enjoy the grandchildren, Austin, Clayton, and Emily. To celebrate our partnership in ministry both in Japan and North America.
5. To accomplish goals in probable shortness of time.
6. To intentionally strengthen ties with our family and expended relatives.
7. To re-examine and celebrate the strong foundation of faith in Jesus, the sinless Son of God, our personal Savior. To recognize His intercession for me at the right hand of God and the Holy Spirit within.

Thought for the Day: *My last breath will be my most important, for it will serve as my transition to the life that is eternal.*

God the Father and the Great Commission

Scripture Reading: Genesis 12:1-3

Key Verse: *... and all peoples of the earth will be blessed through you (Genesis 12:3b).*

Meditation: We must go back to the Old Testament to better understand the biblical foundations on which the Great Commission rests.

God made a new start with the human race through Abraham. God spoke clearly to Abraham that His will included Abraham's being a blessing to the whole world. That plan and promise went beyond the Old Testament era to Jesus Himself.

Adam's sin resulted in the fall of the entire human race. God's original covenant with Adam, making him ruler and lord over all creation, was nullified. The human race was alienated from God. Theologians sometimes use the phrase "total depravity" to describe mankind's inability to restore their broken relationship with God since the fall. This condition of sinfulness and alienation from God makes world evangelism not a matter of debate, but of obedience.

The very uniqueness of the God of the Bible should motivate us to world evangelism. God is the exalted, ultimate Creator of all that exists. As the One lofty Sovereign God, He is not even to be compared with other man-made deities. The fact of ONE GOD, monotheism, is the basis of all missionary work. "For there is one God and one mediator between God and men, the man Christ Jesus, who gave himself as a ransom for all men..." (I Timothy 2:5,6a).

Thought For the Day: *In the Bible we do not find men searching after God; we see God searching after man.*

God the Father and the Great Commission

Scripture Reading: Genesis 3:21-24

Key Verse: *…written in the book of life belonging to the Lamb that was slain from the creation of the world (Revelation 13:8b).*

Meditation: World Missions originated in the heart of God. John 3:16 states "For God so loved the world...," which explains it all. God did not love the world because the world was lovable, but only because God Himself is love. Neither did God elect Israel because Israel was more lovable than other nations, but because God is love. We can insert any name or group in the place of "Israel" or the "world." God loves the world of people.

Our key verse reminds us that God's self-sacrificing love is an eternal principle in the universe. We were all on God's mind before our first parents disobeyed and fell from grace in the Garden of Eden. Christ was crucified 2,000 years ago. Yet our key verse showed the plan of redemption through the slain Lamb was before time as we calculate it. God's intelligence is infinite and nothing catches Him by surprise. God's redemptive purposes are unchangeable; nothing God has purposed will fail to come to pass.

The cross was not some experimental solution to nullify a sinful situation. God's remedy for sin in man was not an afterthought. Redemption is a part of God's original plan for the universe.

Thought for the Day: *God saw the fall of man from eternity and ordered a remedy from eternity.*

God the Son and the Great Commission

Scripture Reading: Galatians 4:1-7

Key Verse: *God sent his Son, born of a woman... (Galatians 4:4a).*

Meditation: Every word in this scripture reading teaches us two truths: First, the biblical philosophy of history. God, in His omniscience operates His redemptive plan in total sovereign freedom. Jesus' coming illustrated God's moving and shaping history.

In retrospect, we can see how the nations unconsciously responded to God's initiative and made a pathway for the coming of the Messiah. Rome made travel easy for the then present world. Greek language communicated everywhere. Jewish synagogues scattered across the Roman Empire provided the destination for missionary work through their pre-evangelism in which "God-fearing Gentiles" prepared to believe in the Messiah.

Second, "God sent his Son, born of a woman." Jesus came, not from a carpenter shop, but from his pre-existent state in heaven. The human channel of an obedient woman made the incarnation possible. In the annunciation of Gabriel to Mary, God asked for her consent to help Jesus be incorporated into humanity. The Holy Spirit conceived Jesus to have a human body in the womb of Mary. "Jesus was verily man and verily God." This very body 33 years later bore the sins of all mankind as it hung on the cross.

Thought for the Day: *Since Adam sinned as a man, Christ had to become a man to redeem all born into Adam's family.*

God the Son and the Great Commission

Scripture Reading: Galatians 4:1-8

Key Verse: *To redeem those under the law (Galatians 4: 5a).*

Meditation: Many different Christian symbols represent aspects of Christ's life and ministry. The church fathers could have chosen the manger for the humility of his birth, a carpenter's bench to identify with manual labor, an apron for service to each other, a stone removed in resurrection power. These are all valid symbols, but they are not central. The heart of the gospel is the fact of Christ on the cross. The actual proclamation of the gospel is the actual death of Christ on the cross for us.

The message of the New Testament, "Christ gave himself for our sins" (Galatians 1:4a), and "Christ redeemed us from the curse of the law by becoming a curse for us (Galatians 3:13a), illustrates the cross used for the death of Christ in our place. Under the law Jews and Gentiles alike were without hope. Christ became a curse for both of us, Jew and Gentile. Christ fulfilled the Old Testament image of the scapegoat in Leviticus 16:5. One goat was killed and its blood sprinkled in the Most Holy Place; the other goat was sent away alive bearing the sins of the nation, symbolizing the removal of the guilt. Christ, dying on the cross, both cleansed and carried away our guilt and our sin.

Every time we think of Christ on the cross we should hear Christ say, "I am here because of your curse, your sin." Oswald Chambers said, "No sinner can get right with God on any other ground. Christ died instead of me."

Thought for the Day: *The missionary message is not "What must I do?" but "Believe in what Christ has already done for you."*

God the Spirit and the Great Commission

Scripture Reading: John 16: 7-11

Key Verse: *...unless I go away, the Comforter will not come to you (John 16:7b).*

Meditation: The four Gospels focus on the redemptive events of Christ's birth, crucifixion, resurrection, and ascension. Luke closes with Christ's promise/command to His followers, "I am going to send you what my Father promised, but stay in the city until you have been clothed with power from on high" (Luke 24:49).

In the five statements of the Great Commission there is reference to the Holy Spirit: Matthew 28:18-20, Mark 16:15-20, Luke 24:46-49, John 20:21,22 and Acts 1:8. Until Christ ascended and the Spirit descended on the church, there could be no valid witnessing or evangelism. On the day of Pentecost, Christ exchanged His physical presence with the disciples for His spiritual omnipresence through the Holy Spirit's outpouring.

Now Christ is no longer limited to one place. He is always present, not confined as in the physical incarnation. Since Pentecost we can be confident that wherever we go in the world, the living Christ, through the Holy Spirit, will accompany us fulfilling that promise, "And surely I am with you always, to the very end of the age" (Matthew 28:20b).

Thought for the Day: *World missions is a divine enterprise directed both from heaven by Jesus seated on the right hand of God, and by the Holy Spirit on earth serving as Christ's vice-regent.*

God the Spirit and the Great Commission

Scripture Reading: John 16:7-11

Key Verse: *I will pour out my Spirit on all flesh... (Acts 2:17a).*

Meditation: The Gospels record all that Jesus began to do and teach. Acts records all that Jesus continued to do and teach. Jesus continues His work today linked to the church and to the world by the Holy Spirit. With this "Divine-human" co-working, we can embark boldly on this worldwide program of evangelism.

On the day of Pentecost Joel's prophecy was fulfilled: God's Spirit came on all flesh, on mankind everywhere. So the missionary does not "take" Christ or the Spirit to the world. They are already universally present. Barriers such as "iron or bamboo curtains" cannot keep them out. No place is without hope and we go to no place alone.

The Holy Spirit is always at work for the hope of conversions and revival. He is active and precipitates a crisis in the unbeliever in regard to personal sin, personal unrighteousness, and the certainty of coming judgment. Judgment is based on unbelief in Jesus and the Holy Spirit who together have provided a way to experience forgiveness and inward righteousness.

Thought for the Day: *The influence of the Holy Spirit in the world is mediated and intensified through Spirit-filled witnesses.*

God the Spirit and the Great Commission

Scripture Reading: Luke 24:45-53

Key Verse: *I am going to send you what my Father promised...*
(Luke 24:49a).

Meditation: The unity of the Trinity is to be modeled in the life of the church. Each person in the Trinity delights to serve the other members. Jesus exalted and glorified the Father. The Spirit glorified Jesus. The Son glorified the Father on earth, and the Father glorified the Son in heaven. The Spirit glorifies the Son in the church and in the life of individual believers.

Luke 24:49 amplifies the unity of the Trinity by telling us of God's supreme promise to give us the Spirit. Jesus stressed that the Holy Spirit is the supreme promise of the Father. God could not give us any other gift more essential that the gift of the Holy Spirit. Having the Holy Spirit is having all of God, not just with us, but in us. Oswald Chambers said that the Spirit releases on us subjectively all that Christ did objectively for us on the cross and through the resurrection. Since this power is from "on high," we are empowered to minister effectively beyond our natural giftedness and in spite of our lack of talent.

The Promise of the Father enables us to witness both locally and cross-culturally as in Acts 1:8. We cannot be an effective witness unless we are operating in the power of the Holy Spirit. We must tarry for the gift of the Holy Spirit who alone makes our works valid in the Day of Judgment (II Corinthians 5:5-10).

Thought for the Day: *Waiting for the Spirit's fullness can be the most fruitful use of our time, for afterwards we will see "the fruit that will remain."*

The Five All's of the Great Commission

Scripture Reading: Matthew 28:16-20

Key Verse: *All authority in heaven and earth has been given to me (Matthew 28:18b).*

Meditation: The word *all* dominates and binds together the words of the Great Commission: *all* authority, a*ll* nations, *all* of Christ's commands, *all* the days of human history embracing the consummation of the present age.

Both the missionaries who go to the world and the sending church must be fully aware of the spiritual resources in Christ available to them. Christ has universal authority on the basis of His incarnation at Bethlehem and His atoning death on the cross. The missionary goes and is sent with the confidence that no power in heaven or on earth operates outside of Christ's permission.

Ephesians 4:8-13 teaches us that during the three days between Christ's death and resurrection He descended to the lower parts of the earth, Sheol, where the Old Testament believing saints were waiting. Apparently Old Testament believers could not be ushered into the Father's holy presence until Christ's death for them was actualized in history. The merits of His death became retroactive for them fully covering all that died with faith in the coming Messiah.

Thought for the Day: *Every power on earth and all evil in the heavenly realm is ultimately under the lordship of Jesus.*

The Five All's of the Great Commission

Scripture Reading: Matthew 28:16-20

Key Verse: *When they saw him, they worshipped him, but some doubted (Matthew 28:17).*

Meditation: The verses of Matthew 28:16-20 embrace all three tenses of human history: The past, the present and the future. They even cover the consummation of history itself. No wonder these verses are called "The Great Commission" by church scholars.

Christ spoke these all-encompassing words to followers who still vacillated between worship and doubt. Jesus did not exorcise their unbelief or give them faith-building exercises first.

Christ did not minimize the importance of "mustard seed-sized faith." He evidently encouraged his followers to expect great things with ordinary faith.

He encourages those of us with hesitant faith to begin to follow God's word. Christ began His Church with fallible workers who simply obeyed while still doubting.

Thought for the Day: *Even "small faith" focused on the words and person of Jesus can produce amazing results.*

The Five All's of the Great Commission

Scripture Reading: Matthew 26:16-20

Key Verse: *...All authority in heaven...is given unto Me (Matthew 26:18b).*

Meditation: When Jesus ascended He passed unhindered through the heavenly realms that are associated with the headquarters of Satan and the power of darkness. Ephesians 6:12b speaks of "the spiritual forces of evil in the heavenly realms." Jesus was not alone; He had all the believing Old Testament saints whom He would lead into the presence of God. When Christ returns the second time, we, too, who are alive will be caught up to be with Him, passing safely through the very territory that Satan once claimed as his own.

According to scripture the church should now view Satan as the dethroned power of the universe. While Satan still exists, he was defeated at Calvary (Colossians 3:15), "And having disarmed the powers and authorities, he made a public spectacle of them, triumphing over them by the cross." Satan's final sentence has not been fully implemented, but the believer can already bind Satan's power in the stronger name of Jesus.

To illustrate from World War II: Historians make a distinction between "D Day" and the invasion of Normandy and "V Day", the end of the war. A period of almost one year elapsed between these dates. But when the allied forces established a beachhead in Normandy, France, that initial victory made the final victory a foregone conclusion.

Thought for the Day: *Since Christ established a beachhead at Calvary, the final implementation of that victory is only a matter of time.*

The Five All's of the Great Commission

Scripture Reading: Matthew 28:16-20

Key Verse: *Therefore go, and make disciples of all nations (Matthew 28:19a).*

Meditation: Serving under Christ's universal lordship, the church is mandated by Christ himself to go into the entire world and make disciples of all nations. According to Matthew disciple-making is the great importance of the Great Commission. Being a convert and being a disciple is radically different.

The word "apprentice" is closer to the original meaning of "disciple." An apprentice attaches himself to a teacher and commits himself to the teacher's priorities. A disciple also keeps on learning by listening and doing until he is able to model and reproduce Christ's lifestyle.

Oswald Chambers stressed that whenever Jesus talked about discipleship, He always prefaced His invitation with "If anyone will come after me." Discipleship is not a group, but an individual matter. We each have a choice in the matter of discipleship. It is optional. Jesus insisted that while many are invited, only a few prove themselves to be chosen. In Luke 9 all three "would-be" followers failed the test of discipleship and became "dropouts."

Thought for the Day: *Many "would-be" followers even today become dropouts for the same reasons: Discipleship is not a secure and glamorous life. It demands the re-ordering of social and family obligations. A disciple must be willing to do ordinary work without looking back.*

The Five All's of the Great Commission

Scripture Reading: Matthew 28:16-20

Key Verse: *...baptizing them in the name of the Father, Son and Holy Spirit (Matthew 28:19b).*

Meditation: Baptism was commanded originally not by the church, but by Christ himself. These words were spoken after His crucifixion and resurrection, reminding us that baptism is irrevocably linked to those two events. In other words, baptism is intended to be a dramatic portrayal both to the believer, and to observers, of Christ's provision for our salvation.

Baptism, according to the Scriptures, is not a condition of salvation, but a witness of the "how" of our salvation. When the mode of baptism is immersion, the meaning is that we are following Jesus to His death (by going into the water) and into His resurrection life (by coming out of the water).

To be baptized into the individual names of the Trinity (the three modes of one God) means that the new believer has now been brought into a direct, personal and dynamic relationship with all the fullness of God. Since the primary movement in baptism is from God to the believer, He not only connects us to the Trinity, but He also connects us to His church in heaven and on earth.

In the early Christian Church they celebrated "White Sunday" in which those baptized came forward dressed in white robes. They thereby witnessed to all present that Jesus had washed their souls from every evil stain. White Sunday was celebrated on the day of Pentecost, 50 days after the resurrection, when the Holy Spirit was given to the church.

Thought for the Day: *Baptism continues to be a strong reminder and portrayal of how salvation was made possible through Christ's crucifixion and resurrection.*

The Five All's of the Great Commission

Scripture Reading: Matt. 28:16-20

Key Verse: *And teaching them to obey everything I have commanded you... (Matthew 28:20a).*

Meditation: Christ continues His lordship over the church by holding us accountable to teach and obey all that He has commanded in His word. Those hearing the gospel would become disciples by the three-fold process: Hearing the Word, believing the Word, and submitting to the Word.

We ask, "Where is this teaching found that we are to deliver to new converts?" It is certainly found in the Gospels, but it is not limited to the New Testament alone. Properly understood, the teaching of Jesus includes all the Old Testament, as well. Jesus often quoted from the Old Testament as an authoritative source and witness to Himself. He linked Himself to Abraham saying, "Abraham rejoiced to see my day" (John 8:56). When He began His public ministry He read from Isaiah 61 about the Messiah's mission and then added, "Today this Scripture has been fulfilled in your hearing" (Luke 4:21). Even after His resurrection, on the Emmaus road, He continued to relate His life to Old Testament teaching.

At the heart of Jesus' teaching are the four gospels, each with its distinctive emphasis: Matthew emphasizes how the Old Testament was fulfilled in the New Testament. Mark, written for the Roman world, spells out the cost of non-Jews following Jesus as disciples. Luke teaches both Jews and Gentiles the universality of God's plan for all people. John emphasizes God's love for all people.

Thought for the Day: *Since all scripture is God-breathed, it must all be taught.*

The Five All's of the Great Commission

Scripture Reading: Matthew 28:16-20

Key Verse: *...And surely I am with you always, to the very end of the age (Matthew28: 20b).*

Meditation: The words, "to the end of the age" assure the church of God's plan, for He is the Lord of history. History is ultimately His Story. History will be consummated at the time of God's choosing. In the meantime, we can rest on His promises and live with the certainty of His ongoing presence with us.

During the 40 days between His resurrection and ascension, Christ had two very important ministries to ensure the future of His church. First, He had to demonstrate the reality of His resurrection so there would be no lingering doubts. The disciples were soon convinced that the Lord had risen indeed. At first they probably did not fully understand how Christ's resurrection was significantly different from that of Lazarus, but they rejoiced that He was back among them as victor over death.

The second important lesson was preparing them for the coming withdrawal of His visible presence. To enable them to realize and comprehend His future abiding invisible presence was much more difficult. As we observe Christ's post-resurrection appearances, we see He would suddenly appear and then just as suddenly disappear as He did on the road to Emmaus. Later He appeared in the midst of the disciples "when the door was shut," only to disappear just as suddenly. He spoke to Thomas words that revealed He was present and listening when Thomas expressed his doubts. The conviction grew on the disciples that the resurrected Christ was with them always. Christ was no longer subject to human needs or natural laws.

Thought for the Day: *After Christ ascended, the disciples returned to Jerusalem with joy, believing Christ would be with them always through the promised and coming Holy Spirit.*

Jonah, the Reluctant OT Missionary

Scripture Reading: Jonah 1:1-3

Key Verse: *Go to the great city of Nineveh... (Jonah 1:2a).*

Meditation: I heard a missionary speaker say, "Some of the best missionaries God ever called never get to the field." In the light of greatness of the harvest and the scarcity of workers, that statement must be true. Some, like Jonah, just run away from God's call, but are turned back by God's strong intervention. The account of Jonah's disobedience is not just a whale of an Old Testament story, but an honest account of the power struggle we may all confront when God calls.

Jonah was not a bad, sinful person. He appears to have been a good moral man, a zealous believer and defender of the God of the Old Testament. He had responded to an earlier call to be a prophet of God. For ten to 15 years he faithfully reported to the people what God said. Jonah was a person who heard and understood God's will and message.

But then he refused to obey God. He reminds us that there could be a "little Jonah" in all of us, at every stage of our Christian lives. I remember hearing a missionary speaker say, "God had to re-call me during each furlough, as I was tempted not to return to the mission field where I worked."

Thought for the Day: *Delayed obedience can quickly turn into willful disobedience.*

Jonah, the Reluctant OT Missionary

Scripture Reading: Jonah 1:1-4

Key Verse: *But Jonah ran away from the Lord (Jonah 1:3a).*

Meditation: Why would Jonah disobey and start running from God? Could he have misinterpreted God's directions because they were unclear? They seemed precise: "Go to the great city of Nineveh and preach against it..." Did Jonah misunderstand the purpose of his mission? That seemed clear: "Its wickedness has come up before me." Did he fear this cross-culture experience in Assyria might end in failure? The later chapters tell us that none of these factors contributed to his disobedience.

Jonah actually feared success more than failure in this divine assignment. Jonah was an isolationist, a very narrow-minded patriotic Jew. He believed that salvation was for the Jews alone, and that Yahweh was the exclusive God of Israel. Since Nineveh, a Gentile city, was beyond the boundaries of Israel, Jonah was determined not to cross that boundary. He "drew a line in the sand" over which he would not cross. He chose the risk of losing everything, his call, and even God's presence in his life.

But let us not give up on Jonah, because God did not give up. Most of us have peoples that we find hard to love. On the screen of our human memories we have names of people for whom we have stopped praying. Perhaps we hope we will not see them again.

Thought for the Day: *When we shut people out of our hearts, striking them from our prayer lists, we may inadvertently be shutting out God as well.*

Jonah, the Reluctant OT Missionary

Scripture Reading: Jonah 1: 1-4

Key Verse: *But Jonah ran away from the Lord and headed for Tarshish (Jonah 1:3a).*

Meditation: Jonah, as the potential missionary dropout, displays the high cost of disobedience. He had a very important position at the king's court. He was a prestigious prophet. He could have easily returned to that position, once he had completed his preaching mission on Nineveh, but that was not to be.

When Jonah refused God's directive to go to Nineveh, everything started going wrong. Out of fellowship with God, he had blocked his ability to hear God's voice, so he was no longer valuable to the king or to Israel. Neither could he remain passive in a place where he once heard the call of God. Too many reminders jogged his troubled memory and made him uneasy. Jonah had to obey or run away. He chose to run. We cannot remain neutral when God calls.

Jonah ran, but God provided an exit route: Jonah found a ship with one opening. Perhaps Jonah thought he was doing the right thing after all. But as we follow Jonah's journey we learn that a mere open door is not necessarily the right door or God's will for us.

Thought for the Day: *Positive human circumstances alone are not always indicators of God's will for our lives.*

Jonah the Reluctant OT Missionary

Scripture Reading: Jonah 1:1-4

Key Verse: *After paying the fare, he went aboard and sailed for Tarshish to flee from the Lord (Jonah 1:3b).*

Meditation: Jonah's saga teaches us we never fully know in advance where our disobedience will take us. Jonah did not land somewhere close to the "Nineveh of God's will" for his assignment. Neither did he have the leisure of glancing over the border should he change his mind.

Jonah finds himself going to Tarshish, a small village in Spain. If he had actually landed, he would have been over 1,000 miles from Ninevah. Someone has said, "Backsliding is turning from the best to the second-best." Jonah now finds himself with second best by willful choice.

Jonah learns that the timing of God's call is very significant. God had actually been pouring out the prevenient grace of His Spirit upon Nineveh, preparing the city for repentance and revival. God's working in Nineveh preceded Jonah's call. Therefore, Jonah's obedience was much more imperative. We are prone to think we have lots of time to obey, but the fact is we do not have our own time schedule. The open door for people to respond to God seems to stay open for only a few years.

Thought for the Day: *If we have enough direction to take the first step, we should take it. Believing that God in His sovereignty will show us all we need to know, we should follow Him immediately.*

Jonah the Reluctant OT Missionary

Scripture Reading: Jonah 1:1-4

Key Verse: *...and sailed for Tarshish to flee from the Lord (Jonah 1:3b).*

Meditation: We tend to focus on Jonah, but God is the key actor in this drama. Jonah, the great missionary textbook of the Old Testament, portrays a God who intervenes. God performs succeeding miracles to turn His runaway missionary back to the city He had sovereignly prepared for repentance and revival.

God's initiative towards us leads to our salvation. The book of Jonah displays the "good news" of the Old Testament. While we may run away from God's call, we are not able to run away from His universal presence. Jonah discovered that God has a very sophisticated radar system, and He always knows where we are.

Jonah reflects the Jewish idea of localizing God to the temple and to Palestine. He wrongly reasoned that God's presence would disappear once he crossed the border of Palestine. Imagine Jonah's surprise when he thought he had escaped, only to have God's presence right with him.

Thought for the Day: *The ultimate springs of love for the world are in God, not in us.*

Jonah the Reluctant OT Missionary

Scripture Reading: Jonah 1:1-4

Key Verse: *Then the Lord sent a great wind on the sea... (Jonah 1:4a).*

Meditation: God has many ingenious ways to get the attention of the disobedient. He sent a great wind on the sea. Then God forced Jonah to join a prayer meeting led by panic-stricken sailors. They exhorted him to pray to his God. Finally, the lot cast by the sailors fell on Jonah. He was marked as the real culprit causing the fierce storm. The sailors cast him overboard at Jonah's suicidal request. God had prepared a great fish to carry him directly to the land of his original calling.

In chapter four are recorded three more occasions when God supernaturally intervened to both teach and get Jonah's attention. God prepares a vine to give the pouting prophet temporary relief from the sun. He took it away quickly with a scorching east wind. God sought to illustrate by the vine how much Ninevah meant to God. Ninevah meant more to God than the temporary vine. God had prepared Nineveh faithfully for years for the positive harvest Jonah helped to reap.

God does not allow anyone who has served Him to fall into oblivion. He will use a variety of circumstances to pressure us back to obedience. He even uses troubles in the journey of disobedience to show us our mistakes.

Thought for the Day: *It is never easy for a Christian to sever his relationship to God.*

Jonah the Reluctant OT Missionary

Scripture Reading: Jonah 3:1-10

Key Verse: *Then the word of the Lord came to Jonah the second time (Jonah 3:1a).*

Meditation: Jonah 3:1 reminds us of the pure grace of God in the Old Testament. Many are too quick to give up on people like Jonah. We adopt a righteous stance and immediately dismiss from our prayers anyone who has withdrawn from God's work and call. The truth is that many are still in the ministry today because of the restoring grace of God. In times of failure and deep dejection, God in His mercy did not cast us aside.

Jonah found his way back into God's favor. He discovered he could still pray, even though rebellious. He remembered the temple where he first heard God's call. He also returned to the place where he began to disobey. Jonah did not have to start all over again; he simply had to obey again at the point of his disobedience. The secret of our recovery is to start back where we began to disobey.

Thought for the Day: *If we find ourselves on the road to Tarshish, we must return to the Nineveh of God's call.*

The First Missionary Sending Church

Scripture Reading: Acts 11:19-26

Key Verse: *...and you will be my witnesses in Jerusalem, and in all Judea and Samaria and to the ends of the earth (Acts 1:8b).*

Meditation: Ten years had passed since the ascended Jesus poured out the Holy Spirit on the 120 persons who waited in Jerusalem. For some reason the twelve disciples focused all their attention on the mother church in Jerusalem. Then, because of the fierce persecution resulting from the death of Stephen, believers scattered as far as Antioch of Syria. The Twelve chose to stay in Jerusalem to guard the mother church at all costs. Apparently, their spiritual horizons were still bounded by the narrow outlook of Judaism.

Spirit-filled lay persons who would not be silenced by persecution launched the task of "world evangelism." At first they limited their witness to "Jews only," but at Antioch of Syria the Jewish Christians took the first major step in Gentile world evangelism. The first Gentile church was born in Antioch of Syria. Thus, the transition from Jewish mission to Gentile mission began, and the leadership of the church changed from Peter and the Twelve to Paul. Most important of all, the major missionary sending church moved from Jerusalem to Antioch.

Notice the sequence of God's working in these chapters. First, God allows the persecutor, Saul, to scatter the church out of Jerusalem. Then, by divine intervention, the persecutor is converted in Damascus, a Gentile city, and he is given a missionary commission to the Gentiles. Finally, he is called to become the senior pastor and first missionary of a Gentile church.

Thought for the Day: *I will not judge prematurely what God permits until enough time passes to see how He uses what He allows.*

The First Missionary Sending Church

Scripture Reading: Acts 11:19-26

Key Verse: *...the disciples were called Christians first at Antioch (Acts 11: 26b).*

Meditation: Antioch of Syria lay 300 miles north of Jerusalem. Incorporated into the Roman Empire in 50 B.C., it had a population of 200,000 people. Next to Rome and Alexandria, it was the third largest city in the empire. Much trade passed through the city, so it was noted for its culture and commerce, but also well known for the pagan temples and immorality associated with temple prostitutes. Even though Jesus never visited or preached there, it was at Antioch that believers were first called Christians. They were called the name out of mockery, but the nickname became a badge of honor that we gladly bear today.

2,000 years later across states and provinces many churches are called Antioch. Even if there are not towns in the vicinity called Antioch, still churches choose that name. We wonder how the name has prevailed to the present? Until the gospel was preached in Antioch, believers were generally referred to as "the people of the way," meaning followers of Christ, the Way. The word "Christian" (Christ+ian) meant "belonging to" or "being a part of Christ." Those who tried to mock voiced an insight into the lives of the believers that perhaps they themselves were not even fully conscious of, "being a part of Christ."

As a pastor of three different churches in the USA, I have always been amazed how much people in the community who never attended church seemed to know what was going on inside the church, both positive and negative.

Thought for the Day: *What is the message about Christ that is going out from your church into your community?*

The First Missionary Sending Church

Scripture Reading: Acts 13:1-3

Key Verse: *...Barnabus, Simeon called Niger, Lucius of Cyrene, Manaen and Saul (Acts 13: 1b).*

Meditation: Yesterday we began to look for distinguishing marks of the first missionary sending church that still serves as a model for the church today. Their radically changed life-styles with constant reference to Christ in conversations earned them the nickname "Christians." Given the diversity of their congregation, they must also have manifested Christ-like love, the first fruit of the Spirit mentioned in Galatians 5:23,24. Someone has said, "The real evidence of Spirit-filled lives is found, not in spiritual gifts, but in the evidence of the fruit of the Spirit which reflect the nine character traits of Jesus himself."

The second mark of the church: The leadership reflected the ethical, social and economic diversity of the city. Antioch comprised at least four ethnic groups: Jews, Romans, Greeks and Africans. The leadership team by their names reflects all of these groups: Saul, a well-educated expatriate Jew and Barnabas, highly sensitized to other cultures. Manaen, a Roman and distant relative to King Herod was no doubt a man of means who could move easily with the upper ruling groups of Antioch. Simeon, from Africa, could identify with immigrants and other strangers. Regardless of one's ethnic, educational or social background, a sympathetic ear could be found in the leadership of the church.

No wonder that Antioch became a missionary sending church, being already involved in cross-cultural missions right in the city. It is no surprise that many of the leaders felt called to go outside of their nation because they were already sharing the prayer requests of the church members for people back in their individual home nations.

Thought for the Day: *Could it be that behind the many immigrants coming to America today there is God's sovereign purpose for them to hear the gospel here?*

The First Missionary Sending Church

Scripture Reading: Acts 13:1-3

Key Verse: *In the church at Antioch there were prophets and teachers… (Acts 13:1a).*

Meditation: The third distinguishing mark of the church at Antioch: The leadership of the church was introduced, not only by name, but also in terms of their spiritual gifts. At least two specific gifts are mentioned: the prophetic gift and the gift of teaching. This church was biblically grounded in Ephesus 4:11b, "when Christ ascended into heaven and poured out His Spirit on the church, He also gave some to be apostles, some to be prophets, some to be evangelists and come to be pastors and teachers."

The two spiritual gifts mentioned here in Acts 13 come from the list of gifts generally called "missionary gifts" or "universal gifts to the church" -- apostleship, the supernatural capacity to found new churches, prophecy, the divine ability to foretell and also speak forth boldly God's will and word. The gift of evangelism, that anointing to enable sinners to believe; the gift of pastoring, that ability to care deeply for individuals and to nurture them in the faith. The gift of teaching, that ability to effectively transmit the full counsel of God to the congregation.

If these missionary gifts mentioned in I Corinthians 12-14 were recovered in our churches today, the gap between clergy and laity would be bridged. Unbelievers would believe that Christ is alive both in heaven and in the church. The church would increase in unity and maturity. Leadership gifts would be encouraged as modeled by Barnabas. Senior pastors would be released for missionary work because of giftedness of others on the team.

Thought for the Day: *Are the leaders and laity of my church in touch with their spiritual gifts?*

The First Missionary Sending Church

Scripture Reading: Acts 13:1-3

Key Verse: *...while they were worshipping the Lord and fasting...* *(Acts 13:2a).*

Meditation: Yesterday we were challenged by the church that intentionally identified spiritual gifts in the leadership team and in the body of Christ. As pastor and missionary field leader, five suggestions have been helpful:

1. Follow the burden you feel for the people of the church and seek to meet that need.
2. Expect some unsolicited affirmation of your giftedness.
3. Notice that you are being able to serve out of your giftedness without exhaustion.
4. Sense divine strength going out from you to meet specific needs.
5. More spiritual growth or understanding seems to happen than you can explain in natural terms.

The fourth mark of the Antioch church was their practice of the spiritual disciplines of worship, prayer and fasting. "Give unto the Lord...glory and strength. Give to the Lord the glory due unto his name" (Psalm 96:7-8a). They discovered the awesome mystery of God, "inhabiting their praises" (Psalm 22:3a). As the Antioch church ascribed to God His mighty attributes, God manifested Himself in the very way they praised Him. The same pattern of God's reciprocal action is portrayed for us in Acts 4 and 12 as well.

Fasting, included in the trilogy of spiritual disciplines, deserves close attention: Jesus seems to emphasize fasting to be very private, and not for men's applause. An act we do "before God," not as a bargaining device, but as a humbling expression by repenting of anything that grieves the Holy Spirit. We also relinquish all dependence on human means and confess our complete dependence on God above.

Thought for the Day: *Whenever our human plans and programs fail, let us immediately return to praise, prayer and fasting.*

The First Missionary Sending Church

Scripture Reading: Acts 13:1-5

Key Verse: *...the Holy Spirit said, Set apart for me Barnabas and Saul for the work to which I have called them (Acts 13:2b).*

Meditation: The fifth distinguishing mark of the Antioch church: When they heard the voice of the Spirit they immediately obeyed. Did they hear an audible voice? Did someone have a revelation? Did someone give a prophetic utterance? We do not know, but most significant was that they collectively obeyed immediately.

Someone has observed that the most important work of the Antioch church was their listening and obeying the voice of the Spirit. If the church today listens to the Spirit, and sends out workers who also hear and obey the Spirit, great results can be expected. I believe the world cannot help but listen to that missionary who has been sent out by a Spirit-sensitive church. A Japanese pastor said to a group of young missionaries, "We Japanese cannot help but listen to the missionary who, like Isaiah has personally heard and obeyed God's call, 'Who will go for us?'"

The sixth distinguishing mark: They observed the importance of identifying closely with the sent missionaries. They "laid their hands on them," a ritual with Old Testament symbolic meaning. When a Jewish worshipper brought a sacrificial animal to the priest, he placed his hands on the animal's head indicating the animal was taking his place. The church at Antioch was saying to Paul and Barnabas, "You are going for us and we are going with you." As they laid hands on them they were also blessing them spiritually and energizing them with their varied giftedness.

Thought for the Day: *At every missionary commissioning service the "sending church" affirms its oneness with the "scattered church."*

The First Missionary Sending Church

Scripture Reading; Acts 13:4-12

Key Verse: The *two of them, sent on their way, by the Holy Spirit...* *(Acts 13:4a).*

Meditation: Saul and Barnabas experienced a two-fold commissioning, one by the church and the other by the Holy Spirit. The results that followed this commissioning should give us a renewed understanding of the vital relationship between the sending church and the Great Commission.

1. Saul's Jewish name was changed to Paul, clearly evidencing his new identity with the Gentile world.
2. They were divinely guided to an untried new effective method of church planning. They went to cities, first beginning at the local synagogue where they found divinely prepared "God-fearing" and sympathetic Jews.
3. A new apostolic spiritual gift seemed to be added, enabling them to minister cross-culturally. Timothy demonstrates a connection between the laying on of hands and the emergence of a new gift (I Timothy 4:14).
4. They were given a renewed confidence that the Holy Spirit was guiding them to all those whom the Spirit was preveniently preparing to be saved.
5. They were supernaturally equipped to wage victorious prayer warfare over all demonic opposition.
6. They preached effectively, baptized and instructed those who believed. They organized these believers into a church and thus fulfilled all the demands of the Great Commission.
7. They had divine wisdom to stand against the legalistic Judaizers within the church in order to make Christianity a visible world-faith rather than a seat of Judaism.

Thought for the Day: *Let us believe in the great potential of our church and every missionary team.*

Prayer and the Great Commission

Scripture Reading: Acts 1:1-8

Key Verse: *...Do not leave Jerusalem, but wait for the gifts my Father has promised (Acts 1:4b).*

Meditation: During the last days of Christ's ministry on earth before His ascension, He indicated clearly that His church would have three distinctives: A spirit of united unceasing prayerfulness, a ministry distinguished by the power of the Holy Spirit, and each member would use his/her spiritual gifts to spread the gospel to the ends of the earth.

Immediately following the ascension, the disciples "all joined together constantly in prayer along with the women..." (Acts 1:4a). The New Testament church understood the duty to wait for the Holy Spirit as God's enduement from on high. They waited for ten days, not only for their own spiritual preparation, but until Jesus was glorified as indicated in John 7:39: "Up to that time the Spirit had not been given, since Jesus had not yet been glorified." The ten days waiting does not apply to us today, since Jesus has already been glorified.

However, we are to wait for the Holy Spirit as Luke 11:13b teaches: "...How much more will the Father in heaven give the Holy Spirit to those who ask him." Jesus spoke this promise before Pentecost and to some extent it was fulfilled by that event. However, it was not recorded until after Pentecost, and there is no indication that the need for intentional asking for the Spirit is now over. While every true believer has the gift of the Holy Spirit, the more serious question is "Are we filled with the Holy Spirit?" A further question is whether the Holy Spirit has all of us, as in Romans 12:1, the crisis surrender to Christ's lordship. Norman Grubb, the late British retreat speaker said, "The problem with a living sacrifice is that it can easily wiggle off God's altar."

Thought for the Day: *The essence of consecration is the giving up forever the right to ourselves.*

Prayer and the Great Commission

Scripture Reading: Acts 12:1-24

Key Verse: *...But the church was earnestly praying to God for him (Acts 12:5b).*

Meditation: In Acts 12 a powerful religious state pounds its fist against the infant church. This strong, unscrupulous power has already killed James with the sword, and now Peter, shut up in prison, expects the same sentence. The church does not know where the next blow will fall. It lies in the path of destruction and possible annihilation. The future looks dark.

Then a battered and persecuted church prays earnestly and unceasingly. With Peter in prison guarded by 16 soldiers, his only hope of escape is a miracle. What chance has prayer against prison walls and locked gates? While the church prayed, their extremity became God's opportunity. A power shift is literally taking place. Suddenly, it is no longer the pompous Herod, but the church on her knees that holds the balance of power in national affairs.

The sovereign hand of God orchestrates the sequence of events in answer to prayer: First, angels come to rescue Peter. Numerous references to angels in Acts remind us that God's special delivery messengers are intimately linked with the Great Commission. Next, the locks and gate open miraculously, by an invisible hand. Finally, Herod is removed from power by divine intervention. While he is being eaten by worms as a result of his acceptance of the peoples acclamation of him as "divine," an even greater miracle takes place: "The word of God continued to increase and spread" (Acts 12:24).

Thought for the Day: *Acts 12 could be repeated today if the church prayed earnestly and ceaselessly.*

Subconscious Factors in Paul's Conversion

Scripture Reading: Galatians 1:11-17

Key Verse: *But when God, who set me apart from birth and called me by his grace, was pleased to reveal his Son in me... (Galatians 1:15, 16a).*

Meditation: Paul is, beyond all doubt, the most effective missionary who ever lived. Evaluated both by the extensiveness of his missionary travels and the effectiveness of his church planting methods, he has no equal. If we use Ralph Winter's model for evaluating cultures, Paul successfully planted churches within the same language and culture, in similar cultures and languages, and also in different cross-cultural settings. Add to that the fact that he wrote 13 of the 27 New Testament books, one-fourth of the total pages of the New Testament. J. Oswald Sanders sums up Paul's life: "Paul is the greatest theologian, the most persuasive apologist and the most tireless traveler of the church he once persecuted."

As serious students of Paul's life, we need to consider a scholars' observation, stated as "Paul's unconscious preparation for missionary work." What were those hidden factors that prepared and shaped Paul to become God's unique instrument? In retrospect, Paul attributes God's sovereign hand in those areas for which he once took credit, like his consuming religious zeal. He then realizes that all his religious aspirations originated not in his own will, but by God's initiative. In our key verse he summed up God's sovereign work in his life:

1. God set him apart from birth.
2. God accomplished his conversion apart from a human agent.
3. God called him to ministry by His grace.
4. God revealed His Son in Paul.

Thought for the Day: *Like Paul, we did not decide on Christ. It was Christ who first decided on us and intervened by the power of the Holy Spirit to make our conversion happen.*

Subconscious Factors in Paul's Conversion

Scripture Reading: Acts 21:37-40, 22:1,2

Key Verse: *...I am a Jew from Tarsus in Cilicia... (Acts 21: 39a).*

Meditation: A person's place of birth plays a significant part in his life. John the Baptist spent his boyhood in the hill country of Judea and in the wilderness. Jesus spent His boyhood in Nazareth and in the countryside. Both John and Jesus showed a fondness for nature and often drew illustrations for preaching from those observations.

Paul grew up in Tarsus and spent most of his life in other great cities of the Roman Empire. Paul makes little use of nature illustrations, but he has a vast knowledge of men, languages, cultures and world religious philosophies. East and West flowed together in Tarsus, capital of Cilicia. The early inhabitants were Greeks and Orientals. Later, Italians migrated there bringing with them the Latin language. Tarsus also had a Jewish colony to which Paul's family belonged.

The Bible Encyclopedia (Vol. 3) gives us other details that show how Tarsus was best suited to equip Paul for his worldwide ministry. Famous for its schools, it nourished in Paul a love for learning. Tarsus provided training in the social, political, intellectual and religious life of the Roman Empire. A cosmopolitan city, Tarsus modeled independence and democratic ideals, with ethnic integration. To be a citizen of Tarsus, and of Rome, was to be a citizen of the world. When Paul said, "I am Roman-born," he was treated immediately with respect and dignity. For God's future world missionary, Tarsus was the most ideal launching place.

Thought for the Day: *God can redeem good from our lives, even from those years before we personally believed in Him.*

Unconscious Factors in Paul's Conversion

Scripture Reading: Philippians 3:4-7

Key Verse: *...of the tribe of Benjamin, a Hebrew of the Hebrews...*
(Philippians 3:5).

Meditation: Family and religious education play a very important place in the life of every person, as it did for Saul. Paul's family was Jewish from the tribe of Benjamin. He was named after the tribe's most renowned ancestor, King Saul, reflecting the family's religious aspirations for their son. Paul confidently refers to himself as a "Hebrew of the Hebrews," assuring his listeners that he is pure Jewish stock from both parents and not a Gentile proselyte. Family blood ties link him to Jacob, Benjamin's father, making him a Jew by birth and by practice.

Since Paul's parents apparently met the property requirements for citizens of Tarsus, we assume they were reasonably well-to-do. A practicing Jewish father would circumcise his son, teach him the Law and teach him a trade. The trade fortified him against laziness and against future adversity. Since Paul learned the art of tent making that he would later use for self-support in missionary work, we conjecture his father also did this work.

Paul's early education took place at home and in the synagogue. Jewish parents did not want their children's minds corrupted by Gentile teachers. Teachers of the Law would answer questions and guide Paul so that he was considered "a child of the Law" at 13. His father would announce to all present that this son fully understands the Law and is now fully responsible for his moral and ethical behavior.

Thought for the Day: *Let us reflect on those things in our background that God is now using for His purpose.*

Subconscious Factors in Paul's Conversion

Scripture Reading: Acts 26:4-11

Key Verse: *The Jews all know the way I have lived even since I was a child… (Acts 26:4a).*

Meditation: Significant people and human circumstances can impact the future direction of a person's life. We have already observed the unconscious factors such as place of birth, family, secular and religious education that shaped Paul's life. In the next two days we look at the need of the young church and how God would use Gamaliel's life as a mentor to mold Paul's life in the direction of the future need of the church.

Acts records how Christianity moved beyond the Jewish boundaries of Jerusalem into Samaria, Antioch, and Caesarea. We observe how unprepared the church leaders in Jerusalem were to deal with the new phenomena. While the Jerusalem leaders seemed genuinely interested in these happenings, they could hardly give wholehearted consent. They did not know how to integrate these "God-fearing Gentiles" into the larger church. They could not easily adapt to the cultured Greeks and the practical Romans or to the uneducated Gentile barbarians who had believed in Jesus.

The fledgling church faced a crisis. Would Christianity remain a small Jewish sect outside Judaism with a fringe of "God-fearing Gentiles" marginalized by Judaizers insisting on conformity to the Law? Would Christianity become a worldwide religion embracing all? Would the Jerusalem leadership of the Church ever be shared with the expatriate Jews who could more easily acknowledge the equality of Jews and Gentiles in God's sight? These questions bring us to the part Gamaliel played in preparing the Church's future most important leader, Paul.

Thought for the Day: *While God can accomplish His work by His own divine power, He usually chooses to work through obedient followers.*

Subconscious Factors in Paul's Conversion

Scripture Reading: Acts 5:33-41

Key Verse: *But if it is from God, you will not be able to stop these men (Acts 5:39a).*

Meditation: The young church needed new leadership. It needed mature guidance to avoid the pitfalls of legalistic Judaism on one hand and on the other, the need to be both knowledgeable and sensitive to other cultures and ethnic backgrounds. These future leaders needed to be well versed in the Law, yet have the ability to discern what is central and what is peripheral to the gospel. To the spiritually sincere Jew, Christianity had to be proclaimed as the fulfillment, rather than the abolition of the Law. To the Gentiles, Christianity must be shared as "good news" with the absence of the accumulated Jewish cultural and religious "baggage."

It appears that Saul was divinely scripted to fulfill that future role. He trained in Jerusalem for the office of rabbi. He had a sister in Jerusalem with whom he probably lodged while attending classes. At the feet of the illustrious Gamaliel, who represented the progressive Pharisees, he began his undergraduate studies. With the Old Testament as his primary textbook Paul studied both the content and application of Scriptures to life. Everything studied had to be proved by Scripture in order to be conclusive. This disciplined Old Testament study would later open doors for Paul in the scattered synagogues in all the major cities of the Empire.

Through the ordering of divine providence, the Rabbinical School of Hillel where Gamaliel taught was considered the most open-minded school in Palestine. He encouraged the study of Greek literature. Paul became a rabbi seated on the Sanhedrin and a teacher in the synagogues. With great promise and zeal he exercised authority to persecute the Church and eradicate Christianity. With that assignment he was destined to be confronted by Jesus, the Lord of the Church.

Thought for the Day: *God's grace transformed the good seed Gamaliel sowed in Paul's mind, enabling him to say, "There is neither Jew or Greek."*

Subconscious Factors in Paul's Conversion

Scripture Reading: Acts 5:33-40

Key Verse: *...Leave these men alone! Let them go... (Acts 5:38).*

Meditation: Gamaliel, the greathearted rabbi from the Hillel school, made an indelible impression on the young Paul. His influence was evidenced in Paul's watchful enthusiasm for the Law, the ultimate authority of Scripture, and the study of the Greek Bible and literature. Paul would be enabled to engage the best minds of the empire. So Gamaliel's defense of the apostles before the Sanhedrin must have caused Paul to have a sense of inner foreboding, self-doubt, fear and possibly guilt.

Stephen, one of the first seven deacons chosen by the apostles to resolve racial tensions in the early church, also significantly influenced Paul. Stephen was a Hellenistic Jew who had adopted the Greek culture and was bilingual. He was a converted member of the local church, a man with a good local reputation, filled with the Holy Spirit and wisdom or sanctified common sense.

Although Paul met Stephen only for a few hours, he heard an unforgettable sermon. Paul masterminded Stephen's trial and stoning. He not only consented to Stephen's death; he arranged it. Behind the sinister arrangement, God was also at work. Paul had planned to vote in the Sanhedrin for Stephen's death. He pretended to be innocent by holding the clothes of those who actually did the stoning and get no blood on his hands. He pretended to be doing only his job as a zealot Jew, but this time he could not go home and forget what he had heard and witnessed.

Thought for the Day: *A man's character, like Stephen's, speaks more eloquently to the unsaved than words.*

Subconscious Factors in Paul's Conversion

Scripture Reading: Acts 9:1-9

Key Verse: *Who are you Lord, Saul asked... (Acts 9: 5a).*

Meditation: Paul's mind must have been in turmoil as he traveled from Jerusalem to Damascus. He had been ordered to stamp out the new sect, "the followers of the Way." But could he ever shake the psychological stress coming from Stephen's stoning and death? Guilt (he had rigged the trial) and anger (the new sect kept growing) nagged him. The sect was now spreading beyond Palestine into the city of Damascus, a place with many synagogues.

During the long journey questions invaded Paul's mind: "Why did Gamaliel suddenly adopt such a conciliatory attitude towards the Christians? What did he mean by suggesting that God may be working outside of Judaism and it would be best not to try to stop the movement lest we be found fighting against God himself?" Flashbacks of Stephen's trial, too, coursed across his mind: Stephen's carefully crafted message of God's historical faithfulness and Israel's unbelief, Stephen's awesome face radiating grace and holiness, his prayer of forgiveness for those stoning him, his vision of the glorified Jesus by God's throne, his peace and calm as he placed himself in God's hands and breathed his last.

On the human side, Paul was tracking Christ's followers, but on the divine side Christ was tracking Paul, waiting for the right moment to confront him. The Lord was setting the stage. When the right moment came He took the initiative, reminding us that preparation for conversion begins with the Lord.

Thought for the Day: *Persecution does not make people into saints, but it does reveal those who are already saints.*

Paul's Conversion and Commission

Scripture Reading: Acts 9:1-9

Key Verse: *Who are you Lord? Saul asked (Acts 9:5a).*

Meditation: While Paul was searching zealously for "the followers of the Way," God was also tracking Paul, waiting for the right time and place to intercept his life. The right time was noon and the place, not Palestine, but Syria. Damascus, a six-day journey from Jerusalem, was populated with a large Jewish community and a number of synagogues that reportedly had been infiltrated with Christian converts. Paul secured warrants from the high priest to arrest defectors from Judaism and repatriate them to Palestine.

Paul did not appear to be a likely candidate for conversion. His transformation on the Damascus road and the following three days has to be a miracle of God's sovereign grace and power. Theologians label his conversion "the prevenient grace of God" or "the effectual calling of the Holy Spirit." Paul did not decide first to follow Christ. God decided for him and intervened dramatically in his life. We are also "dead in trespasses and sins" before God calls us to Himself.

The ingredients of a New Testament genuine conversion are repentance, faith in Jesus, water baptism and the gift of the Holy Spirit. These four acts are really a single stage experience in which we repent, believe, are baptized as a public testimony and receive the gift of the Holy Spirit. After this initiation into Christ other deeper and fuller experiences follow, but these four are non-negotiable essentials.

Thought for the Day: *Our Christian life really began, not with our decision to follow Christ, but with Christ's decision to intervene in our lives by His sovereign grace.*

Paul's Conversion and Commission

Scripture Reading: Acts 9:1-9

Key Verse: *For three days he was blind, and did not eat or drink anything (Acts 9:9).*

Meditation: Luke records Paul's significant conversion three times in Acts. Apart from the life, death and resurrection of Jesus, the next most important event in the New Testament appears to be Paul's conversion. Paul wrote 13 of the 27 New Testament books. Paul reached the Gentile world, a feat that would otherwise probably have taken the church at least a century. His encounter with Jesus convinced Paul of His being the long-awaited Messiah, and validated his apostleship. "Am I not an apostle? Have I not seen Jesus our Lord?" (I Corinthians 9:1b).

With the blinding light of Christ's Shekinah glory and the disclosure of His true identity, Christ certainly could have effected Paul's complete conversion instantaneously. There appear to be at least two reasons for a delay in Paul's assurance of salvation. First, God was working in the church to help them overcome their fear of Paul in order to provide acceptance for him to be a part of the working body of Christ. Second, God did not want Paul to be converted in a vacuum of independence from the church.

Every conversion experience is unique to the individual. We should never feel insecure because our conversion does not fit another mold. The biblical norm of conversion should, however, include a personal encounter with Christ to which we respond in faith and repentance. Our faith is made public by water baptism, being incorporated into a local church or fellowship and by being baptized by the Holy Spirit into Christ's invisible church.

Thought for the Day: *The weakness of the church today is that, while we accept Jesus as our Savior, we postpone indefinitely the decision to make Him Lord of our lives.*

Paul's Conversion and Commission

Scripture Reading: Acts 9:10-19

Key Verse: *...go to the house of Judas on Straight Street and ask for a man from Tarsus named Saul... (Acts 9:11b).*

Meditation: Three people impacted Paul's (Saul's) conversion and subsequent witness and ministry. Stephen's primary role got Paul's spiritual attention. He served as a model of Christ's courage, love and forgiveness. "Lord, do not hold this sin against them" (Acts 7:60). His last words must have left Paul shocked and bewildered.

Ananias was the person Saul (Paul) had planned to apprehend for his identification with the followers of "The Way." Ananias and his friends did not know about Paul's Damascus road experience just two days before. No doubt Ananias was in hiding from Paul when God told him in a vision to visit Paul and lay hands on him in a healing prayer. Though terrified, Ananias obeyed. God prepared Paul for his coming, even telling him his name. Ananias came to Saul in his blindness and helplessness. The warmth of the love of Ananias, his healing touch and his greeting, "Brother Saul" brought both physical healing and spiritual wholeness.

Christ could have completed Paul's conversion, but He chose to work through others. Ananias became Paul's bridge of acceptance to the church.

Thought for the Day: *The power of the Holy Spirit filling Paul's life effected the radical transformation demonstrated in his work and ministry for the rest of his days.*

Paul's Conversion and Commission

Scripture Reading: Acts 9:19-31

Key Verse: *But Barnabas took him and brought him to the apostles... (Acts 9:27a).*

Meditation: The third pivotal person in Paul's early Christian life was Barnabas. As recorded in Acts 4, Barnabas sold a field he owned, brought all the money and trustfully laid it at the apostles' feel to be used for needy Christians who had lost their jobs because of their faith.

Now Barnabas, called the son of consolation, takes the new convert, Paul, and introduces him to the church. Had it not been for Barnabas, Paul could have been easily discouraged to discover he was still regarded as a spy at the mother church of Christianity. Barnabas risked his own reputation to convince the apostles that Paul's conversion was genuine. Again, Barnabas, the expatriate Jew from Cyprus convinced the Jerusalem church that the Gentile conversions at Antioch were works of God. It was also Barnabas who rescued the almost-forgotten Paul after three years of desert experience by inviting him to be his associate at Antioch and launch the world missionary movement.

Many of us are grateful for the Barnabas people God brought to us, especially those who affirmed our conversion. Many of us are Christians or in the ministry because someone saw potential in us which we could not recognize.

Thought for the Day: *In most of our circles of influence there is someone today who needs our intentional affirmation. That person's spiritual gift needs to be encouraged to grow and thrive.*

Paul's Conversion and Commission

Scripture Reading: Galatians 1:17-24

Key Verse: *...but I went immediately into Arabia and later returned to Damascus (Galatians 1: 17b).*

Meditation: Shortly after Paul's conversion he went to Arabia. We wonder if he went out of his perplexity because the believers were still suspicious of his being a spy? He does not tell us explicitly, but we do learn some of what transpired while he was there.

The desert experience where a believer takes time to be alone with God is not unique to Paul. Many leaders who are marked as God's spokesmen have spent time first listening to God. Moses fled to the desert after his initial failure to deliver the people with his own strength. Elijah went into the desert for fear of Queen Jezebel. There he heard the voice of God and regained courage to return to his prophetic task. John the Baptist prepared for his mission by preaching in the desert. Even Jesus, after being baptized by the Spirit, followed the Spirit to the wilderness where Satan tempted Him. Jesus fought His cosmic battle and won a decisive victory both for Him and for us.

The desert for us may not be a geographical reality, but an extended time of being alone with God. During those times we will see, as Paul did, that everything that happened to us, even as far back as our conception, had a divine and eternal purpose. We will also discover significant religious experiences have their origin in God and carry with them a call to serve. For Paul, his conversion and call to ministry were locked together; perhaps they happened simultaneously.

Thought for the Day: *Inherent in our conversion is also a call to service even though the realization of it may not come immediately.*

Paul's Conversion and Commission

Scripture Reading: Galatians 1:11-24

Key Verse: *Now get up and stand on your feet... (Acts 26:16a).*

Meditation: Paul's conversion and commission are closely linked; perhaps they occurred simultaneously. In a sense, each of us who has responded to Christ's initiative with "Lord, what will you have me to do?" will also be confronted with the same commission. The commission has not changed, since man's spiritual predicament before God remains the same since Genesis 3.

What is the inner essence of that two-fold experience that transformed Paul from an apostle of the Jewish Sanhedrin to an apostle of Christ to the Gentile world? First, note the profound dignity of Paul's commission: The resurrected and glorified Jesus appeared to Paul, blinded, groveling on the ground and said, "Now get up and stand on your feet. I have appeared to you" (Acts 26:16a). Between genuine humility before God and inordinate inferiority there is a great difference. Those who cling to their inferiority tend to remain focused on themselves and give a negative impression of the good news of the Gospel. Christ wants His followers to stand erect with profound gratitude and astonishment that "...he had considered me faithful, appointing me to his service" I Timothy 1:12b.

The profound divine-human encounter at Damascus continued as a dynamic reference point that Paul would recall for inspiration and courage. Not only did the encounter change his life, but it also gave him the message to the world. "But when God...was pleased to reveal his Son in me so that I may preach him among the Gentiles (Galatians 1: 6)."

Thought for the Day: *Until God reveals his Son in us by the divine working of the Holy Spirit, we have no message to give to the world around us.*

Paul's Conversion and Commission

Scripture Reading: Acts 26:16-23

Key Verse: *...to appoint you as a servant and as a witness... (Acts 26:16).*

Meditation: Yesterday we learned from Paul's commissioning that our call originates in the initiative of Christ who Himself calls us. We should live in perpetual amazement at our being a divine selection. However, the focus of our ministry must be on Christ and not on ourselves, the called ones.

We are called both to be witnesses and to be servants. A servant in the New Testament does his master's bidding without question. As Christians we can be directed to do something that clashes with our common sense and secular point of view. Or we may be asked to risk everything and take steps with no certain future. A missionary who remains a true servant will love Jesus supremely and keep the adventuresome spirit alive in the heart. Consecration must not be a one-time experience, but an ongoing process throughout our lives.

We are "witnesses of what we have seen of Jesus and that which he will show..." (Acts 26: 16). Until Christ appears to us personally, our witness will be second-hand and unimpressive. Nor can one make himself a witness. Even ordination can only recognize those who have previously been made witnesses by Christ's sovereign interaction in their lives. Before Christ sent the church to witness in the world, He asked them to wait in Jerusalem. In the Upper Room He clearly spelled out the sequence in our witness with these words, "But when the Spirit of Truth comes ...he will speak only what he hears, and he will tell you what is yet to come" (John 16:13). "He will testify about me, and you also must testify, for he has been with me from the beginning" (John 15:26b, 27).

Thought for the Day: *The effective missionary has a personal testimony of conversion and an ongoing experience of the risen Christ in his life.*

Paul's Conversion and Commission

Scripture Reading: Acts 26:17,18

Key Verse: *...to open their eyes... (Acts 26:18).*

Meditation: The third aspect of Paul's commission clearly demonstrates the five-fold task of every missionary. The first three are preparatory to salvation and the last two are the results of salvation. A. Paget Wilkes, a former missionary from England to Japan said, "The mark of a fruitful preacher in a country where there is not knowledge of the Bible can be measured by his ability to discern how much biblical content is necessary before a hearer can make an informed decision for Christ."

Christ clearly defines those steps in Paul's commission as a missionary apostle: First, the necessity of "opening their eyes." The speaker must be convinced of the reality of spiritual blindness and its source as Paul explains in II Corinthians 4:4, "The god of this age has blinded the minds of unbelievers, so that they cannot see the light of the gospel of Christ." Satan intentionally blinds people by keeping them preoccupied with secular things, giving them no time to think seriously of the "age to come." The task of the preacher, through the Word, and in complete dependence on the Holy Spirit, is to make people aware of the futility of all that they are seeking. Sin leads to judgment by the God of creation.

As a young missionary I felt overwhelmed with the challenge of making a sermon logical in one hearing by the people. I would ask those who remained for prayer, "Do you understand?" to which they replied, "I see." Finally, I realized that even if they could not follow my logic, they could actually see Christ dying for them, atoning for their sins and they desired His forgiveness.

Thought for the Day: *Whenever authentic missionary apostolic preaching takes place, Paul assures us in Galatians 3:1, Before your very eyes Jesus Christ was clearly portrayed as crucified.*

Paul's Conversion and Commission

Scripture Reading: Acts 26:15-18

Key Verse: *...and turn them from darkness to light... (Acts 26:18).*

Meditation: The second task of the missionary-apostle is to turn the listeners from darkness to light. From a human perspective, a prolonged period of instruction would be necessary before an intelligent turning could take place. But that limits the illuminating power of the Word of God and the direct ministry of the Holy Spirit to dispel darkness in human hearts.

When I first arrived in Japan on a two-year assignment, I was assigned, without language study, to a team of seven Japanese pastors and evangelists. At one of the nightly tent meetings I preached with an interpreter beside me. So good was he that I almost forgot I was preaching to Japanese. I gave a typical American invitation: "If there is anyone here who would like to accept Christ, please raise your hand and we will come and pray with you." To my amazement, a senior high school student in his black uniform immediately raised his hand. "What do I do now, Lord?" I prayed, as my interpreter and I went to him.

I assumed he had attended church before, but I found this to be his first time. He had not read the Bible before. All the spiritual preparation he had came from his high school English teacher teaching him to sing Silent Night, Holy Night in English at Christmas. He told us he could not understand the meaning of the words, but he could not forget the tune. He had heard singing at the tent meeting and felt compelled to come inside. Even more amazingly, after a careful walk down the "Roman road" (3:23, 6:23 and 10:9-13), he himself prayed to receive the forgiveness of Jesus.

Thought for the Day: *Christ the true light that shines into the world is at work in the whole world through the Holy Spirit who is actively preparing people to receive the gospel.*

Paul's Conversion and Commission

Scripture Reading: Acts 26:17,18

Key Verse: *...from the power of Satan to God... (Acts 26:18).*

Meditation: While we should be careful about non-biblical superstitions about the devil, the Bible plainly teaches Satan's real and personal existence. As a chief angel he rebelled against God and tried to usurp His power and glory. He fell from his lofty position, but took with him one-third of the angels who were also disobedient and now serve under Satan as emissaries of evil in our world.

Satan caused our first parents, Adam and Eve, to sin in the Garden of Eden. This fall from favor with God would impact all subsequent generations. We are all "born in Adam" into a state of sin and loss of innocence, with no exemptions. In writing to Christians in Ephesians 6, Paul tells us that even those "born again" by the Holy Spirit, continue to be engaged in spiritual warfare. We do not engage in combat with difficult people, but against Satan and his demonic subordinates who serve in his evil empire.

Those called as missionary-apostles must be aware daily of the human condition from which people must be redeemed. Christ has provided a radical provision to move people out of their bondage to Satan and over to God. That provision is the cross of Jesus. At the cross through the dying of Jesus in our place, the redemptive power of God was released in the world. Through the cross forgiveness is available for all people, past, present and future generations.

Thought for the Day: *Whenever the message of the cross is proclaimed and believed the real presence of God is released again, causing the hearer to turn from Satan to God.*

Paul's Conversion and Commission

Scripture Reading: Acts 26:17,18

Key Verse: *...so that they may receive forgiveness of sins (Acts 26:18).*

Meditation: The biblical word for salvation covers all three tenses of our human existence. **Past**: A Christian has been saved by the merits of Christ's atoning death on the cross. **Present**: He is being saved now from the power of sin by the indwelling Christ and the cleansing and empowering of the Holy Spirit. **Future**: Every Christian will ultimately be saved from the presence of sin by death or by the Second Coming of Jesus. This great word, salvation, includes justification, sanctification and glorification.

Peter, in his sermon at Pentecost, promised two immediate blessings to every person who believes in Jesus: The forgiveness of sins and the gift of the Holy Spirit. In Paul's conversion these same two results are recorded, the forgiveness of sins and a place among those who are sanctified by faith in Jesus. Until even the religious person receives these two blessings, he is too weak to start living the Christian life. Oswald Chambers used to caution his workers with these words, "Don't expect anything from seekers until they have first received something from God."

The sense of forgiveness usually follows justification. Once we agree with God that the only basis of our justification and forgiveness is due to Jesus' paying the wages for our sins, we can fully feel God's forgiveness of our sins. John's promise of forgiveness to those who confess (I John 1:9) carries with it not only the assurance of forgiveness, but also the subsequent act of continuous cleansing from the very pollution of sin itself.

Thought for the Day: *Sin is a debt that Christ forgives upon our confession that results in cleansing and initial sanctification.*

Paul's Conversion and Commission

Scripture Reading: Acts 9:17-19

Key Verse: *...Immediately, something like scales fell from Saul's eyes, and he could see again. He got up and was baptized... (Acts 9:18).*

Meditation: If you agree with God's diagnosis of our sinful condition, both the acts of sin and the principle of sin, and confess them, two wonderful results will follow. God will forgive our acts of sin and continuously cleanse us from the stain and pollution of sin. In other words, according to Christ's commission to Paul, our missionary task is incomplete until both forgiveness and heart cleansing is experienced. John also ties conversion and initial sanctification together, and so must we.

The same pattern of the Holy Spirit's dynamic ability was demonstrated in the conversion of Paul at Damascus. When Ananias laid his hands on Paul, scales fell from Paul's eyes and he was filled with the Holy Spirit immediately. Paul's personal Pentecost here recorded qualified him for his apostolic role. Cornelius and his household experienced a similar phenomenon. While Peter spoke, the Holy Spirit came on all present. Here the Spirit's coming was also accompanied with gifts of the Spirit. This special instance certainty showed the church that uncircumcised Gentiles, too, were rightful heirs of all the blessings of salvation, including the gift of the Holy Spirit.

From Acts we learn that conversion is unique to the person. In some cases, the Spirit's fullness happened simultaneously with conversion. At other times the Spirit's fullness was delayed until the believer experienced something of the Romans 12:1 crisis of consecration. Paul's and Cornielius' experiences may not be the norm for the church, but the principle is that there is an inseparable relationship between conversion and the beginning of the holy life.

Thought for the Day: *Ephesians 1:4 describes our election in these words: For he chose us in him before the creation of the world to be holy and blameless in his sight.*

Paul's Missionary Guidance to Europe

Scripture Reading: Acts 16:6-10

Key Verse: *...having been kept by the Holy Spirit from preaching the Word in the province of Asia... (Acts 16:6b).*

Meditation: Different people interpret history differently. Many embrace a cyclical view of history that civilizations rise, wane, fall and disappear, followed by another civilization cycle. Believing that events just happen, they see no divine purpose. The biblical view of history affirms God at work in history with a purpose and a goal towards which God is shaping everything that happens. History will be consummated in Christ's return. In the meantime, we are active participants in the movements of the world as Paul demonstrated in Acts 16.

Acts 16 describes a watershed event where God intervened, charting the future course of Christianity. Had Paul prevailed in his intention to go to Asia, he would have missed God's ordained open window of opportunity in Europe. The Golden Age in Greece had passed. The Greek people worshipped a pantheon of deities who glorified human heroes. Rome and her citizens hardly fared any better. Two-thirds served as slaves for the others, or were "foreigners." For them, emperors were presented as divine beings. Romans 1 and 2 portray Roman civilization and explain why so many turned to Christianity. God knew Europe would expand their empires all over the world. On those journeys missionaries would be on each ship to share the gospel in the new land.

Thought for the Day: *Sometimes we may be guided by God even though it appears we are being hindered in our plans.*

Paul's Missionary Guidance to Europe

Scripture Reading: Acts 16:6-10

Key Verse: *So they passed by Mysia and went down to Troas (Acts 16:8).*

Meditation: Acts 16 gives us three profound missionary principles: Christ, the Lord of the Harvest, knows best which fields are ripe; the Holy Spirit knows how long that window of opportunity will remain open; and God in His omniscience knows which countries will be more receptive to the Great Commission. Thus we understand why God stopped Paul from going to Asia. The demise of the Greek culture made the Greeks more responsive to the Gospel. The Romans, with their brutality and depravity, created in people a longing for a truly loving God of Christianity. God set the stage for this strategic historical moment. Even though Asia needed the message of hope, Europe was more ready. Asia would be evangelized later, but now the harvest waited in Europe.

No doubt Paul puzzled over God's negative guidance repeated twice, "You cannot go there." Paul kept moving towards Asia. Leaving Asia, he was pushed by the Spirit towards Troas, still not clearly understanding God's plan. But he learned, as many of us, that God can elevate a second or third human choice and make them more fruitful and fulfilling than we could ever have imagined.

God opened a strategic door from Troas proving that He never leads us into dead ends or blind alleys. God opened cities like Phillipi, Thessalonica, Berea, Athens, Corinth and ultimately Rome. Paul trained new workers, expatriate Jews and even Gentiles, to bring in to one body both Jews and Gentiles.

Thought for the Day: *When our human choices lead us to a dead end, look for God's open doors.*

Paul's Missionary Guidance to Europe

Scripture Reading: John 4:35-38

Key Verse: *Do not say four months more and then the harvest...*
(John 4:35b).

Meditation: Japan illustrates the three strategic missionary principles:
The Lord of the harvest knows best when the fields are ripe; the Holy
Spirit knows how long the opportunity remains available; God knows
which nations are most apt to share the Gospel with the world.

On August 15, 1945 Emperor Hirohito, long considered a divine
descendant, spoke as a human being for the first time to the nation.
The people listened in psychological and religious shock as he
announced, "Let us accept the inevitability of defeat and bear the
unbearable, lest we be wiped off the face of the earth." Hiroshima and
Nagasaki were decimated by the atomic bomb. Though the Japanese
had fought with faith in the emperor's supremacy, now they had no
divinity emblem.

General MacArthur, appointed as Supreme Commander of the Allied
Powers, directed the change in Japan from a dictatorship to a
democracy. The speedy transfer of power to the Japanese people
continues as a celebration of freedom by Japan today. Few people,
however, know that General MacArthur embraced the ideals of
Christianity and asked for 10,000 missionaries and a million Bibles to
fill the spiritual void in the hearts of the Japanese people and facilitate a
spiritual reformation in Japan. This may be one of the few instances of
a military leader also taking a Christian initiative in a non-Christian
country.

Thought for the Day: *God has the big picture in mind and continues
to prod us in that direction.*

Paul's Missionary Guidance to Europe

Scripture Reading: Acts 16:6-10

Key Verse: *...we got ready at once to leave for Macedonia, concluding that God has called us to preach the gospel to them... (Acts 16:10).*

Meditation: Paul responded twice to the Holy Spirit's restraint in his guidance to Europe. He needed to discern the important difference between Satan's obstruction and God's closed door. That spiritual discipline in our lives will help to keep us on track with God's plan for us.

Paul willingly accepted guidance that surprised him. He wanted Asia, but God gave him Europe. William Carey planned to go to the South Seas Islands, but the Holy Spirit led him to India. Adoniram Judson aimed for India, but God led him to Burma. God gave Paul, during a time of deep uncertainty, a vision of Macedonia's spiritual need. Paul obeyed and all the continent of Europe heard the gospel.

Paul's traumatic experiencing of abruptly changed plans reminds me of the missionaries to China in the late 1940's when the Communists took control in September 1949. Many missionaries funding for China gave up altogether the idea of going to China. Some on the field left disenchanted, as they had felt called to China. Some, however, changed their travel bookings to Japan and walked into the open door there. Now we refer to them as "old China hands" who joined us for exemplary and fruitful work on a second divine appointment.

Thought for the Day: *Do not let one closed door blind you to the possibilities of another door God is sovereignly opening.*

Paul's Missionary Guidance to Europe

Scripture Reading: Acts 16:6-10

Key Verse: *...concluding that God had called us to preach the gospel to them (Acts 16: 10b).*

Meditation: Paul obeyed the guidance of the Holy Spirit, the most important lesson of the Christian life. Even though the plan does not appear to fit our human logic, God's plan gives the great opportunity. God's outlook reflects His sovereign ability to know the strategy and outcome of every movement.

On this occasion God chose to guide Paul by a vision. God does not always choose the same method to direct us; He does what He knows best. Generally, supernatural manifestations for guidance are exceptions and should not be demanded. Never dictate to God how He should confirm His guidance. Neither should we expect Him to conform to our timetable. God is very creative in confirming His guidance, and while it may be necessary to wait, He is never late. We are not told how long they waited in Troas -- one day, one week or one month. But it always saves time to wait on God at His Troas rather than move ahead on our own without Him.

We can summarize God's guidance in this chapter: He guided negatively by saying "no" twice and by closing two doors. He guided by withholding a sense of peace, by divine restraint. He steered them towards Troas, a step in the right direction, but not their final destination. He was guided by a providential sign for Luke, a Greek, appeared to join them as Paul's doctor and as a future writer of Luke and Acts. He guided them by a unanimous team concurrence that "...God had called us to preach the Gospel in Macedonia."

Thought for the Day: *The Holy Spirit often guides us not by supernatural phenomenon, but by His inner nudging.*

Paul's Missionary Guidance to Europe

Scripture Reading: Acts 26:19-32

Key Verse: *So then King Agrippa, I was not disobedient to the vision from heaven (Acts 26:19).*

Meditation: Someone has suggested that the ultimate test of a vision is that it will cause us to expect God to do more in the future than we have experienced in the past. We must not debate the pros and cons of the vision, but obey immediately. Thus we will retain the initial impression and our lives will remain open for further manifestations of God's will.

Look closely again at Paul's vision of the man from Macedonia that caused the most important turning point in history, directing Paul to the West, to Europe. Paul had the vision while he was sleeping. Perhaps God had more access while Paul's conscious barriers were gone. Even while we are sleeping the Lord of the harvest is actively working.

Notice what Paul did not see: He did not see a hospital, a school or even a rice paddy. Surely need existed then for medical facilities, improved education and agricultural methods. Apparently these needs alone were not to be the primary emphasis. We are to care about the whole man, but never forget that the first and primary need is spiritual.

Thought for the Day: *The Holy Spirit delights to activate vision in the church for God's work in the world.*

Paul's Missionary Guidance to Europe

Scripture Reading: Acts 16:6-10

Key Verse: *During the night Paul had a vision... (Acts 16:9).*

Meditation: Paul received this vision when he was sound asleep. Ray Stedman observes a difference between a mere human dream and a vision from God. A dream, Stedman says, is usually about us, where we are the focus. In strong contrast, a vision is about God and others. By this criterion we know Paul had an authentic vision originating with God himself and resulting in a radical new focus for the church, from the Jew to the Gentiles.

The focus of the vision on a person reminds us that missions are primarily about reaching individuals with the gospel. The man in the vision was not a Jew but a Gentile, requiring the church to move from its comfort zone to embrace others. The man in the vision is standing, beckoning for help denoting great urgency, "for how can they believe in the one they have not heard?" (Romans 10:14b). While the man in the vision was an individual, he was a representative of the world. The center of the vision appeared to be human, but the message was God's unmistakable divine initiative and authority.

Few of us will ever be challenged by a vision that will result in the opening of a whole continent for the gospel. Yet individuals and people all around us need Christ. Some may be in other countries and others across the street. Some may speak Greek and others English with a Chinese or Japanese accent. Wherever that person lives or whatever language he speaks, he is a person who needs Christ and salvation.

Thought for the Day: *We should always hold our plans lightly, ready to submit them to God for His acceptance and modification.*

Paul' Missionary Guidance to Europe

Scripture Reading: Acts 16:6-10

Key Verse: *...we got ready at once to leave for Macedonia (Acts 16:10).*

Meditation: The church should never underestimate small beginnings birthed by God's initiative. Four men on a ship with an Invisible Presence ultimately changed the spiritual direction of the whole continent of Europe. Christ led this vanguard of men when He brought them together with their diversified ethnic backgrounds and spiritual gifts to spearhead the advance of the gospel into Europe.

The members of the team included Luke and Timothy. Luke met the team in Troas by sheer coincidence, for the team had no prior intention of going to that city. His appearance coincided with Paul's vision of the man from Macedonia. Luke was a Greek as well as a physician. No doubt he would be a great asset to Paul during his many bouts with illnesses. Someone has said, "When we pray, coincidences happen; when we do not pray, they do not happen." Timothy's father was a Greek and his mother a Jew. Paul had him circumcised to allay needless opposition from local Jews in order to have an effective ministry to both Jews and Gentiles.

Silas, one of the two initial members of the team, was a Jew with Roman citizenship, an important asset to an itinerant missionary in the Roman Empire. One of the trusted leaders of the Jerusalem church, he was commissioned to accompany Paul to read the guidelines for the Gentiles at Antioch and encourage the believers there. He backed Paul's vision for Gentile evangelism. Paul, the team leader, had now been in ministry for 20 years and had completed his first missionary journey, planting many churches and mentoring men like Titus, Timothy, Silvanus and others. In fact, he was on his second missionary journey to strengthen the churches with Silas and Timothy when God sent him to Europe.

Thought for the Day: *All lasting missionary work begins, continues, and ends in the Holy Spirit.*

Paul's Missionary Guidance to Europe

Scripture Reading: Acts 16:11-15

Key Verse: *The Lord opened her heart to the Gospel in response to Paul's message (Acts 16:14b).*

Meditation: Luke highlights three first converts in Europe who each had significantly different backgrounds: A businesswoman who was a Jew or God-fearing Gentile; a Roman slave girl in spiritual bondage to an evil spirit of divination; and a jailer. Lydia, a tender soul, the slave girl, a tormented soul and the jailer, a tough soul who needed an earthquake and the imminent prospect of death to make him aware of his need of salvation. The gospel saved each of these different types of people.

The first two converts were women. A Roman man did not speak publicly to a group of women. Christianity in Europe immediately demonstrates the equality of genders in the kingdom of God. In I Corinthians 11:2-16, women are featured as prophets and leaders, reminding us today of the revolutionizing aspect of the gospel regarding the status of women. Lydia was also a woman of influence and means. Her conversion appeared quiet and unspectacular, yet she would impact her whole household with the gospel with all her servants and employees being baptized. She provided hospitality for all those who ministered to her. She brought all the social groups together to start a church in her home.

In every genuine conversion there is always a divine side and a human side. In Lydia's salvation the human side was Paul intentionally sharing the gospel with her, and the divine side was the Lord opening her heart to respond to Paul's message.

Thought for the Day: *Whenever the gospel is preached a supernatural power is released, opening blinded eyes to see and the heart to believe.*

Paul's Missionary Guidance to Europe

Scripture Reading: Acts. 16:16-24

Key Verse: *...in the name of Jesus Christ I command you to come out of her! (Acts 16:18b)*

Meditation: The second prospective charter member of the new church in Europe is described as a slave girl having the spirit of divination, the ability to foretell future events by occult means. Socially, her slave status made her property of Roman merchants. Economically, her owners exploited her for her sooth-saying, but she shared none of the profits. Spiritually, demonic forces controlled her. From a human evaluation, this girl does not appear to be charter member material. Her spiritual extremity prompted God's opportunity to affect a chain of events that would impact the whole city with the gospel.

God chose several times in the book of Acts to arrest the attention of a city through supernatural intervention. The exorcism of the demon proved to be such an event that would be followed by an earthquake. This teenage medium had followed Paul several days shouting "These man are the servants of the Most High God who are telling you the way to be saved." She spoke the truth, but the source was demonic and Paul could not tolerate this kind of publicity that would lead to compromise and misunderstanding.

Ray C. Stedman observes that Satan attacks the church in two ways: One is an apparent alliance, the other, an outright attack in some way. Paul sensed an alliance to be more dangerous because it appears so innocent in the beginning, but the truth would be compromised by the connection in the end.

Thought for the Day: *There are only two recorded conflicts in Acts between the Gentile pagans and the church and the issues were not doctrine, but money.*

Paul's Missionary Guidance to Europe

Scripture Reading: Acts 16:16-24

Key Verse: *...a slave girl who had a spirit by which she predicted the future... (Acts 16:16).*

Meditation: Paul's personal walk with God enabled him to discern quickly the spirit of deception at work in the girl. He cast out the evil spirit with the authoritative command, "In the name of Jesus I command you to come out of her." The evil spirit left her immediately and so did the spirit of divination, rendering her unprofitable to her unscrupulous owners. When Satan realized his first approach, apparent alliance, did not work, he resorted to the outright attack.

Times have changed in the revelation of evil, but the presence of evil is still a reality in our "sophisticated" world. While disbelief in Satan is more fashionable in many academic circles, schools and churches, it does not change the reality of evil all around us. The Bible nowhere seeks to deny the existence of Satan and his hierarchy of evil spirits. It does stress that Satan was decisively dethroned at the cross and that he is presently operating with divine restraint until the Day of Judgment. Satan does still act as the pretender to the throne, but his power is primarily limited to those who do not believe in God.

Next we learn that Paul's authority to cast out demons was not in himself, but was Christ-centered, derived directly from Jesus himself. The seven sons of the chief priest, Sceva, attempted to imitate Paul by casting out demons "by the Jesus that Paul preaches" only to have the demons turn on them and viciously attack and humiliate them (Acts 19:10-12). While they tried to imitate Paul, they lacked a personal relationship with Christ and an intimate walk with Him.

Thought for the Day: *Merely imitating the words of others without a personal growing relationship with Christ will render us unprotected and vulnerable before the enemy of our souls.*

Paul's Missionary Guidance to Europe

Scripture Reading: Acts 16:19-40

Key Verse: *...the magistrates ordered them stripped and beaten (Acts 16:22b).*

Meditation: Paul discerned that the first Satanic attack on his ministry at Philippi would be followed by a more violent one, and he braced himself. The early church, unlike much of Christianity today, did not avoid suffering or persecution; they actually welcomed it. Their suffering "for Christ" enabled them to enter into a deeper more profound "fellowship of his suffering" (Philippians 3:10). They regarded suffering as an inevitable consequence of faith in Jesus, but they fully understood that only Christ's suffering had an expiatory effect. Whenever Satan uses violence against the church, it is a sign of desperation. Provided the church remains faithful to Christ, Jesus will use the very violence to provide a wider witness for the gospel.

Two divine interventions are recorded in this chapter: The exorcism of the demon in the girl, and the prison earthquake that opened closed doors and loosened chains, all without collapsing the building. The third miracle was the singing and praising God by those two men who were falsely accused, wrongly beaten, and cramped in stocks. Someone has said, "The gospel entered Europe by two men prisoners giving a sacred concert that brought the house down."

The reason for their joy: They fully believed their suffering served a redemptive purpose. They were confident Satan would be thwarted and the gospel would spread. They expected God to manifest Himself according to the level of their praise. The results: The jailer sought salvation with his whole household; God used their suffering to secure the future safety and respect of the church; the earthquake brought diversity in gender to the church; they never forgot Paul or the Christ he proclaimed. Paul and Silas finally met the man they had seen in the vision at Troas.

Thought for the Day: *Biblically speaking, suffering is to be viewed as a gracious gift from Christ reminding us of His redemptive suffering for us.*

Paul's Great Missionary Sermon

Scripture Reading: Acts 17:16-34

Key Verse: *I even found an altar with this inscription, TO AN UNKNOWN GOD... (Acts 17:23).*

Meditation: Paul came to Mars Hill with special preparation for cross-cultural ministry. His background included factors important both to Jews and to Gentiles

1. Paul's Jewish heritage, giving him knowledge and acceptance by the community. He did free himself from the limitations of the movement, so he could reach all the people. 2. Paul's Roman citizenship served as his international passport to all the countries of the Roman Empire. 3. Paul's academic training in Hellenistic culture prepared him to meet the best minds in the empire. Since he spoke fluently both Hebrew and Greek, he was probably the most versatile man in the New Testament.

Paul saw the altar to the Unknown God and preached with his understanding of the different cultures so that the people would comprehend his message. He shows that the Unknown God could be known. He insists that the Unknown God is God the Creator and that they should seek Him as He is revealed in Christ.

Paul uses concepts known to his listeners, such as altars, poets, and gods. Then he builds on these ideas to appeal to them for the message of the Gospel.

To better understand the communication of the gospel to different peoples, a process we call "missions," we will view man's condition and God's response as Paul has written in Romans. Then we will study our responsibility to take the message to any culture, for we believe God is available to every person.

Thought for the Day: *Mankind searches for peace: Jesus came to show them the God who created all of us.*

Seven Steps from Monotheism to Paganism

Scripture Reading: Romans 1:21-25

Key Verse: *For although they knew God... (Romans 1:21a).*

Meditation: Scripture does not support the theory that mankind is evolving upward morally, intellectually or spiritually. History witnesses that wherever the Gospel of Christ is not embraced, the pull of human nature is downward. Natural man is not moving towards, but away from God. The human race did not begin with idolatry, but with monotheism. Paul traces man's descent in seven simple steps. Even nations once considered Christian might be moving down this slippery path to paganism.

1. For although they knew God, they neither glorified him as God... (Romans 1:21a). Primitive man knew God from creation and in his own conscience. Creation itself discloses God's power and deity. When man fails to recognize the clear revelation of God in nature, the mind substitutes human speculations. God will judge man, not for inadequate knowledge, but for his inadequate response.

2. ...nor gave thanks to him (Romans 1:21b). God dislikes ingratitude immensely. Paul's preaching always stressed God's generosity that calls for a grateful response. Paul at Lystra in Acts 14:17 relates God's goodness to man. He *has shown kindness by giving you rain from heaven and crops in their seasons; he provides you with plenty of food and fills your hearts with joy.* But verse 18 goes on to say, *Even with these words they had difficulty keeping the crowd from sacrificing to them.* The people thought Paul and his friends were some kind of gods.

Thought for the Day: *God wants to be our recognized Creator.*

Seven Steps from Monotheism to Paganism

Scripture Reading: Romans 1:21-25

Key Verse: *...but their thinking became futile... (Romans 1:22b).*

Meditation:
3. Evil progresses. First, God is neglected, then ingratitude for His blessings. Inevitably, futile thinking about God results. When religious truth is ignored and not put into action, the person loses that truth and replaces it with erroneous human reasoning. Whenever man makes a substitution for God, he ends up with something less than the Creator God. In today's world we have inordinate expressions of humanism where the man himself, as an example of futile thinking, replaces God on the throne of men's hearts.

4. Their foolish hearts became darkened (Romans 1:21b). Rejecting the true message and nature of God causes confusion in the human heart. Man turns from recognizing the Creator God and makes idols. The abandonment of the true God leads to inferior objects of worship.

5. Although they claimed to be wise, they became fools (Romans 1:22). Man's unaided search for truth leads to foolishness from God's perspective. I Corinthians 1:21 says, "the world by its wisdom knew not God." The "world" is that system of thinking that has no place for an absolute God or for His Son Jesus. The spirit of the world is the evil one who seeks to cut off communication with God.

Thought for the Day: *When truth is neglected, then errors quickly multiply.*

Seven Steps from Monotheism to Paganism

Scripture Reading: Romans 1:21-25

Key Verse: *...and exchanged the glory of the immortal God for images made to look like mortal man and bird, and animals and reptiles (Romans 1:23).*

Meditation: "In all my travels around the world, I have yet to find a beautiful idol," so observed Dr. Harold Greenlee, one of my seminary professors. Most of the idols I have seen attest to that; they are grossly distorted caricatures of God. God greatly honored man by making us in His own image.

6. For us to try to make God into the image of His own created beings, such as birds or animals, dishonors Him. God did not condone the idolatry of the Old Testament people; how can He approve of the actions of our people today? According to the prophetic scriptures, in the end of human history mankind shall once more be confronted with the choice of worship of man/beast or of God himself. The writer of Revelation 13:18 cautions us, *This calls for wisdom. If anyone has insight, let him calculate the number of the beast, for it is man's number. His number is 666.*

7. They exchanged the truth of God for a lie, and worshipped and served the created things rather than the Creator... (Romans 1:25a). Idols are actually a lie, for they portray God to be someone totally alien to the scriptural revelation of God. Idols have a form, but God is a Spirit. The idol concept assumes someone or something is to be venerated in place of the true God. Perhaps the most dangerous lie of all is that people are now being programmed by idolatry to fall for the "man of lawlessness" when he will be revealed at the end of human history and demand to be worshipped.

Thought for the Day: *Idolatry is not men using an idol to worship God, but rather using other objects in the place of God.*

God's Response to Intentional Paganism

Scripture Reading: Romans 1:24-32

Key Verse: *Therefore, God gave them over...to sexual impurity... (Romans 1:24a).*

Meditation: Repeating this refrain three times in these verses emphasizes God's response to the outrageous sinful conduct of people who knew but ignored God's requirements. God lifted His restraining hand and allowed them to experience the ugly results of their own sins in their own lives.

Paul addresses first the use of temple prostitutes to expect the gods to bless with a bountiful harvest and to increase the herds. But by this willful exchange of worshipping the "created thing" rather than the Creator, they banished God from their lives.

Next, God "gave them over" to total perversion in human sexual relationships. The sexual deviation contains its own penalty for flagrantly ignoring the seventh Commandment "You shall not commit adultery" (Exodus 20:14).

"He gave them over," repeated the third time, refers to those people who intuitively knew God, but willfully refused to acknowledge Him lest it impede their preferred evil living. The depraved mind described in Ephesians 4:14, "As having lost all sensitivity, they have given themselves over to sensuality so as to indulge in every kind of impurity, with a continual lust for more." The depraved mind people can no longer form right judgments because they have abandoned themselves to sin.

Thought for the Day: *The ultimate end of idol worship: Man becomes incapable of discerning the glory of God the Creator and worships the created things only.*

Four Principles of God's Final Judgment

Scripture Reading: Romans 2:1-4

Key Verse: *...God's judgment...is based on truth (Romans 2:2b).*

Meditation:
1. God's judgment is based on truth (Romans 2:2). God's judgment of the world will be carried out without any partiality. The Jewish people cannot claim exemption because of chosen status. The Gentiles will not be spared because of God's patience or goodness. God expects them to repent. Man's partial judgment based on inadequate information cannot compare with God's judgment. From God's viewpoint nothing is overlooked, including the hidden matters of the heart. David, in Psalm 51:6a, reminds us, "Surely you desire truth in the inner parts." God expects not only outward virtue, but inward purity. Only those who love and practice truth inwardly will escape God's final consequences of judgment.

2. God will give to each person according to what he has done (Romans 2:6). Paul, standing before Cornelius, the Gentile, and his household, made a startling statement about the relationship of good works and acceptance before God: "I now realize how true it is that God does not show favoritism, but accepts men from every nation who fear him and do what is right" (Acts 10:34,35). The two conditions are "those who fear Him," and "who do what is right." Cornelius, the Gentile, practiced a life of quiet prayer, generosity and belief in the gospel when he heard it preached.

Thought for the Day: *Whoever practices righteousness will receive eternal life; whoever practices unrighteousness will receive the wrath of God.*

Four Principles of God's Final Judgment

Scripture Reading: Romans 2:5-16

Key Verse: *...not those who hear the law, but those who obey the law will be declared righteous (Romans 2:13).*

Meditation:
3. Obedience, not knowledge, determines the judgment. Pagans, enlightened by conscience, are as informed about God as those with the Mosaic Law. They will not know all the requirements of the Mosaic law, but missionary pioneers and anthropologists have discovered many peoples who were never in contact with Christianity, who nevertheless agree and practice most of the Mosaic commandments that relate to man's relationship with man. In fact, Paul observes that Gentiles sometimes excelled the practice of the Jews, even though the Jews had a higher set of standards in the Old Testament.

4. God will judge man's secrets through Jesus Christ... (Romans 2:16). In the final analysis, God is just and will judge righteously. He will judge according to the revelation available to people and their obedience to that understanding. Neither will the Gentiles be judged by the revelation they did not have. Those who have allowed their conscience to become seared will be held accountable for what they have heard or known. The Jew who knew the law but did not keep it will be held responsible for his knowledge. People who refused to believe and follow Christ will still be held answerable. God sees not only the visible acts of sin, but also those hidden evil desires that were not expressed, and holds both responsible on the Day of Judgment.

Thought for the Day: *The greater our privileges the more severe will be the judgment.*

Paul: Man's Predicament before God

Scripture Reading: Romans 1:18-32

Key Verse: *...so men are without excuse (Romans 1:20b).*

Meditation: Paul addresses primarily two groups of people here. The first is those who do not have access to special revelation, the Scriptures. Many ask, "How can a just God condemn those who have had no opportunity to read the Bible or to hear the Gospel?" Paul, however, does not hold this category of people guiltless. They have two channels of truth concerning God.

First is physical creation. "For since the creation the world God's invisible qualities, his eternal power and divine nature, have been clearly seen, being understood from what has been made, so men are without excuse" (Romans 1:20b). God reveals distinct truths about Himself in creation. The majesty of the physical universe eloquently witnesses to the God who both calls man and demands his worship.

In Psalms David teaches a God communicating through creation. God speaks, literally shouts at us, so we may hear and respond to His revelation. The universe is God's natural Bible, constantly revealing knowledge about Him. That revelation is everywhere, universal. There is no place where nature's voice is silent and no time when it cannot be heard.

Thought for the Day: *The sun, moon and stars are God's traveling evangelists so that everyone in the world can see and hear, leaving all of us without excuse.*

Paul: Man's Predicament before God

Scripture Reading: Romans 2:14-20

Key Verse: *Since they show that the requirements of the law are written on their hearts... (Romans 2:15a).*

Meditation: Not only does the physical universe shout about God to all of us, but also the witness of our conscience shows us what God expects. Paul indicated that even those Gentiles who do not have an external written revelation of the law still do instinctively know what the law requires.

How can we explain not having the law and yet obeying it? Paul explains that since God created man as a self-conscious moral person, we demonstrate this behavior that the requirements of the law still remain, however faintly, written on our hearts. Even today anthropologists and missionaries find people who honor parents, who recognize the sanctity of life, are loyal to spouse, practice honestly and speak the truth, covering at least five of the Ten Commandments.

The active knowledge with the conscience speaking warns man against wrong behavior. We see triple proof that the Gentiles will be held accountable to God: The conduct of some who show the evidence of God's law written on their hearts; the action of conscience condemning wrong behavior; and their thoughts constantly reminding them of the most required behavior.

The standard of judgment for the Jews will be the Law of Moses. The standard for the Gentiles will be the law of conscience. The standard for the Christian will be the Gospel.

Thought for the Day: *The greater our knowledge of right and wrong, the greater our accountability before God.*

Paul's Theology of Salvation (1)

Scripture Reading: Romans 8: 29-39

Key Verse: *For those God foreknew... (Romans 8:29).*

Meditation: Paul describes the meaning of salvation in Romans 8 by beginning, not with man, but with God. He does not spell out in detail the demands on man, but rather emphasizes what God has already done. Paul portrays our salvation from the divine side, beginning with the eternal past and extends to the eternal future. God has always been thinking and will always be thinking of us, planning for any contingency.

In my boyhood I recall a preacher pacing as he gave us the story of Adam and Eve sinning in the garden. His pacing gave us the impression that God was so distressed He did not know what to do. But we never surprise God. And He is never without an alternative plan. The Scriptures show Jesus as.. "the Lamb slain from the creation of the world" (Revelation 13:8b).

In Romans Paul outlines God's divine initiative towards us. None of these actions originate in us, but all flow out of God's redemptive love towards us. God still moves irresistably towards us, drawing us to Him and then keeping us to the end of our earthy life. He wants us to fully glorify the full culmination of God's plan of salvation for us. I used to be concerned about doing my part in my conversion, but God showed me through the communion time, "I know you are worried about your lack of spiritual preparation for your conversion as a Christian in 1947. I want you to focus on what Jesus did for you at Calvary 2,000 years ago. That is what makes the difference."

Thought for the Day: *At the heart of the Gospel, the Good News, is the message of what God has already done for us in Christ.*

Paul's Theology of Salvation

Scripture Reading: Romans 8:29-39

Key Verse: *For those God foreknew... (Romans 8:29a).*

Meditation: Let's look at the prior divine actions of God towards us in salvation. Someone has called them the Five Golden Links. Salvation includes these five actions: *Foreknowing, predestining, calling, justifying,* and *glorifying.* The word salvation in the Bible covers three tenses: Salvation reaches into the past; it embraces the present and extends into the future. Salvation comes freely to us as a gift. Jesus Christ's death on the cross provided everything necessary for forgiveness. What then must we do? We need only bow before God in repentance and by faith receive His free gift of forgiveness.

God knew me long before I became a Christian in 1947. David says "God knew me from the womb." God's *foreknowledge* expressed itself in the purpose of redemption of the human race. God knows each of us individually. He chose us to be saved. When God sent Jesus to the cross, He went for us.

Our common understanding of *foreknowledge* means to know something in advance. *Foreknowledge* in the Bible means much more than just knowledge. It means God's closeness, His intimacy, and His personal affection towards us. In fact, the *foreknowledge* of God is the same as being fore-loved by God.

Thought for the Day: *God in His foreknowledge made the provision for our salvation even before Adam sinned.*

Paul's Theology of Salvation

Scripture Reading: Romans 8:29-39

Key Verse: *...and those he predestined... (Romans 8:30a).*

Meditation: The five actions depicting God's salvation are written in the Greek New Testament in the aorist tense, conveying completed action. In God's heart these acts are already done, awaiting only our personal reception. We can respond to God's initiative with expectant faith.

While theologians disagree about the interpretation of predestination, if understood Biblically, it brings much comfort to us. The word *predestination* in the Bible is never addressed to the unsaved. Rather it assures Christians that when God saves us He will also care for us right to the end of our Christian pilgrimage.

Notice the distinct purpose of our *predestination,* essentially the same as election "...to be conformed to the likeness of His Son." Paul teaches us that we are "to be holy and blameless in his sight." These verses teach us that we must cultivate both deep humility before people and a careful walk in holiness before God.

II Corinthians 3:18a says that we will increasingly "with unveiled faces reflect the Lord's glory." God wants us to be characterized by Christ-likeness. God's desire and redemptive provision of each of His children is that the image of Christ be superimposed over every area of our lives. That is the kind of destiny He has preplanned for us and made possible through Christ.

Thought for the Day: *God predestined us because He loves us, and He loves us not because we are lovable, but because of His agape love.*

Paul's Theology of Salvation

Scripture Reading: Romans 8:29-39

Key Verse: *...he also called (Romans 8:30a).*

Meditation: *Calling,* the next salvation act of God, confronts us much more than a pastor's invitation at the close of a sermon. Theologians call this "the effectual calling" reflecting certain characteristics:

First, this *Divine calling* is so full of the Holy Spirit's energy that the sinner intuitively knows he could get saved at that moment that he makes his spiritual needs known to God in a prayer of repentance. Second, this *Divine calling* is perceived very personally. God seems to be calling us by name. Third, the *calling of God* has a compelling sense of urgency to act now.

Billy Graham calls his radio and television programs The Hour of Decision. For 40 years he did not change the title to the Years of Decision. His title reflects biblically sound basis that now is the only one good time to be saved. That time is when the Holy Spirit strives with us. Paul reminded the Galatians that their moment of decision came when "...before your very eyes Jesus Christ was clearly portrayed as crucified" (Galatians 3: 16).

Sometimes evangelists stress the importance of the "now of decision" as though they know that exact time of the effectual calling of the Sprit. I want to say that no one except that individual himself really knows the voice of the Spirit who speaks not once, but many times. However, if the person continually resists the voice of the Spirit, causing "hardening of the heart" or "searing of the conscience," the ability to respond becomes more difficult.

Thought for the Day: *The danger of postponing the Spirit's intense* **now** *is that it may end in being* **never.**

Paul's Theology of Salvation

Scripture Reading: Romans 8:29-39

Key Verse: *...he also justified.... (Romans 8:30).*

Meditation: A recent convert loved to tell how wonderfully God had brought him to his dramatic conversion. After a spontaneous testimony in church a more legalistic elder said to him, "Young man, since salvation is 'part us' and 'part God,' would you tell us more about your part in being saved?" The young convert apologized for the omission and said, "My part was sinning and running away from God, and God's part was following after me until He found me."

Christ not only pardons us; He *justifies* us. He puts us in a relationship with God not subject to change. "Nothing can separate us from the love of Christ" (Romans 8:39). The president of the United States has authority to pardon anyone, his friends, or otherwise, who have broken the law. The "easy pardon" may compromise the integrity of both the president and his office. But God did not compromise His own righteousness by handing out easy pardons for us sinners. Rather, He allowed our sins to be placed on His sinless Son on the cross. Jesus was literally charged with our sins, as in II Corinthians 5:21, "God made him (Jesus) who knew no sin to be made sin for us, so that we might be made the righteousness of God." As we personalize our sins to Him, He personalizes our righteousness before God.

Thought for the Day: *In Christ we stand before God just-as-if-we-never-sinned, an act of grace and secured once for all.*

Paul's Theology of Salvation

Scripture Reading: Romans 8:29-39

Key Verse: *...he also glorified... (Romans 8:30b).*

Meditation: God's final redemptive action towards us: He *glorified* us. Probably the most daring statement of faith Paul records, he is so certain of the God who *foreknew* us, *predestined* us, *called* and *justified* us, will also *glorify* us. In fact, so certain is he that he writes the word in the past tense, *glorified*.

Paul is indicating that we are already made glorious by the indwelling of the Holy Spirit. We may find that hard to believe. Just look at all of our weaknesses and imperfections, " Who, me, already glorified?" we respond incredulous. But we are made temples of the Holy Spirit in our conversion. We are each already a miniature Holy of Holies. While we realize that ultimate glorification has not yet taken place, we are all waiting with great anticipation for that day of His appearing. "For when he appears we shall be like him, for we shall see him as he is" (I John 3:2b). At the precise moment of His Second Coming, every Christian shall stand glorified with the same kind of glory Jesus manifested on the Mount of Transfiguration. "...His face shone like the sun, and his clothes became as white as light" (Matthew 17:2).

Paul affirms in many of his writings that the God who initiated salvation and who continues in the present, will consummate it in glorification. In Ephesians 4:30 he speaks of the Holy Spirit as "the seal and guarantee of that future day of deliverance." None of us knows what tomorrow may bring, but the Christian can live with assurance that even death itself cannot prevent the successful goal of salvation, *our glorification.*

Thought for the Day: *If God's provision for my salvation has been completed, then all I need to do is to receive all as unmerited gifts.*

The Missionary Call

Scripture Reading: Matthew 9:35-38

Key Verse: *Ask the Lord of the harvest, therefore, to send more workers... (Matthew 9:38a).*

Meditation: Every believer serves God. In addition to natural talents, God gives us "spiritual gifts." These gifts produce unity, wholeness among those who love God, and a powerful impression on those outside the church.

The reality of the great imbalance between the huge harvest and the scarcity of workers on the mission fields of the world demands some corrective thinking about God's call. There are, however, misconceptions about the *"missionary call."*

The first misconception: *More people would go to the mission field if they were more dedicated to God.* While some truth is reflected in this miss-concept, it suggests there are different levels of dedication: One level for a missionary, another for a pastor and yet another for a layman. During 500-1100 AD Christians were challenged to enter the monastic life, more harsh and austere than that of the average Christian. Personally, I have never considered myself as being more dedicated than a faithful pastor at home or a farmer who rises early to milk his cows to support the local church and the cause of world missions.

Thought for the Day: *Our mandate for more missionary workers is not by a deeper dedication, but by praying to the "Lord of the harvest to send forth workers."*

The Missionary Call (2)

Scripture Reading: Judges 6:11-18

Key Verse: *The Lord turned to him (Gideon) and said, Go in the strength you have and save Israel out of Midian's hand (Judges 6:14a).*

Meditation: The second misconception: *The need or the open door is the call and we need nothing more.* A similar thought, *We should go where the need is the greatest.* These concepts contain half-truths. We should be concerned about the three billion world people who have not heard enough biblical truth to make an informed decision. We should be aware of the remaining 4,000 distinct language groups that do not yet have a portion of the New Testament in their language.

However, primarily those who have a personal sense of calling, or special personal guidance will persevere through language study and other crises. Adam Clarke, theologian of early Methodism, wrote that one of the gifts needed by everyone in God's service was to have a confident sense of being commissioned by God to go and testify of His grace.

The Scriptures record that while there are many different methods by which God calls persons into his service, yet in each instance what matters is a personal sense of being called: Abraham (Genesis 11,12), Moses at the burning bush (Exodus 3), Gideon (Judges 6), Samuel as a child (I Samuel 3), Elisha as he plowed (I Kings 19), Isaiah in the temple (Isaiah 6), Paul on the road to Damascus (Acts 9). None volunteered before they heard the call of God.

Thought for the Day: *Inherent in every genuine call is a sense of "Woe is me if I don't do it."*

The Missionary Call (3)

Scripture Reading: Acts 7:20-22

Key Verse: *Moses was educated in all the wisdom of the Egyptians and was powerful in speech and action (Acts 7:22).*

Meditation: The third misconception about the missionary call: *Anyone can be a missionary regardless of preparation.* Some believe that mission boards should accept and send out all who apply for missionary service. Amazingly, these are people who require a certain level of preparation for ministers, but not for missionaries who have an even more complicated assignment to engage in cross-cultural communication that involves the self-discipline of learning a complex language.

Missionaries rarely go to illiterate peoples, and even if they do, the culture requires respect and study. Most people have migrated to large cities of five to 25 million. The greatest challenge lies in training leaders of those cultures who will reach their own people. Academic preparation in one's own country gives credibility and often an immediate hearing from those in the receiving culture.

Those of us who served in Japan were beneficiaries of three pioneers sometimes called the famous triumvirate of the late 1800's: Dr. J. C. Hepburn who prepared a Japanese-English dictionary and a Bible dictionary. He also assisted in the first translation of the Bible. Dr. S. R. Brown established the first English school using the Bible as the center of study, and Dr. G. F. Verbeck, a gifted linguist, evangelist, orator and brilliant statesman.

Thought for the Day: *Personal spiritual and academic preparation and previous experience can help determine a missionary's usefulness on the field.*

The Missionary Call (4)

Scripture Reading: I Corinthians 9:16-23

Key Verse: *Woe is me if I do not preach the gospel (I Corinthians 9:16).*

Meditation: I endorse this definition of a missionary: A *person with a strong inner witness from the Holy Spirit calling that person to cross-cultural ministry.* Often this urge is accompanied by a strong sense of urgency. Paul expressed that urge as "Woe is me if I do not preach the gospel." In another place he expresses the urge as being entrusted with a divine stewardship for which he was directly responsible to God.

Usually the missionary call unfolds in a progression: Few people know immediately God's total plan for their lives. In hearing about a certain country, a specific ministry or a particular mission, their hearts are touched with the need. (Of great importance is being connected to an organization that is compatible doctrinally, has sound financial policies, is suited for giftedness and burden for ministry, clear about children's education and pastoral care of the missionaries.)

The nature of the missionary call is unique to each person. No one can duplicate the experience of another. Some see a vision and feel called, but the two should not be equated. Some receive a challenge for a field, but may not go in person, yet pray for those people for the rest of their lives. Some people think they hear an audible call, go and find themselves in impossible situations. Going step by step, following established avenues of guidance gives that peace that leads to the place God wants us to be.

Thought for the Day: *When we feel a great pressure to act immediately we should pause and "test the spirits."*

The Missionary Call (5)

Scripture Reading: I Corinthians 4:1-5

Key Verse: N*ow it is required that those who have been given a trust must prove faithful (I Corinthians 4:2).*

Meditation: Hearing a missionary message or reading a biography challenges many people, but a challenge and a missionary call are not necessarily synonymous. Every missionary should have an inward call that Martin Luther called, "God's voice in the soul." No one else can tell you that you are called. They can encourage you to listen, and may affirm your spiritual gifts, but only God can make the call clear to you. God calls and equips us for missionary work.

Beyond the initial "inner call" God will confirm your leading: Your evangelical home church will recognize God's call on you and should encourage you in prayer, giving and nurture. The other confirmation would be when a valid mission organization would accept your application and give you the avenue to use your spiritual gifts in a ministry that could be for many years.

Many people serve for a short time on a mission field location. This exposure gives a good opportunity for the Holy Spirit to show you whether you are equipped or could get equipped for a ministry there. Be aware of the mission's record of growth and their long-range goals. Interact with the field missionaries and national leaders to test your acceptance of them and your comfort in working with them.

Thought for the Day: *If a missionary call is authentic one should expect both divine and human confirmation.*

The Missionary Call (6)

Scripture Reading: Judges 6:7-19

Key Verse: *...If I have found favor in your eyes, give me a sign that it is really you talking to me (Judges 6:17b).*

Meditation: In seeking confirmation of a missionary call, some question the legitimacy of the "fleece" (sign). The Old Testament examples, as in today's scripture, show how people looked for a sign of God's guidance. Some wonder if we need a sign today since we have the indwelling presence of the Holy Spirit.

I believe that God still accommodates Himself to our occasional need for a sign, provided we follow certain guidelines and recognize their limitations:

1. A sign is not for additional information, but for obedience. A sign should not be sought in any matter to which you have not yet committed yourself.
2. Do not ask for a sign for anything that is contrary to the basic teaching of the Bible.
3. Do not dictate to God what the sign must be. God is creative and we will recognize His revelation.
4. Do not insist on your timetable. God will not be put in your box of thinking. Should God choose to use people to answer your prayer, as in provision of funds, the people may not act as quickly as you expect. God is still working, but the people have to respond before you see the result of His working.
5. Do not use a sign first, but learn to trust the inner voice of the Holy Spirit, providential circumstances, the Word of God either strengthening or weakening the impression and the input of mature Christians.
6. Like Gideon, test the results several times.
7. Do not expect a sign to insulate you against future doubts and normal anxieties that accompany decision-making.

Thought for the Day: *God, in His infinite patience, often accommodates Himself to our concerns. He does not chide us for incorrect choices provided we are open to His correction.*

The Missionary Call (7)

Scripture Reading: Ephesians 1:3-14

Key Verse: *For he chose us in him before the creation of the world to be holy and blameless in his sight (Ephesians 1:4).*

Meditation: Seven biblical portraits should reflect the lives of all those set apart for missionary work:

1. A bowed head, indicating reverence and worship of God. "Worship the Lord in the splendor of his holiness..." (Psalm 96:9).
2. Knees bent in prayer, with humility and dependence on God. "And for this reason I kneel before my Father..." (Ephesians 3:14-16).
3. A listening ear fine-tuned to hear God's voice. "Speak, for your servant is listening" (I Samuel 3:10b).
4. A renewed mind through the Word and the Holy Spirit. "...be transformed by the renewing of your mind" (Romans 12:2b).
5. A Spirit-filled heart, issuing in a love-motivated ministry. "...As God has poured out his love into our hearts, by the Holy Spirit, whom he has given us" (Romans 5:5b).
6. A disciplined eye, to see past the temporal to the eternal world. "...by faith Moses persevered because he saw him who is invisible" (Hebrews 11:27b).
7. A surrendered will, that continually acknowledges Christ's Lordship over every area of our lives. "For the earth is the Lord's and everything in it" (I Corinthians 10:26).

Thought for the Day: *Many are called but few are chosen (Matthew 22:16). Only the ones who make Jesus Lord become the chosen ones.*

The Missionary Invited to Stay

Scripture Reading: Acts 20:25-38

Key Verse: *What grieved them most was his statement that they would never see his face again... (Acts 20:38a).*

Meditation: "Whatever happened to that vanishing breed called *Missionaries for Life?*" read one periodical article recently. I believe our present generation of young people is just as dedicated to Christ as past ones, but the fact remains that there are only a few who apply as missionaries for life. Looking at the few laborers for the abundant harvest we come to these conclusions:

Perhaps we have not emphasized in our presentation of the missionary challenge the importance and value of a lifetime commitment. In my most recent assignment working on college and seminary campuses, I am surprised at the student reactions when they learn I have spent over 30 years in Japan. Amazed, they respond, "Thirty years in one country!" Learning the language and earning the trust of the people takes time, and career missionaries will tell us that the effectiveness and outreach of their ministry is nearly doubled with each succeeding period of time spent in the country.

In early days of missions back to the 1860's missionaries did not return to their home countries very often; some stayed ten years or longer. Those beloved by the people of their adopted country retired there and even were buried where they had worked.

Thought for the Day: *National Christians want to feel that the missionary's heart will always remain in his adopted country.*

The Missionary Invited to Stay

Scripture Reading: John 3:1-15

Key Verse: *...You must be born again (John 3:7b).*

Meditation: The national church still eagerly welcomes missionaries with certain characteristics:

1. **Those with an authentic, "born again experience."**
Being "born again" is a given requirement by every evangelical mission organization and is on every application form. Yet I am surprised at how little emphasis is put on our conversion, which is the pivot upon which everything else turns in our Christian life once we get to the country. I have noticed this lack of emphasis particularly in those who were saved as young children. A childhood conversion can be genuine, but somewhere in our spiritual journey this experience should be updated with our adult knowledge of the scriptures.

We need to articulate our understanding of Jesus' death on the cross in our place in order to take our sin, both personal and Adamic, and make us born-again children of God. This personal application to our lives gives us the passion to preach about the cross and share our own testimony. Thus we find ourselves identifying with the listeners and there is a leveling of all mankind that takes place. The message of the cross, Calvary theology, ignites the evangelistic zeal in our own hearts and in those who hear this message.

Thought for the Day: *Since the Holy Spirit inspired Luke to record Paul's testimony three times in the book of Acts, then each missionary should be aware of the importance of a personal testimony of redemption in sharing the gospel.*

The Missionary Invited to Stay

Scripture Reading: Acts 13:1-5

Key Verse: *Set apart for me Barnabas and Saul for the work to which I have called them (Acts 13:2b).*

Meditation: The missionary who will stay will:

2. Have a vital spiritual tie with the home church.

Serving on the committee that interviewed prospective career missionaries, I was totally unprepared and puzzled to find that a significantly large percentage had no vital connection with a church. Those who were saved through the para-church ministries were particularly unaware of the value of the church body. To consider being involved in church planting overseas, one would have to know what a church means in your personal life. How can anyone work in a church if that person does not know what a church is? Paul and Barnabas did not just volunteer to become messengers of the gospel; they were chosen and sent by the church.

An authentic fulfillment of the Great Commission, "Go into all the world and preach the gospel, baptizing, making disciples" (Matthew 28:18,19), means there will be a body representing Christ that will demonstrate His love and salvation to the community. Passing out tracts or preaching should result in decisions by individuals followed by their baptism, discipling and becoming witnesses as they participate in the fellowship of the body of Christ. Not only does God give His Holy Spirit to each believer, but also He gives spiritual gifts that must be used in the context of the church for mutual edification and accountability.

While there is no mandate in the scriptures for a church building, experience has demonstrated that the believers need a visible or permanent place to gather, particularly in countries where temples and shrines symbolize worship.

Thought for the Day: *Two are better than one..If one falls, his friend can help him up... (Ecclesiastes 4:9,10).*

The Missionary Invited to Stay

Scripture Reading: Acts 6:1-7 and 8:5-8

Key Verse: *Brothers, choose seven men from among you known to be full of the Spirit and wisdom... (Acts 6:3a).*

Meditation: The missionary who stays will:

3. Have some experience in ministry in the homeland before embarking for the field.
 To try to master a new language and then start a new ministry can be a daunting challenge. Only one thing could be more formidable: To attempt to do something in a new language that you had not done before, ever. National Christians and leaders expect the missionary to come prepared and experienced. Invariably we are asked, "How did you handle this kind of problem in your church work back home?"

Philip demonstrates the prepared missionary. He had served as one of the seven deacons in the mother church, having proven his spiritual and character qualities, "Known to be full of the Spirit and wisdom." He served effectively in the role of team player and, together with the other six men, he resolved crises with the direct result that "the number of disciples in Jerusalem increased rapidly and a large number of priests were obedient to the faith" (Acts 6:7).

During a time of increasing persecution of the church in Jerusalem, Philip went to Samaria as the first great missionary of the faith to a people that the Jews had purposely avoided because of their past marriages to pagan Assyrians. A great revival broke out with demons fleeing before the power of God in Philip. Then God called Philip away to a lonely desert appointment to witness to a single Ethiopian man. This man became, next to Paul, the most strategic convert in all the book of Acts (8:26-40).

Thought for the Day: *A spiritual success in a present ministry may be God's signal to move you overseas.*

The Missionary Invited to Stay

Scripture Reading: Romans 12:3-8

Key Verse: *We have different gifts... (Romans 12:6a).*

Meditation: The missionary who stays

4. Knows his/her own spiritual gifts and affirms the giftedness of others.

King Saul failed as the first king of Israel because he never accepted his own divine giftedness as king. His deep insecurity caused him to be threatened by David and jealous of him, even though David tried to support the king. Even when people said positive things about David, King Saul internalized those remarks as criticism of himself, resulting in a paranoid determination to be rid of the only one capable of helping him.

Our western culture teaches us to compete with each other, trying to get to the top regardless of the people who are hurt or pushed aside in the process. This cultural rivalry can follow us, subconsciously even to the mission field. Conditions on the field will bring that individualistic spirit to resurface unless we are sensitive to the Holy Spirit's bringing it our attention. New missionaries sometimes think their innovative strategies are the answer to winning the national to Christ. Meanwhile, they are frustrated by the demands of the rudimentary language study and the humility required to be faithful at the assigned task.

The missionary who accepts direction with humility, understands his gifts, but affirms others, especially national pastors and believers, will discover a reciprocal level of trust and an ever widening ministry opportunity.

Thought for the Day: *An unwillingness to recognize our own giftedness causes us to inhibit the gifts of others and can weaken the whole organization.*

The Missionary Invited to Stay

Scripture Reading: II Corinthians 11:23-33

Key Verse: *Three times I was beaten with rods... (II Corinthians 11:25a).*

Meditation: The missionary who stays will

5. Have a strong sense of guidance and calling to the adopted country.

This two-fold sense of calling and guidance are both essential for staying power. A brief visit to a country and a long stay are not synonymous at all. Staying brings the challenges of the daily task and consists of very few of the romantic moments of the brief, more tourist-like visit.

A journalist interviewed a medical missionary in Africa, "Do you enjoy your work and do you really love the people here?" he asked. The doctor's response may surprise us, "To be very honest with you, I have to say that much of the time I, humanly speaking, would rather be working with highly trained professionals in a sanitary building in my own country. I feel the isolation and lack of consultant support here. My human love cannot keep me here."

The journalist, amazed, continued "Then, please tell me what it is that keeps you coming back term after term?" The doctor explained, "This is my calling; I cannot leave these people here to die without some medical help." This honest confession reminds me of a senior missionary to Japan saying, "You know, my wife and I need a new call to return to Japan each term." Paul said, "I was not disobedient to the heavenly vision," suggesting that there were times when he himself struggled with the demands of his calling. While it may have been exciting to be God's pioneer to the Gentiles, yet that entailed a list of over 25 hardships with this culminating sentence, "Besides everything else, I face daily, that pressure of my concern for all the churches."

Thought for the Day: *Ultimately every missionary's ministry will be measured by whether or not he/she was obedient to the vision from heaven.*

The Missionary Invited to Stay

Scripture Reading: Romans 5:1-10

Key Verse: *...While we were yet powerless, Christ died for the ungodly... (Romans 5:6b).*

Meditation: The missionary who stays will have

6. A disciplined commitment to study the history and culture of the adopted country.

The missionary must leave behind the idea that one's own country centers the universe, and that one's own culture demonstrates some kind of superiority. Unless this attitude of humility directs the adjustment, the person will always be comparing experiences with "how we do things back home." Being willing to learn from the national pastors and people allows identification with the new culture and understanding of cross communication.

Every organization has weaknesses and the outsider may be even more aware of them, but should not impose his/her measurements and assessments. Only longer experience gives the perspective to make an accurate judgment and the right to suggest corrective measures. One person encountered racial prejudice in the national church. A national pastor asked, "What makes you think that Christianity will do more in another country than it has done in your own nation?" We must join E. Stanley Jones who confessed, "Much of Christianity in the west does not thoroughly reflect Christ."

As we prayerfully study the adopted culture God will show us natural points of contact for the gospel. As we follow these insights we will be amazed how people will actually come to Christ directly. We must remember the difference between presenting the gospel to those who grew up with biblical concepts and those who are hearing for the first time.

Thought for the Day: *The gospel is good news only to those who hear it within the context of their culture.*

The Missionary Invited to Stay

Scripture Reading: I John 1:5-2:1

Key Verse: *...And the blood of Jesus his Son, purifies us from all sin (I John 1:7b).*

Meditation: The missionary who stays will have

7. A joyful, Spirit-filled and anointed ministry.
One of the character traits of Galatians 5:22,23 describing the Spirit-filled life is joy. The *fruit* of the Spirit described in Galatians (rather than the plural word, *fruits*) suggests all nine traits listed should be manifested simultaneously. We are all called as Christians to witness to the good news about Jesus. I am convinced also that we should "look like good news." We should not dress and act like we are at a funeral, but our demeanor should reflect the happy news of the gospel.

Being a Spirit-filled demonstrating Christian means we have moved beyond the crisis of sanctification into the process of becoming a mature Christian. We need the crisis of total commitment and infilling of the Spirit which is a recorded experience, but the process of maturing and reflecting the fruit of the Spirit will take our lifetime. To remain a Spirit-filled, growing Christian demands total honesty to walk in the light that God brings into our life through study of the Bible, interaction with others, and prayerful appreciation of others' reactions to us and to our ministry. As we confess our needs, Christ is faithful and just to cleanse us, continuously.

Missionaries should be humbled by the expectations of the inviting churches. Christians there pray and believe that seekers would be born again, young people would be called to ministry and the human interactive problems would be solved. The only way these prayers can be answered is through the special and fresh anointing each time on the message and the messenger who brings God's Word to them.

Thought for the Day: *The cleansing of Christ's blood promised in I John 1:7 is written in the present tense and embraces ongoing cleansing both for the act and the principle of sin.*

History is Moving Toward a Goal

Scripture Reading: 1 Thessalonians 1:2-10

Key Verse: *And to wait for his Son from Heaven... (I Thessalonians 1:10a).*

Meditation: On the first day of December we should each take a forward, as well as, a retrospective look at the meaning of Biblical history. As we do this, especially during this season, we will be reassured: "Just as Christ was born into human history as the prophets had predicted, we can be just as certain He will come again to consummate history." This is the living hope by which we live. The fact of Christ's "imminent return" also helps us to order our priorities daily. G. Campbell Morgan once said, "I never began my work without thinking that Christ may interrupt that work to begin His own, for His last words to the church are – 'Occupy until I come.' "

I once had an unforgettable experience in Japan while preaching on the hope of Jesus' return. As I was emphasizing the Biblical view that all of history has a purpose and goal, and is even now moving towards a climax, the lay pastor of the church, who was also a medical doctor, stood up and interrupted me saying, "Schultz Sensei, please repeat that again for it is so important to us Japanese Christians and I want to write it all down."

Why was Dr. Taguchi so struck by this new way of looking at history? The Japanese secular view of history is cyclical. Civilizations are born, rise and then fade away into oblivion. Then, another civilization is born, but again it follows this same cycle with no movement, purpose, or goal. In other words, to them, history is not going anywhere and so all we can do is observe it passively.

But, if history is linear and moving irresistibly toward its God-ordered goal and consummation, then we cannot passively observe history any longer. We must surrender to the One who is moving history, and actively cooperate with Him to "hasten His return."

Thought for the Day: *History is His-story, Christ's story.*

God Prepares the World for Christ

Scripture Reading: Galatians 4:4-7

Key Verse: *But when the time had fully come... (Galatians 4:4a).*

Meditation: As the time approached for Christ to be born, some amazing things began to happen. In fact, Christian historians tell us that never was such a propitious time, before or since, for Christ to be born and for Christianity to be spread around the world.

Paul refers to this time in history as "the fullness of time." God was actually using pagan nations for His own purpose. First, there was the Greek Empire, which made a great intellectual and cultural contribution. This clear and precise language would later become the language of the New Testament. Even the Old Testament Hebrew was translated into Greek by the second century B.C. Although Greece fought and lost against Rome, their language was retained and spoken from one end of the empire (Spain on the west and Persia on the east) to the other. Paul and the other missionaries did not have to go to language school, for Greek language and culture was universally accepted. Even today after about 2,000 years linguists still refer to the Greek Bible for the most accurate translation of Scripture.

The Roman Empire, too, would be used of God for the spreading of Christianity. Rome, by force, intentionally welded together into one empire many smaller nation-states. They built the Roman Road, a highway that would be used by Paul and other ambassadors of the "King of kings." It could be written after only two decades, "The Lord's message rang out from you, not only in Macedonia and Achaia – your faith in God has become known everywhere" (I Thessalonians 1:8). This miraculous spread of Christianity was made possible by one language spoken in the then known one Roman world.

Thought for the Day: *The invisible hand of God is always at work even though we may not perceive it except in retrospect.*

God Prepares the Jewish People
for Christ's Coming

Scripture Reading: Luke 3:1-18

Key Verse: *The people were waiting expectantly... (Luke 3:15a).*

Meditation: Yesterday we observed how God, in order to prepare the world for the coming of Christ, divinely intervened in the affairs of secular nations like Greece and Rome. But, we also ask, "What about the Jews, God's chosen people? Was God also preparing them?"

While we are tempted to generalize that all of the Jews were much like those who opposed Jesus, that is not the total picture. Many sincere Jews had tenaciously held on to the hope of the coming Messiah. Even though the prophets who had spoken of the Messiah had been dead for 400 years, the whole nation remained tense with expectation. When John the Baptist and others appeared on the scene, the first question people asked was, "Tell us, are you the Messiah?"

Not only was this sense of expectation high among the Jews residing in Palestine, it was high among scattered Jews as well. The fact remains that the Jews were literally scattered all over the then known world. Wherever they went they built a synagogue that served as a temple, except they did not have an altar upon which to offer sacrifices. Laymen who were more inclined to accept Christianity and open doors to God-fearing Gentiles directed most of the local synagogues.

No doubt God used the presence of a local synagogue to teach the Persian wise men about the coming of a King. Also, Paul later used the scattered synagogues with their God-fearing groups of Gentile converts as stepping stones for spreading and universalizing the Gospel. In fact, God used these scattered Jews as His pre-evangelists who encouraged the Ethiopian eunuch and many other Gentiles to visit Jerusalem where they heard about Jesus and were filled with the Holy Spirit.

Thought for the Day: *Even when God seems to be hidden, He is silently working preparing His next witness.*

The Significance of an Insignificant Place

Scripture Reading: Micah 5:1-6

Key Verse: *But you Bethlehem...though you are small among the clans of Judah... (Micah 5:2a).*

Meditation: The author of the textbook for my Ancient World History course seemed intent on impressing us with the wonders of the past great empires: Babylon, Greece, Persia, Rome and others. Each empire had a corresponding great leader such as Nebuchadnezzar, Alexander the Great, the various Caesars, who each ruled the world from the capitals of their day. These civilizations and leaders were viewed as the authentic movers of history.

In strong contrast, the Bible seems to bypass all these empires, capitals, leaders and their impressive conquests. The focus of biblical history seems to converge on a very insignificant village called Bethlehem hidden in the hills five miles south of Jerusalem.

The wise men somehow lost sight of the star as they inquired of Herod and the scribes about the birth of a king. They appear to have recovered the star as they went to Bethlehem. Then the star stopped, not over a king's palace, but over a manger with a helpless babe poorly clothed.

This was not exactly man's way of staging an important event. Yet, in retrospect, all of the great rulers and glittering civilizations have faded away, but the name of the Child who was born in a humble manger is on the lips of two billion people today.

Thought for the Day: *The most significant happenings in our world today may not make the headlines; they rarely do.*

Christ's Identification with Us

Scripture Reading: Hebrews 2:14-18

Key Verse: *For this reason He (Christ) had to be made like His brothers in every way… (Hebrews 2:17a).*

Meditation: A farmer chose to stay home rather than go with his family to the Christmas Eve candlelight service. He viewed the Christmas event on the same level as the story of Santa Claus, a kind of harmless entertainment for children. He sent the family away cheerfully, glad for a quiet evening in front of the fireplace.

He stoked the fire with a large armful of fresh wood. Just as he was starting to relax he heard a strange "thud" against the bay window. Within seconds he heard that strange sound several more times so he reluctantly got up to investigate. Nothing could be seen from inside the house, so he put on his overcoat and braved the snowstorm outside.

With a flashlight in hand he soon discovered a flock of misguided birds who, in the storm, had been attracted by the light in the house only to hit the window pane. Some of the birds still seemed bewildered and stunned by the impact against the house. Anxious to save the birds caught in the storm, he turned on the lights in the barn and hurriedly built a smudge fire to warm the place. He tried to shoo the birds toward the barn but they refused to go inside. Next, he tried using a large blanket, but again he failed to get them to the safety of the barn. After repeated tries, in exasperation, he burst out saying, "If only I was a bird, I could tell them what to do." At that very moment the midnight bells from the church rang out with "Thou didst leave thy throne and Kingdom's crown, when Thou camest to earth for me…"

Suddenly the farmer understood the real meaning of Christmas! Jesus had to become like one of us in order to talk to us and lead us to believe in God. This He wasn't able to do from Heaven; He had to come down to where we are in our lostness.

Thought for the Day: *Jesus had to come down to where we were to lift us to God by the way of the cross.*

A Light is Still Shining

Scripture Reading: John 1:1-12

Key Verse: *The light shines in the darkness... (John 1:5).*

Meditation: It was a cold, rainy December night in Japan. Our tent was damp and sagging between the poles with the added weight of the moisture. It was my turn to preach; I wondered how many people would brave the cold to attend. As always, I drove the sound truck around the community streets as my Japanese co-worker, using the public address system, announced the "Happy Sounds" (Gospel) meetings.

The tent was about half full. Among the listeners was a high school student in his black school uniform with gold buttons. He listened attentively both to me and to my interpreter. (I had recently arrived in Japan and relied on my interpreter, who understood English very well). At the close of the message I asked those wanting to know more to raise their hands. Almost immediately the high school student put up his hand and I went to talk to him.

Since he had responded so quickly, I assumed he had some church background or had been reading the Bible. But, much to my amazement, I found this was his first personal contact with a Christian or with the Bible. He said, "In my English class at school our teacher taught us the first verse of 'Silent Night' in English. I do not know the meaning of Christmas or even the words of the song, but I cannot get the melody out of my mind. Please explain the meaning of this song to me."

After explaining the song and the plan of salvation, I prayed the sinner's prayer with him. Then with the interpreter's urging, he began to pray his own prayer of confession and faith in Jesus.

Thought for the Day: *Jesus, the Light of the World, is still shining; we can witness with hope and confidence.*

The Uniqueness of the Birth of Jesus

Scripture Reading: Isaiah 9:6-7

Key Verse: *Unto us a child is born (Isaiah 9:6).*

Meditation: During the time I lived in Japan there were four new ambassadors appointed from our country. Each time before the official announcement was made in Japan, our government sent credentials and other documents in advance. In a sense, this is what God did in the Old Testament. Through revelations to the patriarchs and prophets God was sending advance notice to the world and to Israel about what Jesus would be like.

From a historical viewpoint, Jesus is the only world religious leader whose birth was predicted in advance. Not only was the exact place announced 700 years earlier, but also the details of His virgin birth. Jesus could later confront the religious leaders with "These are the Scriptures that testify about me" (John 5:39b). No other person has ever made a similar claim.

Another distinct feature of the birth of Jesus is His dividing history into two periods, B.C., before His birth, and A.D., after His birth. Even those who are unbelievers must date their letter in reference to Christ. In Japan a historical period covers only the time from one Emperor's coronation to his death. Christ's period begins before His birth and continues forever.

Another extraordinary factor is that Christ was born to die. But unlike other great teachers, His teaching did not end with His death, but His death caused His teaching to spread around the world. "The Lamb of God was slain from the foundation of the world" (Revelation 13:8). By divine intention, Jesus was slain in the heart and plan of God before He was born, and even before Adam and Eve ever sinned.

Thought for the Day: *The best way to understand the meaning of Christ's birth in history is to look backward from the cross.*

The Song of Angels is Still Being Sung

Scripture Reading: Luke 2:8-12

Key Verse: *Suddenly a great company of the heavenly host appeared with the angel, praising God... (Luke 2:13a).*

Meditation: There are four persons who lived on three different continents almost 200 years apart, but who became intimately linked in singing the Biblical story of Christmas in Japan: George F. Handel (1685-1759) a European, Homer A. Rodeheaver (1880-1955) an American, Ugo Nakada (1880-1965) and Washio Yamazaki (two Japanese).

George Handel wrote the famous oratorio entitled *Messiah,* which continues for 200 years to be the most performed major choral work in all of history. The uniqueness and durability is obvious from the fact that it consists of only carefully selected scriptures with the background of majestic music. The focus of the Word is on the birth of Jesus and the future coming of His Kingdom.

At the turn of the twentieth century, Homer Rodeheaver, the well known song evangelist of Billy Sunday, visited Japan and other countries to recruit promising song evangelists to train at his School of Sacred Music in Winona Lake, Indiana. The Japanese person selected was Ugo Nakada, the son of the co-founder of OMS International and the Holiness Church in Japan. At that time he had already written a number of indigenous hymns and translated many from English and other languages.

One of the choral works which deeply moved Mr. Nakada, was Handel's *Messiah.* Upon hearing that a fellow Japanese pastor, Washio Yamazaki, was in the process of translating it, he dreamed of the day when this majestic musical would be heard all over Japan. Little did he realize then what changes he would soon be facing when he returned to Japan, and how long he would have to wait to see the full realization of his vision.   (to be continued...)

Thought for the Day: *Even God-given dreams often require much patience, hard work, and time before they are realized.*

The Song of Angels

Scripture Reading: Luke 2:8-12

Key Verse: *...and on earth peace to men on whom His favor rests (Luke 2:14b).*

Meditation: When Rev. Nakada returned to Japan, he sensed the growing political turmoil in his country. Militarists were taking over. Before long democracy was displaced by a military dictatorship. This military dictatorship "used" the emperor as a "front" to motivate the people to unparalleled hardships and sacrifices for the "just cause of the war."

It became apparent to Rev. Nakada and his fellow pastors that their message about the Second Coming of Jesus would bring them into confrontation with the emperor. The emperor, the high priest of Shinto worship, was elevated to such a level in the minds of the people it was considered unthinkable that he would have to bow before Jesus. The inevitable happened the day after the surprise attack on Pearl Harbor. Rev. Nakada and all his fellow pastors were imprisoned and their churches locked up for the duration of the war. This was hardly the atmosphere in which to sing the *Messiah*, except in their hearts.

However, on that first December after the war, Rev. Nakada received permission from the U.S. occupation army to sing the *Messiah*, in English, at the U.S. Chapel Center in downtown Tokyo. The choir was made up of U.S. servicemen and those Japanese who spoke English. In the years that followed, both English and a Japanese choir would sing the *Messiah* each Christmas.

One Christmas after Norma Jean and I had moved from Tokyo to Sendai, in northern Japan. We were experiencing those *Christmas-away-from-home-blues* when we turned on the Japanese educational TV channel. To our amazement, a 50-voice Japanese choir was singing the *Messiah* in Japanese! Just before the singing of the Hallelujah Chorus the choir re-positioned itself into the shape of the cross!

Thought for the Day: *The message of the Great Commission is best preached and understood at Christmas.*

The Song of Angels

Scripture Reading: Luke 2:8-12

Key Verse: *...Do not be afraid, I bring you good news of great joy that will be for all people (Luke 2:10b).*

Meditation: In the summer of 1953, an evangelistic team of seven Japanese Christian workers and I were assigned to start a new church in Sakado City, Japan. The strategy we followed had proven so successful everywhere else, we just assumed it would also work here. During a period of one month we would visit every home within a radius of ten miles and leave a witness and a gospel tract. In the evening we would conduct evangelistic meetings, using a tent. By the end of the month we expected 20-25 would be seeking baptism.

However, by the end of the first month our attendance had dwindled to five and the majority of the team members were ready to "shake the dust off their feet" and move to the next town. To our surprise, our team captain, Rev. Hara, challenged us with these words, "While we have worked hard, we have not prayed hard with fasting. We must do both before we can leave." Gradually the attendance began to pick up. After another four weeks 20 people were prepared for baptism and a church was organized.

Because of the unforgettable "birth-pains" of this church we felt a special attachment to the people there. We would revisit them often. Of our many visits to this church the one that stands out is Christmas of 1994. The city hall had been rented and standing on the platform was a choir of 50 voices; below them an orchestra of 25 musicians. They were performing Handel's *Messiah* in Japanese!

My mind was transfixed on the original team of eight Christian workers who would have given up except for those words of challenge, "But we have not yet prayed hard or fasted."

Thought for the Day: *Perhaps there are new things that could happen in our lives and in the church if we, too, would follow this Japanese pastor's advice.*

He Must Increase

Scripture Reading: John 3:27-30

Key Verse: *The friend who attends the bridegroom waits and listens for him, and is full of joy when he hears the bridegroom's voice. That joy is mine and it is now complete. He must become greater; I must become less (John 3:29,30).*

Meditation: When Zechariah sang his song of joy over the birth of his son, John the Baptist, he prophesied only of the privilege John would have to go before the Lord to prepare the way for Him. Zechariah knew nothing about what the future might hold, in addition, for his son, the chosen messenger of God.

Faithfully, John the Baptist carried out his commission, to call the people to repentance with the public acknowledgment of their change from an old life to a new life that would prepare them to follow Christ. Even though John was a cousin of Jesus, he does not appear to have expected any special favor. Only once did he ask for reassurance, "Are you the One that was to come or should we expect someone else?" (John 7:19). John had been preaching the coming of a King and he was seeking reassurance that indeed Christ would establish His rule as foretold.

Jesus sent John's inquiring disciples back with the validity of his Messianic authority: He opened the eyes of the blind, made the deaf to hear, the lame to walk, and those who could not speak to sing. Jesus asked John to trust His kingdom to come in God's time.

John did not live to see Christ's kingdom on earth and neither may we. But we have His kingdom in our heart. That is what we need to remember when our lives are in peril, perhaps not from evil rulers, as in John's case, but from other assaults that are the result of living in a fallen world. God's plan will be fulfilled as His kingdom increases in our hearts. Someday we will join Him when the kingdoms of this world become the kingdoms of God.

Thought for the Day: *And blessed is the man that does not fall away on account of me (Luke 7:23). Our ways are not His ways.*

Light in the Darkness

Scripture Reading: Luke 1:67-79

Key Verse: *The Lord has anointed me...to comfort all who mourn...to bestow on them the oil of gladness instead of mourning (Isaiah 61:1-3).*

Meditation: Zechariah sang of the salvation to come through Christ (Luke 1:78,79). He celebrated the fulfillment of the promise given him by Gabriel in the temple, which he could not believe and so was smitten with lack of speech.

Sometimes we find great obstacles to believing the promises of God. Our daughter at five years old was diagnosed with an "incurable blood disease," aplastic anemia. We were advised by the physician "not to spend any money on this child." We sought, in prayer, the path we should take. Both my mother-in-law and I (Norma Jean) were given the promise, "Fear not, only believe, and she shall be made whole" (Luke 8:50).

But she was not healed instantly. She was diagnosed in October and treated with blood transfusions and medicines. By the first of December we were advised to put her in the hospital for a period covering the Christmas season. That year we had an "early" Christmas. We have pictures of our family under the tree opening presents on December 12 because the next day she would be in the hospital. On Christmas Day a friend relieved me in the hospital so I could go home and have Christmas dinner with my husband and other daughter. Our friend helped our sick daughter draw pictures of the dinner and imagined those around the table where she could not be present.

We were, like the people in Isaiah, experiencing darkness and tempted to despair, but Jesus had promised the oil of gladness instead of mourning and instead of despair, a garment of praise. By Easter she had started to make her own blood components and we have another picture -- our "resurrection" celebration.

Thought for the Day: *God gives us promises to be fulfilled in His time and for His purposes. He wants us to celebrate in faith based on hope in His wisdom and promised purpose for our lives.*

Becoming One in Christ

Scripture Reading: Luke 2:13-20

Key Verse: *Glory to God in the highest and on earth peace among men on whom His favor rests (Luke 2:14).*

Meditation: Early in our missionary career in Japan we lived in a Japanese community in northern Japan. A grandmother neighbor asked me (Norma Jean) to teach her and her friends American cooking in my western-type home. I agreed on the condition that I could have devotional time before the classes.

I found, also, in an apartment next door, a lovely young mother with her baby daughter. Down the road was another mother with a daughter and a husband who belonged to a very radical "new" religion that promised health, wealth and power. He had, however, a great interest in English, so we became friends, even though he knew I was encouraging his wife to consider Christ.

Another avenue was opened for ministry and witness as I welcomed young wives to English and devotions, like the cooking class.

We thought Christmas time would be a perfect season to bring all these people together. We planned a party. All of my friends, students, and contacts were invited to appear at 6:30 p.m. The time arrived, but only about half of the invited persons came. After an hour they excused themselves and the other guests arrived in a group. The groups seemed to have divided themselves in social and economic levels, of which I had not been aware.

I learned that the message of the angels is not understood quickly in another culture, or even, in ours. While there was no open animosity between these people, they felt more secure in their own social groups. Those who have truly come to know who Christ is can eventually include all peoples in the salvation Christ offers. God is patient with us.

Thought for the Day: *Christ came to bring peace in the hearts of men who honor Him, but our social systems provide many obstacles to His simple message.*

The God of Hope

Scripture Reading: Romans 15:8-13

Key Verse: *May the God of hope fill you with all joy and peace as you trust in Him so that you may overflow with hope by the power of the Holy Spirit (Romans 15:13).*

Meditation: The God of Hope: A benediction closes the doctrinal section of the epistle of Romans, but it is not a formal word; the benediction carries promise of great possibility. We are covered with the blessing of a God who sees a future for us.

God planned this future before He formed the world. God has made His plan known through the Bible and when we study it carefully, we understand how He is developing His plan to include all of us who will recognize Him as Lord and Savior. God said to Abraham, "I will bless those who bless you, and whoever curses you I will curse; and all peoples on earth will be blessed through you" (Genesis 12:3).

God chose Abraham to form the nation of Israel through whom Christ would come to earth. But He also made arrangements for all of humankind to be included in the blessings of this choice. The oratorio, *Messiah*, magnificently conveys the total plan of salvation for all mankind by its inclusion of all the major prophecies of the Old Testament culminating in their being fulfilled in the coming of Christ to our world and being "for all people."

During the Christmas season, perhaps more than any other time, we celebrate the Hope of Israel, but He is the HOPE for all people, including you and me.

Thought for the Day: *We are included in God's plan: He gives us directions for our lives now and hope for the future.*

The Shining Light

Scripture Reading: Isaiah 60:1-7

Key Verse: *Arise, shine, for your light has come, and the glory of the Lord rises upon you (Isaiah 60:1).*

Meditation: Continuous clouds and dark days make us long for the sunshine. Some people actually sense depression as a result of not being exposed to the sunlight, and purchase special lights to simulate the rays the give them hope.

During Old Testament days the people whose lives are recorded were under more times of darkness than of light: "For behold, darkness covers the earth, and thick darkness is over the people (Isaiah 60:2a)." When we are in a plane on the ground, we are often under a cloud cover and it appears as though we are going to be buffeted by clouds as we ascend to 35,000 feet. But once we get through the condensations of moisture we find ourselves in the clear and brilliant sunlight. We can look down and see the clouds, but they are no longer oppressing us. "The Lord rises upon you and His glory appears over you. Nations will come to your light and kings to the brightness of your dawn" (Isaiah 60:2,3).

In God's plan of salvation to lift us from the darkness of our sins to His light, He has included us. We do not have to live under a cloud of uncertainty and dread. We are invited to praise God for His great love to us: "Praise the Lord, all nations! Extol Him, all peoples. For great is His love toward us; and the faithfulness of the Lord endures forever. Praise the Lord!" (Psalm 117:1,2).

Thought for the Day: *If we are living in darkness of any kind, we can come to Jesus, the Light of the world.*

The Triad

Scripture Reading: Romans 12:1-21

Key Verse: *Be joyful in hope, patient in affliction and faithful in prayer (Romans 12:12).*

Meditation: The threesome described here epitomizes the Christian's ideal life and conduct. We know the way we should view our life circumstances, but we do not often model the ideal. God is more patient with us than we are "patient in our troubles," and He waits for us to "get it all together."

In an earlier reading we noted that the God of hope will fill us with joy and peace, as we believe. That is a magnificent fact anytime, but particularly during the Advent season. We can open up the fount of joy and peace by trusting in God. Then God adds the promise of the Holy Spirit's power to keep us going. We all have to keep buying batteries for our toys and technical gadgets because their power gives out. But God promises us power that is continuously effective. If the power is not at our disposal, then it must be we who have shorted out!

The last essential of the triad is "pray all the time." That must be the key to an open power line: We are to keep the prayer going and God will keep the power flowing. Then we will have hope and the hope will keep us joyful. Prayer is often considered a duty and a task. But God makes it hope flowing into our spirits and driving out the fear and doubt.

Thought for the Day: *"My soul glorifies the Lord, and my spirit rejoices in God my Savior," (Luke 1:46b), was Mary's song as she visited Elizabeth.*

Peace to the Nations

Scripture Reading: Zechariah 9:9-12

Key Verse: *Rejoice greatly, O daughter of Zion...He shall proclaim peace to the nations (Zechariah 9:9,10).*

Meditation: A promise that we do not yet see fulfilled, described in these verses, impacts us personally. We do not yet see peace in the nations, we are subjected to daily reports of conflicts, atrocities, famine, want and disease in many nations. Those who live in the places of upheaval are suffering unbelievable agonies. We who live in "safer" countries cannot truly empathize with the sadness of others. In the Christmas story we often overlook the suffering of those families who lost their infant sons to the cruelty of Herod as he sought to eliminate the "king of Israel" by killing all the baby boys under two years old.

Yet the prophetic scripture admonishes the country and people of Israel to have great joy at the promised coming of the Messiah who would give peace to all the nations. We know now that Christ brings peace into the heart of that person who receives Him as Savior, and in that experience strength comes to meet the distresses of the everyday world. This is a miniature peace, but it carries the promise of a yet-to-be-realized universal peace of Christ's kingdom in the world.

Our own community world is often torn with violence. A young Christian woman randomly shot and paralyzed from the waist down says, "I am going to keep trusting in the Lord, and I have to have hope." Her parents say, "We have anger, but we are not going to let it destroy us. We believe in the Lord and we must trust in Him."

Christ came to a world torn in the same places as ours. What difference has He made? We now have the power of His life in us to meet the insanity of wickedness in our world.

Thought for the Day: *The one who is in you is greater than the one (the evil one) who is in the world (I John 4:4).*

Fear Not

Scripture Reading: Luke 1:26-38

Key Verse: *Do not be afraid, Mary, you have found favor with God (Luke 1:30).*

Meditation: I wonder what Mary would have thought if she had read first, "God has not given us the spirit of fear, but of power and of love and of a sound mind" (II Timothy 1:7). It probably would not have made any difference. Being confronted by the messenger angel of God with the news that she was to be the bearer of the Son of God was enough to scare anyone, to make the bravest heart fear.

The angel called her the "favored one." From a human viewpoint the task was unthinkable and incomprehensible. The sense of awe and fear must have been overwhelming. Isaiah felt it when he saw the glory in the temple and cried, "Woe is me, for I am lost." Peter, seeing the miraculous haul of fish under the power of Jesus cried out, "Depart from me for I am a sinful man." The power of God usually shows us our inadequacies. Only by His supernatural power can we do God's work and will in our world.

"You have found favor with God." The angel answered "The Holy Spirit will come upon you, and the power of the Most High will overshadow you so the Holy One to be born will be called the Son of God" (Luke 1:35). Whatever power necessary to bring Jesus into the world to be our Savior would be afforded to Mary's body. God's power will show us our weaknesses, sins and insufficiencies. But He has a job for us to do in our world and will come upon us with the power of the Holy Spirit so we can be the instruments He wants.

Thought for the Day: *Yielding our weaknesses to Him opens us to His Spirit's power.*

The Call to Bethlehem

Scripture Reading: Matthew 2:1-12

Key Verse: *We saw his star in the east and are come to worship him (Matthew 2:26).*

Meditation: If you had been living during the time of Christ's birth, how many days would you have been willing to spend in search of the Christ child? How many miles would you have been willing to travel to find Bethlehem? What would be your reaction when the star stopped over a stable, rather than over a palace?

Those who went to Bethlehem had to travel a distance with a very conscious decision and effort to see Jesus. We, too, must make a determined effort to find Jesus either for the first time or in a continuing growing relationship. Like the wise men we, too, have a vision of God's plan for our lives. Often there is a significant lapse between the vision and the decision to take the road to its fulfillment.

The wise men made significant preparation for their journey. No doubt there were family responsibilities that had to be delegated and unexpected illnesses or inconveniences. When I prepared to go to Japan as a single missionary for the first time, I remember the ache in my heart as I left my aged parents to carry on the farming and the harvest. How pulled I was between the vision and the duty!

Thought for the Day: *Only a small minority of those who have seen Christ's star (vision) actually will arrive in their appointed Bethlehem.*

The Call to Bethlehem

Scripture Reading: Matthew 2:1-12

Key Verse: *When they saw the star they were overjoyed (Matthew 2:10).*

Meditation: The experiences of the Wise Men on their way to Bethlehem help us in our school of obedience and faith. No doubt many nights they could not see the star due to weather fluctuations. Fording rivers, going through mountain passes, crossing deserts must have been enormously taxing. Like Abraham they probably were tempted to stop at some Haran and wait until the star appeared again. Perhaps they were tempted to turn back. But if they had not persevered, they would have missed the Son of God born in Bethlehem.

Think of the disappointment they probably received from doubting folks along the way. Why would anyone follow a star to find a baby? Even though people looked for a Messiah, they were not looking for him as an infant. The people nearest to Bethlehem did not go there themselves. To note this apathy could have trivialized the Wise Men's 1,500 mile journey and unnerved their determination.

The final test of their faith lay in the location of the star stopping over a stable, the cheapest rental in Bethlehem. We would not blame them if they had dropped their heads in disappointment and turned their camels toward home.

Thought for the Day: *After seeing the vision we must be prepared for those days and nights when the sky will be overcast and the guidance not clear at all.*

The Call to Bethlehem

Scripture Reading: Matthew 2:1-12

Key Verse: *...they bowed down and worshipped him (Matthew 2:11b).*

Meditation: The Wise Men did not bow their heads in disappointment when they found the star had stopped over a lowly stable. Rather, they bowed their heads in worship.

The Wise Men reflect the faith of many of our heroes in the Bible: Joseph's dream and vision promised a great future for him. But his family did not accept him as God's choice and turned against him. Joseph was literally in the pit or a succession of pits and prisons over 30 years. We must look for God in the pits and stable experiences of our lives. God's plan can be fulfilled as easily in a stable as in a palace. God's kingdom depends not on our resources but on His faithfulness.

We even lose sight of Jesus in the scriptures for 12 years after His birth. We see Him briefly as a child prodigy and then not for another 18 years. Nothing is recorded about Him during this time. Apparently He was doing God's will in the commonplace surroundings of His life. At the end of the years of silence God affirms Him with "You are my Son, whom I love; with you I am well pleased" (Luke 22). The Father approved as did the people of Nazareth who knew "He went into the synagogue as was His custom" (Luke 4:16).

Thought for the Day: *God is pleased with common people who do their common tasks faithfully in hidden places.*

The Call to Bethlehem

Scripture Reading: Matthew 2:1-12

Key Verse: *Then they opened their treasures and presented him with gifts... (Matthew 2: 11c).*

Meditation: God's kingdom has two sides: The side of humility and the side of splendor. A bright star announced His birth in a humble stable. A choir of angels heralded His birth to humble shepherds. The child is homeless and soon to be a refugee in another country. When Jesus is crucified one of the thieves asked to be remembered when Jesus came into His kingdom.

Jesus appeared helpless in the manger, but the Wise Men worshipped him. On the cross He appeared defenseless, but the thief recognized royalty and resurrection in Him. Jesus may seem to be helpless to us when our prayers are not answered the way we expect. Our western culture espouses self-reliance and we may feel guilty over our inability. But Christ identified with us in our sense of helplessness and aloneness as He hung on the cross, forsaken by the Father. "Although He was a son, yet he learned obedience from what he suffered" (Hebrews 5:8).

Amazingly, Jesus came from nine months in the womb of a human mother. He had parents in a family setting. He did not appear suddenly from heaven in blazing power and glory. He followed years of public ministry. This period of 33 years on earth assured us that He identifies completely with us in our earthly stable experience. Just as the Father was faithful to Him, so will Jesus be faithful to represent us before the Father.

Thought for the Day: *Let us give God our best gifts in our "stable experience" here, and we, too, will get a glimpse of God's presence here even as the Wise Men experienced.*

Jesus' Becoming Like Us

Scripture Reading: Hebrews 4:14-16

Key Verse: *...we have one who has been tempted in every way, just as we are, yet without sin (Hebrews 4:15b).*

Meditation: Every Christmas we are struck anew with the awesome mystery of Jesus, God's Son, becoming man. How could Jesus be made "very man" and yet remain "very God?" Most of all we wonder how did two natures, the divine and the human, play themselves out in the next 33 years of Jesus' life, especially as He faced temptation? Were His temptations like ours, or did He face them on an entirely different level?

Jesus was tempted and subjected to the same pressures that any of us experience. The writer of Hebrews tells us that in the days of His flesh, Jesus offered up prayers and supplications with strong crying and tears. Jesus resisted the insinuations of Satan, not with a short quiet prayer, but with strong crying out to God for deliverance (Hebrews 5:7,8).

Mark tells us that Jesus was deeply distressed as He faced the cross (Mark 14:33). Authentic human agony caused Him to recoil from the cross. His sorrow literally threatened premature death. He prayed for the Father to take this cup from Him. How could He desire something so contrary to the Father's will? The answer: Jesus was both divine and human. As a man He had willed to limit His knowledge. As a man He was merely looking for some other way of fulfilling the requirement of the death penalty for the sin of man. As a man Christ cried for escape from the cross death.

The sinlessness of Jesus did not preclude Him from genuine temptation. Sinlessness did not protect Him from enticements, but Jesus never consented or yielded to any of them. Because Jesus faced the full force of temptation as a man, He continues His ministry of intercession for us as our sympathetic high priest who identifies with our weaknesses.

Thought for the Day: *There is no temptation we will ever confront that Jesus did not face and conquer, not only for Himself, but also for us.*

What to Give, What to Keep at Christmas

Scripture Reading: Matthew 2:11,12

Key Verse: *But Mary kept all these things and pondered them in her heart (Luke 2:19).*

Meditation: Christmas secular culture displays extravagant giving. An average family spends over $800 at this time of the year. As a corrective to the excesses of our materialistic culture, we need to reconstruct that first Christmas and, like Mary, keep and ponder these essential things in our hearts.

Let us discipline ourselves to keep the simplicity of that first Christmas. Jesus was born in a stable with the animals, not the news reporters, surrounding Him. No banners announced His entrance into the world. No trained medical personnel ministered to Mary, just an anxious Joseph.   No sterile sheets, but only strips of cloth, wrapped the newborn baby. In this humble setting God's divine Son came to us. No wonder Paul wrote, *Though he was rich, yet for your sakes he became poor, so that you through his poverty might become rich* (II Corinthians 8:9b).

Let us determine to keep the awe and wonder of that first Christmas. Charles Wesley wrote, *"Oh, where shall my wondering soul begin,"* and *"Lost in wonder, love and praise,"* when he referred to his experience with Christ. We must recapture our sense of awe of the Almighty becoming a baby for us so we will have the perspective and power to impact our cynical world again.

Man, by the permissive grace of God, has accomplished great things, even to exploring the moon and outer space. But nothing we have ever done impacts the human race like the transforming power of Jesus, who entered the earth space in Bethlehem.

Thought for the Day: *God Himself has visited our planet.*

The Difference Christmas Makes

Scripture Reading: I Corinthians 15:12-28

Key Verse: *If I had not come... (John 15:22).*

Meditation: Years ago a Christmas tract depicted a minister who had a dream on Christmas Eve. In the dream he saw a world without Christ. On Christmas morning there were no decorations, no tree and no Christmas cards. The house was so empty he decided to walk to church around the corner. But when he got to the location, he found no church building, just an empty lot covered with weeds. Confused, he returned to his house and sat in his study. He looked at his library and realized all the books on the New Testament were missing.

The doorbell rang. His neighbor asked him to hurry to this house to pray for his dying mother who was not ready to meet God. He grabbed his Bible intending to ready comforting verses from John's Gospel. At the house he opened his Bible (in his dream) to discover it ended with Malachi.

Later, in his dream, at the funeral service he wanted so much to give words of hope but found himself saying, *We are sorrowing as all others for we have no certain hope of salvation or resurrection. Our good-byes today may mean good-bye forever.* When he saw the sad faces of the family and friends he collapsed in one of the seats saying, *I can no longer be a minister, for if Christ has not come I have no message to give.*

His sobbing awakened him from his dream and with a great shout of relief he cried out, *Christ has come and that changes everything!*

Thought for the Day: *Christ's coming changes everything for us now and in eternity.*

Christmas Lessons From the Shepherds

Scripture Reading: Luke 2:8-14

Key Verse: *I bring you good news... (Luke 2:10a).*

Meditation: In contrast to the Wise Men, the shepherds represented the opposite end of the social and educational scale of that day. Most of them did not own the flocks, but served as *tenant shepherds.* Just as God included the Gentile wise men at the first Christmas, He equally represented the poor. The church must never forget God's love for those who do not have the wealth of others. Abraham Lincoln said, "God must have loved the common people because he made so many of them."

Why did God choose the shepherds to symbolically represent the poor of at the birth of His son? Could it be that they were the most spiritually sensitive in the region? Sheep were used as sacrifices at the temple in Jerusalem. The shepherds knew the value of caring for the sheep so they had no blemish and would be fit for the special sacramental use, symbolizing the "Lamb of God" for whom they waited. On the other hand, because the shepherds worked with animals they were considered unclean and were shut out of the temple. Ironically, these who cared for the sacrifices were not allowed to be close to the ceremony for which they provided the required lamb.

On Christmas God chose those shut out for centuries to be included in the greatest event of all time. He even honored them with the annunciation of angels, "Do not be afraid. I bring you good news of great joy that will be for all people." No doubt the shepherds had always lived with the fear that their sheep would not meet the standards of the temple. Now they heard the song of great deliverance, *Fear Not.*

Thought for the Day: *The good news of Christmas frees us from fear, making us adequate through Christ's including us with Him in God's presence.*

Christmas Lessons From the Shepherds

Scripture Reading: Luke 2:8-20

Key Verse: *And all who heard it were amazed at what the shepherds said to them (Luke 2:18).*

Meditation: The shepherds did not doubt or question the message of the angels. They did not relate the royalty annunciation to their poverty. They did not postpone their obedience with even legitimate concerns like weather or safety of the flocks. Their unanimous response, "Let us go to Bethlehem and see this thing that has happened," reminds us that true faith is born both from hearing the word of God and obeying it. Delayed obedience can so easily turn into disobedience.

We would not have faulted the shepherds even if they had been tentative about going to Bethlehem. Great risk involved their leaving the flock, for it represented their entire livelihood both for them and their families. I do not encourage people to follow every voice without testing its validity. Many have done that and have caused themselves great humiliation and disappointment. But once we have tested the voice, we should not be afraid to take the faith risk believing that God can protect the sheep we leave, whatever that may mean for us, when we follow God's direction.

God rewarded the obedient risk of the shepherds. They found "God" lying in a manger. Their eyes beheld the long anticipated *"Lamb of God that takes away the sin of the world."* Not only did they see and believe, but also they immediately spread the word concerning what had been told them about the child. Someone has observed that the weakness of the church today is that so much of our faith is based on hearsay. We must individually experience the birth of Jesus in our hearts and go out to proclaim the good news to the world.

Thought for the Day: *After seeing Jesus most of us will return to our tasks, like the shepherds, but we will never be the same again.*

Lessons From the Wise Men

Scripture Reading: Matthew 2:1-11

Key Verse: *We saw his star in the East and have come to worship him (Matthew 2:2).*

Meditation: For the first time I see God's intervention in the lives of those living far away from this geographic location of the divine act. I am reminded that God is a "missionary God" who determined that among the worshippers at the birth of his Son there would be representatives of the Gentile world.

In an art gallery in Birmingham, England the painter Burne-Jones depicts the three Wise Men bringing their precious gifts to Jesus. One is an Aryan, white-skinned; the second is a Semite, bronze-skinned and dark-bearded; the third is a black-skinned person. Whether the artist rightly portrayed the first three Wise Men or not, we can be sure that he read correctly the intent of God's heart. Even the promise to Abraham in Genesis 12 signified worldwide involvement. John 3:16 and Mark 16:15 continue that same theme of God's love and the gospel being preached to the entire world.

The coming of the Wise Men to Bethlehem began in God's heart. They studied the movement of the planets expecting effects on earth. But they looked for more than mechanical cause and effect. Many apparently believed that God was speaking to them personally. When they saw the new star they followed it to find the God who put it in the sky. They saw in the "new star" the birth of a King and brought gifts that symbolized Jesus and His mission in the world to the human race.

Thought for the Day: *When God loved, He loved the whole world, and when God gave his only Son, He gave Him for all the people of the world.*

Lessons From the Wise Men

Scripture Reading: Matthew 2:1-11

Key Verse: *Then they opened their treasures and presented him with gifts... (Matthew 2:11a).*

Meditation: The Wise Men brought gifts to worship a king. Gold, the most rare and expensive metal, indicated their faith in the royalty and kingship of Jesus. The frankincense used by priests in the temple suggests their faith in the prayers and intercession of Jesus. The myrrh spices, used to embalm the dead, pointed to the forthcoming sacrificial death of Jesus.

How can we explain this knowledge and timely presentation of prophetic gifts by non-Jewish persons? Charles Spurgeon, commenting on Psalm 19, observes that God has two books, two bibles! One of God's created world that is His natural revelation. He made man to be an erect being so he could always be observing the natural world. God's natural Bible speaks to us of His power, greatness and glory and can be clearly read in every place and in every language of the world.

Even if governments closed all churches, took away all Bibles and silenced people, yet God's voice would not be silenced. God's choir of the sky, the sun and the stars and moon would continue to "bubble forth speech about God." No person is ever without some spiritual light and no one is ever without some accountability to God. Someone has said, "God's natural revelation may get us as far as Jerusalem, but we need a personal revelation, like the Wise Men, to get us to Bethlehem." The Bible is our final guide to Jesus.

Thought for the Day: *If God could get three men from a pagan country to travel 1,500 miles to find Jesus, let us continue to pray and believe for those who would only have to walk across the street.*

Lessons From the Wise Men

Scripture Reading: Matthew 2:1-11

Key Verse: *...where is the one who has been born King of the Jews? (Matthew 2: 2a)*

Meditation: God accommodated Himself to the Wise Men's understanding in their spiritual search. Their work directed them in the study of the stars. That is the place where God revealed Himself to them. When God wanted to speak to mankind, He sent Jesus. J. B. Phillips expresses the incarnation as God scaling Himself down, down, down as a helpless baby to identify with us. Jesus did not wear His humanity like a costume to look like us; He actually became one of us.

Just as God revealed Himself to the Wise Men from geographical distance, God is still searching and seeking people everywhere. An elderly Japanese mother told us how she found the God of the Bible. At the end of the World War II she and her two daughters were repatriated from Taiwan, formerly a colony of Japan. She had lost her husband in the war and her son had been sent to Siberia as a prisoner of war. She returned to Japan destitute, and found her country in the same condition. Hopeless, one day in deep despair she had a vision and heard a voice.

She saw in her vision a Christian church with a cross on the steeple. The voice told her to find it and believe. She began walking, searching and asking. Finally, she found the church, the exact replica of that one in the vision. She knocked, went inside and was led to Christ by an evangelical pastor. Within a year her son returned from Russia where he had been indoctrinated with communistic ideology. Somehow, after awhile, his mother's testimony won him to Christ and he sensed God's call to ministry. I worked with this pastor for many years, and his children are also in the ministry.

Thought for the Day: *If God can use a star or a dream to bring people to Jesus, He will bless our efforts and accommodate our strategies to "by all means win some."*

Lessons From the Wise Men

Scripture Reading: Matthew 2:1-11

Key Verse: *...We saw his star in the East and have come to worship him (Matthew 2:2b).*

Meditation: What an amazing story of God's divine intervention to bring these three Wise Men to the feet of Jesus, the King of the Jews and the Savior of the World. Could there be another ingredient in the background of their revelation?

The book of Esther records that there were scattered all over Persia enclaves of Jewish people from the dispersions. Wherever there were 12 Jewish males, a synagogue would be erected for the reading of the Law and the Prophets. Perhaps at some time these Wise Men intersected these devout Jews steeped in messianic prophecies and in the hope of His imminent birth. Perhaps they had joined them in worship with other God-fearing Gentiles as were present in Jerusalem on the festival of Pentecost. I believe there was a connection between a synagogue, a star and the coming of the Wise Men to Bethlehem. God has never left Himself without a witness to collaborate His book of nature. In this case it could have been a synagogue and a few messianic Jews.

In England there was a church built overlooking a harbor. It could be seen miles away. One night a powerful hurricane hit the coast and destroyed the building. Members gathered, assessed the damage and agreed they would never be able to rebuild their church. But within a few days a representative from the British navy came asking them to rebuild. He insisted, saying, "The church spire is on every Navy chart and map. The ships of the world are depending on this church. It is this church that guides our ships safely into the harbor."

Thought for the Day: *Even though we may think we are insignificant, God has a special plan that includes us in guiding many people to Him.*

HELMUT SCHULTZ
(A Brief Biography)
by

Ed Erny

In the poem on a tablet at the base of the Statue of Liberty, the lady, called the Mother of Exiles, cries out:

> *Give me your tired, your poor, your huddled masses, yearning to breathe free. . . . Send those homeless, tempest-tossed to me. I lift my lamp beside the golden shore.*

Though Ewald and Hertha, the parents of Helmut Schultz, immigrated to Canada, not the United States, these words from the poetess Emma Lazarus could have been penned expressly for them.

Their ancestors were among the masses of Germans who flocked into Russia in the 18th century in response to the invitation of Russia's Empress, a German princess, Catherine II. To encourage these fellow countrymen, she issued a magnanimous bill of rights for German immigrants coming to Russia which included, among other privileges, free land, freedom from taxation and exemption from military service.

The political climate of Russia had changed, however, by 1871 when Czar Alexander II revoked all of the German settlers' preferential rights. Then, suddenly, with the outbreak of World War I in 1914, and the initial fierce conflict between Russia and Germany, the German-Russian population overnight became objects of special abuse and persecution. Their men were drafted and placed on the front lines to slaughter fellow Germans. Farmers, among them Helmut's grandparents and their children, were driven off their lands. In the hellish years of wandering that followed, many died of exposure, hunger, and persecution. Others were imprisoned and perished in slave-labor camps in Siberia. When Hertha and Ewald Schultz married in 1919, life was hard beyond belief. In her brief family history, Hertha writes:

"Our daughter, Ella, lived one year and one month; then came Alfred, who lived ten days. Then Emma, she lived three weeks. Then Irmgard who lived two months."

Selling what few possessions they had left, Ewald, 30, and Hertha, 26, immigrated to Canada, accepting the Canadian Pacific Railroad's offer of a homestead of 160 acres at $11 an acre in vast prairie lands of Alberta. They located near a small village, New Sarepta. Their first home was a derelict old building, actually a renovated granary. "Our new life," said Hertha, "began with breaking the soil and cutting the bush."

In the blessed new land of freedom and with the first, small beginnings of prosperity, additional children were born— twins, Margaret and Norman, in 1929, Helmut in 1931, and finally Gertrude in 1934. In time, the family moved out of the old granary and built a two-story framed house. "There was no insulation in the walls," Helmut recalled, "but this gave us a sense of living 'close up' to nature, and Mother made thick feather comforters that kept us from freezing in the winter."

Though the children attended the local one-room school, long hours of hard farm work were the main features of their lives. There were required chores early every morning before school and then long hours of work upon their return home. During the harvest season, many of the children were excused from school to help their parents bring in the crops. "I cannot remember doing any homework from grades one to eight," Helmut once remarked. "Ours was an austere life, but I am grateful to this day that I early acquired an appreciation for the value and dignity of hard work."

Helmut's mother, Hertha, was a remarkable woman. "Amazingly tough," Helmut said. "She could work along side any man." She also wrote poetry in German, had a beautiful voice and played the autoharp. She loved the Bible, had an amazing knowledge of scripture and taught a Sunday school class. His father, Ewald, more retiring, was renowned as a story teller, but most of all he enjoyed hunting with his brother, Ted.

Helmut's favorite teacher in the South Busenius one-room elementary school was Mrs. Fields. She had a great influence upon her young pupil and must be given large credit for early implanting in the lad a deep thirst for learning that would one day make of him a lover of books and a true scholar. Strong, raw-boned and athletic, Helmut was a budding athlete who, in the annual track and field day competition, regularly garnered blue ribbons. "Of course," he admits, "the school was very small and just about everybody got some kind of ribbon."

Before immigrating to Canada, the Russian community in which Ewald and Hertha lived had been deeply impacted by a mighty revival movement, led by German Lutherans called Brubers. As a result, both of Helmut's parents had come to a personal knowledge of Christ, which naturally brought them into fellowship with other evangelicals. In Canada they began attending the Evangelical United Brethren Church which, at that time, still had German services. Helmut traces his conversion to meetings held by Reverend A. E. Stickel (for the full story see the July 5 reading). At the invitation his friend, Herman Hueber, grabbed his trembling arm and said, "Helmut, let's go forward and get saved." Hand in hand the two boys went forward to kneel at the altar. The pastor knelt beside them, quoting I John 1:9, "If we confess our sins, he is faithful and just to forgive us our sins and cleanse us from all unrighteousness."

Two months later (see July 6 reading) while attending a Moravian church, Helmut heard what seemed to be an audible voice saying, "I want you to be a minister." This alarming directive was further confirmed when his church youth leader, Sadie Kublick, drew him aside one Sunday and said, "Helmut, isn't the Lord calling you to preach?"

The notion that God was calling him to preach the Gospel, Helmut found profoundly disturbing. Wrestling mightily against increasing conviction over the next two years, he finally yielded to the pressure of the Holy Spirit and testified to his parents and before the entire church congregation that God had indeed called him to the ministry. The next year Helmut enrolled in Hillcrest Bible College supported by the Evangelical United Brethren in Medicine Hat, Alberta. (How God marvelously provided for his financial needs despite a terrible hailstorm which destroyed their crops is beautifully told in the July 8 reading.)

Arriving on the campus of Hillcrest in 1947, Helmut discovered that a revival was in progress. It had started in the girls' dorm and now the movement of the Spirit had begun to have an impact on the boys as well. Dividing themselves up into teams of two, the students found quiet places in the dorm to pray and wait on God. Helmut's prayer partner, Art Brown, was not long in asking his new friend if, since his conversion, he had experienced the deeper cleansing, filling and empowering of the Holy Spirit. Helmut admits, "I didn't know what he was talking about." (See July 9 reading.) Even more disturbing, Art then went on to inquire if Helmut would be "willing to answer God's call to missions."

"I finally said yes," Helmut writes (July 10 reading), "acknowledging God's lordship over my life." There was no immediate surge of emotion, but the next morning when he awakened, he recalled, "I had a vision of the glorified Jesus who seemed to be looking down at me with love and acceptance." Immediately he got out of bed and fell on his knees repeating over and over, "Jesus, I worship you. I love you."

The Hillcrest years were a vital period of spiritual and academic growth in the life of the young man. The shy, awkward farm boy was developing power and confidence as a speaker and preacher. On weekends he served in local churches or on evangelistic teams. In class he was distinguishing himself by his scholarship and intense love for God's Word, but above all, it was his love for people that most endeared him to his fellow students.

A classmate at Hillcrest was Alice Huff, who would later follow him to The Oriental Missionary Society and serve for many years as the executive director of the mission's Prayer Circle Department, later named World Intercessors. "During Spiritual Emphasis Week," Alice recalls, "I remember how Helmut's face shone as he told how he had yielded his life to God and been filled with the Holy Spirit. He had a great love for people; he looked for opportunities to serve them. The first time I met Helmut was in the college laundry room where I saw him pressing trousers, not his own, but those of his dormitory buddies."

His senior year at the Bible college, Helmut was elected class president. By this time he was convinced that God was calling him to missions. His testimony in the yearbook begins, "Little did I realize when I joined the student body at Hillcrest that God would call me to be a witness in the needy Orient."

Missionaries occasionally visited Hillcrest, and from them Helmut first heard of The Oriental Missionary Society. About this time a friend sent him the OMS magazine, *The Standard*. On the back cover in bold letters was a plea for 21 young men to join the new Every Creature Crusade. The first crusade, called the Great Village Campaign, was begun in 1911 by Charles Cowman and Ernest Kilbourne. Their vision was to put the Gospel in every home in Japan. Young Bible school students from the United States joined teams of Japanese evangelists to complete this task in 1918. "The task is finished!" announced *The Standard*. "The Gospel has been placed in more than 10,000,000 homes in the Japanese empire, reaching 50,000,000 people." Now, in the post World War II years, OMS was launching a second crusade to reach a new generation in Asia. Helmut sensed God calling him to join this venture, but the thought of himself becoming a foreign missionary seemed quite incredible. In order to "prove" his call, he devised a Gideon-like scheme to make certain of God's direction.

Wesley Wildermuth, OMS missionary in Japan and later the field leader, remembers the day the field committee reviewed the application from the young Canadian. "As the committee looked over the application, we had some serious questions about this boy's qualifications. The form was filled out in pencil, barely legible and difficult to read. Answers to questions were vague. In response to the question, 'What experience have you had in Christian work?' he had written, 'I once taught a Sunday School class.'" Upon the advice of their field leader, Dr. Roy Adams, the committee all voted to reject the application of Helmut Schultz.

For some reason, never fully explained, OMS headquarters did something unusual and possibly unprecedented: They overruled the decision of the Japan field committee and accepted the young candidate. OMS further advised them that Helmut Schultz would be arriving in Japan in a few months to join the Every Creature Crusade. "When we received this intelligence," Wes Wildermuth recalled, "we were furious. Why did OMS even send us the application if they refused to honor our decision?"

The day came when the missionaries went to the wharf to meet Helmut's ship. "Down the gangplank he came," remembers Wildermuth, "a gangly, self-conscious, blond young man who spoke with a marked German-Canadian accent. Could this youth actually be missionary material?"

"All our questions were answered at that first weekly missionary prayer meeting when we heard Helmut pray," says Art Shelton. "His fervent passion clearly indicated a wonderful familiarity with his Lord." "All our doubts," adds Wesley, "were dissolved. Then as we sat listening to his testimony, we were amazed at his spiritual depth. Later as we witnessed his love for the Japanese and their language, we wondered with a sense of shame how we could have ever been so blind as to turn down his application. He later told us he had deliberately filled out his application in such a way as to appear unimpressive, asking God that if it was His will for him to go to Japan, He would somehow overrule and He did."

The original Every Creature Crusade plan, which was very simply to place Scriptures in every home in a nation, had been considerably refined by the 1950's. Young crusaders from the U.S. and other Western nations joined teams of

Japanese evangelists, all graduates of the Tokyo Bible Seminary, to travel from town to town throughout Japan, utilizing Army surplus tents for living quarters and evangelistic services. During the day they systematically distributed Gospel literature explaining the way of salvation to every home in an area. At the same time, they invited all they met to the evening services. The program each night commenced with a children's meeting; this was then followed by the evangelistic service which began with singing of simple Gospel choruses, concluding with a Gospel message, usually from a Japanese team member. Occasionally, however, the Western crusader would preach, with a Japanese colleague interpreting. Many of the crusaders admitted that their Japanese interpreter vastly improved upon their original sermon. After the service, seekers were counseled and later visited in their homes. Once a congregation of believers was formed, a team member was appointed as pastor of the new church. The others then moved to a new location where the campaign was repeated. During the McArthur years following World War II, Americans and Christians had acquired considerable esteem in the eyes of the Japanese. Large crowds attended the tent meetings and many received Christ as Savior.

The same qualities that had endeared Helmut to his fellow students at Hillcrest now combined to make him a most effective young missionary evangelist. His teammates soon discovered that here was a man who was not only given to long hours of prayer, but a fervent preacher. More than this, he was a real Christian brother who truly loved them and every Japanese he met. This deep love he expressed with naturalness and humor, unabashedly throwing his huge arms around the shoulders of the colleagues.

"I remember in the early days of our time in Japan when Helmut was a crusader," says Art Shelton, "he often invited me to his tent meetings. One I particularly remember was at Sakado City. It was the closing night of a two-week campaign, and many young people from high schools had been saved. One after another stood and gave their testimonies. This was followed by their teacher, who commented that, although he was not yet a believer, he had seen a remarkable change in the lives of his students and this deeply impressed him."

Helmut's two crusade years were full of joys and God gave much fruit that remains. During this time, three churches were established by his crusade team. As the two-year term drew to a close, Helmut sought God's direction for his future. One day Field Director Roy Adams, who had become a mentor to the young man, took him aside. "Helmut," he said, "you must return to Japan and help us, but two things you must do. First, you need to get additional training and then, secondly, find a good wife." In fact, returning to Japan was something that Helmut had been praying about for the past two years. Now there was the sweet, settled conviction that God had called him to the great, island nation. As for the matter of a wife, it was a subject that he had, in fact, pondered from time to time.

Back in the United States, the summer of 1954, Helmut attended the OMS International Convention, held at that time in Winona Lake, Indiana. Bob Erny, son of the mission president Eugene Erny, later to be OMS field director in Hong Kong and Indonesia, says, "I first met Helmut at Winona Lake. He had just returned from the Crusade in Japan. He shared his experiences, I recall, with tremendous fervor. I was deeply impressed. He also helped organize a night of prayer, interceding for an outpouring of God's spirit upon the convention. I still remember the passion of his praying."

Helmut had intended to enroll in a college in Oregon where he had been offered a scholarship, but after visiting the campus of Asbury College he was convinced that God would have him apply there. He entered as a sophomore in the fall of 1955.

At this time I was a senior at Asbury. OMS crusaders were then returning from Japan and zealously recruiting other Asburians to take their places. The previous year Lowell

Williamson had returned and had a profound influence on my roommate, Grant Nealis. Following graduation that spring, Grant joined the ECC and prepared to leave for Japan. (Lowell and Grant would later serve as OMS field leaders in Taiwan and Hong Kong.)

All of this had generated great interest on campus in these audacious young men who had dedicated two years of their lives to reaching every home in Asia with the Gospel. (This was long before the advent of Operation Mobilization and Youth with a Mission and other like organizations that regularly send short-termers overseas.)

That fall Helmut appeared. This big, blond man of German descent was hard to miss. His huge smile and friendliness somehow reminded me of an over-grown puppy who was so delighted to meet us and become a friend that welcome oozed out of him from every pore. But none of this was superficial. Earnest inquiries about one's life, family, hopes and plans for the future convinced us immediately that here was a man somehow saturated with the love of Christ.

For a time Helmut lived off campus away from dorm life, in the home of an Asbury professor. This provided him a quiet environment, free from typical dorm disturbances, where he could devote long hours to prayer. Those who overheard him praying commented on his intensity and passion as torrents of intercession would pour forth.

Helmut was elected president of the Asbury College chapter of Student Volunteers. This redoubtable movement begun a century earlier by Moody, John R. Mott, Robert Speer and other missionary leaders, had been used by God to enlist thousands of collegians in the cause of foreign missions. Now, a century later, Student Volunteers, though all but defunct elsewhere, was still very much alive and well on the campus of Asbury College. Helmut had never studied *Robert's Rules of Order* and hardly knew how to conduct a proper business meeting, but all that was forgotten when he preached. He threw himself into carefully prepared and prayed-over messages with a passion we had seldom seen.

He would thunder exhortations and warnings and then follow with ecstatic commentary on the wonders of God's love and the glory of the blessed Gospel. From time to time he would lean over the pulpit, pausing as though so overcome by emotion that he hardly knew how to proceed, his face bathed in heavenly light. Now and then something would strike him as humorous. Tears would come to his eyes and he would tremble with holy laughter. His unabashed emotion would at times leave some of the hearers a bit uncomfortable, but whatever opinion they had of this kind of preaching, there was no question but that it left a profound impact upon every hearer and was impossible to forget.

Helmut became an older brother and, indeed, a mentor to us younger students who attended those meetings. At times he would draw me aside, drape a big arm across my shoulders and offer a few words of counsel, some new spiritual discovery or a word concerning my devotional or love life. All the while, he had not forgotten the two admonitions of his own mentor, Dr. Roy Adams. He was hard at work now getting the suggested "additional education," but not so studious as to neglect Roy's directive to "find a good wife." Helmut had decided that the ideal woman for him must be, not only a sincere Christian with a missionary call, but also a nurse.

My brother Bob was at this time across the street from the college in Asbury Seminary. His wife Phyllis was enrolled in the School of Nursing at the nearby University of Kentucky in Lexington. Through the OMS campus fellowship Bob and Phyl had made Helmut's acquaintance and, as it happened, one of Phyllis' very best friends in school was a devout young lady, Norma Jean Hickerson, an honor graduate of Kentucky Mountain Bible Institute, who boldly professed a call to be a missionary.

"I remember the day I met Helmut," says Norma Jean. "He and I were introduced on the sidewalk in front of Asbury Seminary after a missionary conference session in which Dr. Eugene Erny spoke. Bob's car had a flat tire and we were all standing around watching as he fixed it. That was when I first noticed Helmut. He was hard to miss, actually—tall, with striking clear blue eyes. Somehow we all wandered down to the local drugstore for ice cream and sodas, laughing and talking as a group. A few days later I got a call from Helmut, asking for a date that Sunday. "I'm afraid that is not a good night," I told him. "I'm scheduled to speak in Paris, Kentucky, at the Church of God. 'Oh, that's all right,' he broke in. 'That'll be fine. I'll just come there.'"

Helmut kept his word and when I saw him walk into the church that evening, I was suddenly more nervous than I cared to admit. The ushers apologized for the fact that their regular pastor was absent and "a young woman will be speaking tonight." Helmut just smiled and said that would be fine. "He always said he remembered my sermon that night about the cross, but the fact is, I can hardly remember a thing I said."

When I finally introduced Helmut to my family, they immediately took a liking to the big Canadian. He was easy to talk to and familiar with work which impressed my father. It was not long before we were deeply in love, and I felt sure he was thinking of engagement, as I was.

Helmut was, indeed, in love and thinking of marriage but what no one knew was that he was still petitioning God for a sign that Norma Jean was the woman He had chosen for him. During my sophomore year I had, with my roommate, Earl Andrews, begun pastoring a church in Shelbyville, Kentucky, about 50 miles from the college. (The next year, Earl married and took another pastorate, and Bob, my brother, joined me as co-pastor of the Shelbyville mission.) People's Chapel of Shelbyville had been opened during the great 1950 Asbury revival movement. The little work ministered primarily to a class of people who would have felt uncomfortable in the city's mainline denominational churches, which attracted the more reputable citizens in the community.

Leaving campus Saturday afternoons, we would drive the 50 or so miles to Shelbyville and hold street meetings in the afternoon, followed by an evangelistic service that night.

Sunday, after a long day of visitation, a jail service and two regular services in the chapel, we would head home.

One weekend Earl and I invited Helmut to preach for us at the Shelbyville mission. Both morning and evening Helmut spoke with unusual anointing and at the invitations the little altar was crowded. That Sunday evening Clara Lambert, a troubled teenager with whom we had been working, was soundly converted.

Some time later Helmut cautiously inquired if it would be all right if both he and Norma Jean joined us for a weekend's ministry at the Shelbyville mission. Of course we were delighted. That Saturday afternoon the four of us piled into my old and very unreliable '41 Dodge. All of the tires were bald and the clutch, I suspected, was about to give up the ghost. We had a glorious weekend with more coming to Christ under Helmut's preaching. As we started home that night, wending our way over the mountains and hills that stood between us and Asbury College, it soon became apparent that the palsied clutch was slipping badly and about to succumb to old age. We hit on a scheme, however, that we hoped would save us from total breakdown in the Kentucky mountains at midnight. With Norma Jean at the wheel, Earl, Helmut and I would push the old car up to the crest of a hill, at which point we would jump in and coast part way down one hill and half-way up the next. When we lost momentum, we would jump out, push and repeat the process. In this fashion we managed to traverse the 30 or so miles from Shelbyville to Lawrenceville, where we agreed that there was nothing now to do but give up on the old jalopy, junk it and phone for help.

We took refuge in a local hotel lobby where I telephoned my brother Bob, explained our plight and asked him to please come and get us. As we waited for rescue, I commenced profound apologies to Helmut and Norma Jean for this shabby treatment of our honored guests. I was not far into my speech when Helmut put an arm around me and drew me aside, out of earshot. In a voice barely above a whisper, he said, "Ed, don't apologize." And then with a twinkle in his eye, "This whole thing is of the Lord. I'm thinking of marrying Norma Jean, and I've been asking the Lord to put us in a tough situation where I can observe her and see whether or not she's missionary material. Well, this is it." Evidently Norma Jean passed the test, for shortly thereafter they were engaged and married. Bob's wife, Phyllis, appropriately served as Norma Jean's bridesmaid.

Helmut graduated from Asbury College in June 1958, and by that fall he and Norma Jean were on a ship bound for Japan. During the voyage they celebrated their first wedding anniversary. The Japan to which Helmut returned was quite different from the country he had left four years earlier. Reconstruction, a new constitution and a surging economy had wrought striking changes. Evidences of prosperity were everywhere and for the first time in years, plentiful consumer goods. All of this would make Japan a country that some have called the most materialistic nation on earth. For missions, the post-World-War-II harvest years were about over. Although the crusade continued, crowds now had diminished and the apparent hunger for the Gospel seemed to be ebbing.

It soon became clear that Helmut and Norma Jean had chosen to serve God in one of the most difficult of Asian countries. The Japanese language is a formidable challenge with a complex grammar and honorifics that are a bafflement to foreigners. Few missionaries ever master it. In this, both Helmut and Norma Jean evidenced their tenacity and love of scholarship so essential in the conquest of a difficult foreign tongue. In time, Helmut became both an effective teacher and preacher in the Japanese language.

An even greater challenge, however, lay in the fact that historically Japan has been a truly resistant and sometimes hostile field for missionary laborers. Although retaining some perfunctory reverence for the old religions, Bhuddism and Shintoism, the modern Japanese is usually, for all practical purposes, an atheist. Today after 150 years of Christianity, less than one percent of Japanese are Christian. The typical church has fewer than 25 members.

While on the OMS compound and Bible school campus during their language study years, they mentored three young crusaders, Kemp Edwards, Dick Amos and Kelly Toth. The boys frequently stayed in their home on their day off and precious bonds of friendship were forged that continue to this day. Kemp, Dick and Kelly would all return to Japan as field missionaries.

Following the completion of their language study, the Schultzes were assigned first to the Tohoku district which included Sendai where with OMS missionaries, Charles and JoAnn Dupree, they helped to plant a church, later raising funds for the purchase of land and erection of a church building. The fledging missionaries now set about to acquire an in-depth understanding of the Japanese people—their history, their actions and their culture. How well Helmut achieved this is evidenced in his masterful thesis entitled, "Communicating the Gospel to the Japanese," which he used for orientation of new missionaries.

In Japan, as elsewhere, Helmut and Norma Jean soon won the hearts of their Japanese colleagues. Helmut's unabashed friendliness and affection for every human being, whether pastors, students, church members or strangers on the street, spoke volumes to the nationals. Norma Jean became a true friend to women in the church and with her skills, both as Bible teacher and nurse, she proved a constant helpmeet to her husband.

OMS missionaries who frequently meet together or visit in one another's homes comprise an intimate and tight-knit community. It is remembered that Helmut soon became a favorite "uncle" to the MKs. Art Shelton recalls that their son Allan "couldn't pronounce *r's* so Helmut often minced his pronunciation of *refreshing* as *reweshing*." He also told their daughter, Deanne, that she could be his girlfriend until she was 12 years old and later advised her not to date anyone until she found out if he had a call.

Wes and Margaret Wildermuth recall that Helmut proved a great friend to their teenage daughter, Charlene, who was then studying German in the Christian Academy of Japan (CAJ). "She was having a difficult time with the grammar," he remembers. "Neither Margaret or I knew enough about the language to help her, so she called Helmut for some advice. He was already proficient in the Japanese language. Helmut took one look at her sentences in German and burst out laughing. 'Charlene,' he said, 'you're writing German words, but using Japanese grammar.' Charlene never forgot the patient instruction from one of her favorite missionary uncles."

Helmut also had a mischievous streak and became something of a legend for his love of outrageous humor. Art Shelton, however, remembers a time when his joking backfired. "We had a young man from Montana," he recalls, "who had come to help for several weeks. Helmut took him to the Kumagaya Church where he teasingly announced that Ervin was looking for a wife. The next day two young Japanese ladies appeared at Helmut's door, announcing that they were offering themselves as prospective brides for young Ervin. Helmut learned that day there are some things that in Japanese culture are not acceptable subjects for humor." Students still talk about the day that Helmut, in the midst of a lecture in the Bible seminary, discovered one of his students, Kobayashi, was sound asleep. Upon the utterance of a particular salient point, he paused, thunderously slapped his hand down on the desk and shouted, "Isn't that so, Kobyashi-san?" The bewildered young scholar woke with a start and, no doubt, after that thought twice before allowing himself the respite of slumber in Dr. Schultz's class!

Coming to the end of that first term in Japan, Helmut was more and more feeling the need of additional theological training. So upon their return to the U.S. in 1963, the Schultzes requested a four-year study leave. Living in Kentucky, in the Wilmore and Lexington area, Helmut enrolled in Asbury Theological Seminary, earning first a BD and then a Master of Theology degree. Later (1976) he enrolled in Lexington Theological Seminary where he earned a Doctor of Ministry degree. From 1963 to 1967 he also pastored a church in Graefenburg, Kentucky. During this time Norma Jean completed a degree in Education at Asbury College, after which she taught in the School of Nursing at the University of Kentucky. These years saw an increase in their family with the addition of two lovely daughters, Malita born in 1965 and Juli in 1966.

The Schultzes returned to Japan in 1967, where they were again assigned to one of the outlying areas for a period of three years. Then in 1970 Helmut was appointed OMS Japan field director. Now they would be at the mission headquarters in Tokyo. In addition to his responsibilities as field leader, he continued preaching in the churches, as well as teaching in the OMS Tokyo Biblical Seminary. Norma Jean, while continuing to employ her nursing skills, taught cooking classes, an effective means of making friends with Japanese women in order to win them to Christ.

In 1970 began a three-year ordeal in which Helmut and Norma Jean exhibited both the grace of God and also the holy tenacity which kept them on the field long after others would have opted to return to the homeland. Their daughter Malita, eight years old at the time, took ill with a mysterious disease later diagnosed as aplastic anemia. A well-known blood specialist was called in for consultation. After examining their daughter, he bluntly said, "I suggest you not waste money on treatment for your daughter. I can give you no hope." Stunned, Helmut remembers, "We left that hospital with feet of lead."

For the next several months, Malita was completely dependent on blood donors (see June 27 reading) and hospitalized continuously from November 1970 to April 1971. At the lowest point in this awful travail, Helmut and Norma Jean remember a visit from Mrs. Sekiguchi. She was a woman who, with her husband, had passed through some terrible trials and, as a result of answered prayer, had known miraculous deliverance. This godly woman prayed with them. Before leaving, she placed a card in their hands. When they opened it they read the words, "What is impossible with men is possible with God." God did indeed answer prayer, the prayers of family, missionaries and, above all, dear Japanese friends who stood with them during these difficult months. Gradually, Malita began to recover. Eight years later she was taken off all medication.

When the Schultzes returned from furlough in 1972, they were once more back in Tokyo where Helmut continued his duties as field leader and professor in Tokyo Bible Seminary. He also preached regularly in churches of the Japan Holiness Church. Norma Jean served on the board of CAJ, the school where both Malita and Juli were enrolled. She also taught English in the seminary and used nursing skills in a ministry to students, pastors and missionary families.

Toward the end of this term, Helmut accepted the position of OMS Vice-President of Homeland Affairs and in 1981 the family moved to Greenwood, Indiana, where mission headquarters are located. Working now under his direction at OMS was his former classmate at Hillcrest College, Alice Huff, Director of World Intercessors.

"At headquarters," Alice recalls, "I noted again qualities that I had first observed during his student days. Helmut believed in the Spirit-filled life, lived it and preached it with great conviction. I'll always remember a powerful message on holiness he gave at a large ministerial meeting in Canada. His tender servant heart was still there, none of the cynicism and professionalism that so often mark people who have turned ministry into routine. He cared for friends and supporters and loved to visit and spend time with them. He made it a point to express gratitude and wrote notes of encouragement to those under him. And as always, there was a humility about him that was no put-on. He knew very well his limitations and acknowledged that the source of his strength was from above. As my leader, I also appreciated his decisiveness and ability to make decisions, every one carefully thought out and thoroughly prayed over."

The office of vice-president of homeland affairs was responsible for all OMS regions in the U.S., the regional directors, all furloughing missionaries and mission outreach to local churches—a tremendous task and heavily weighted with administrative duties. In time, Helmut came to feel that these demands, important as they were, were keeping him from the full use of his ministerial gifts. Since there had now been a change in OMS field leadership in Japan, he was convinced that, in the interest of pastoral ethics, it was best that he not immediately return there. About this time an invitation came to take the pastorate of World Gospel Church (WGC) in Terre Haute, Indiana. This outstanding mission-minded church founded by Carl Froderman, followed by associate Charles Lake, was now clearly in need of strong leadership sympathetic to the initial mandate of vision of the founders—to take the Gospel to the whole world.

The Schultzes, with reluctance, resigned from OMS in 1981 and began a fruitful eight-year ministry in Terre Haute. The church drew a good number of students and professors from local colleges and universities. This was a challenge that Helmut accepted with great zest, and under his anointed leadership the church grew during his tenure from an attendance of 150 to more than 400. The folk at WGC warmed to their new pastor and his wife, and he soon won their hearts.

Mrs. Hester Pilcher, one of his parishioners recalled her first impression of the Schultzes. "We soon discovered," she said, "that Helmut and Norma Jean really deeply, genuinely, cared about us. Helmut greeted everyone with his huge bear hugs. When our son, Foster, was presented his Eagle Scout award, Helmut and Norma Jean made it a point to be there. Growing up on a farm, there was still in Helmut the farmer's love of the soil. He had an amazing garden and shared with us from his abundance huge quantities of cucumbers and plump zucchini."

Helmut's preaching ministry was deeply appreciated and everyone remembers that often at a climatic moment he would pause, especially when speaking of the love and grace of God. And then, totally overcome by emotion, he would burst out with a thunderous "Wowee."

Another member, Robert Wray, recalled that Helmut, like Christ, came "not to be served but to serve." He says: "When we moved into the neighborhood we were so busy that I had neglected to mow the lawn. Imagine my chagrin when I returned one day to find the lawn perfectly mowed. 'Who mowed the lawn?' I demanded of my wife. 'Your pastor,' she smiled. 'Helmut came, got the mower and did the whole job himself.' Talk about embarrassed—my pastor, a man of God, mowing my lawn! Somehow Helmut got the idea that we needed, in fact had to have, a garden. He gave us a little lecture on the joys and blessings of gardening. I demurred, not sure I wanted that much work. Then one day when I came home, the news from my wife was, 'Well, now we have a garden.' We do? How come we have a garden? 'Well,' she explained, 'Helmut came over today, he spaded the garden and planted the seed and now we have a garden.'"

The Pilcher's teenage son, Foster, who would later joined OMS as a graphic artist, was deeply influenced by Helmut's life and ministry. "Helmut never knew a stranger," Foster recalls. "He hugged everyone and as much as he loved to preach, people were always his priority. He not only loved people, he was passionate about people and he was kind and gentle, never rude, always looking out for the interests of others. Though during the Terre Haute years he was not on the foreign field as missionary, his vision was undiminished. He was always urging on us the responsibility and the privilege of sharing Christ with the world. There was never any pious posturing as with so many ministers. More than anyone I knew Helmut Schultz was real, authentic."

While in Terre Haute, Malita and Julie finished high school. Juli enrolled in Asbury College where she majored in elementary education. Malita went to nearby Indiana State University for three years, then transferred to Azusa University in California for her final year. She received a full scholarship to the University of Kentucky where she earned an MA in International Studies after which she worked for the U.S. State Department for 12 years. During these years, Norma Jean worked as visiting nurse and nursing clinical director. She also completed a graduate degree in counseling at Indiana State University. In 1988 Juli married Brian Hubbard, an Asbury classmate from Virginia. They have three children and live in Virginia where Juli teaches elementary school.

In 1990 Helmut and Norma Jean resigned from World Gospel Church to rejoin OMS. Helmut was named vice-president at large. In this role he and Norma Jean were free to travel to OMS fields throughout the world in a ministry to both missionaries and national churches. In 1994 they returned to Japan to fill the role of interim field director for two years while helping younger missionaries transition to leadership.

They moved to Kentucky in 1996 where Helmut accepted the pastorate of the Missionary Church in Wilmore. They also continued to serve part-time with OMS in a ministry to churches and campuses, as well as accepting occasional overseas assignments.

In 1998 Malita married Henry Kim. Henry's parents had come to the U.S. from Korea when he was five. His mother is a business woman in New York and the descendant of an "attachee" or "interpreter" to the Korean emperor. Malita and Henry took a position with the U.S. State Department in Indonesia from 1998-2001.

In 1990 Helmut had been diagnosed with prostate cancer, still in the early stages. By 1999 doctors had decided that surgery was required. Preliminary tests prior to the surgery yielded a startling discovery. Helmut also had colon cancer, already in an advanced stage. In less then diplomatic fashion, the young doctor informed Norma Jean, "Don't worry too much about the prostate cancer; your husband will die of colon cancer." Norma Jean, a nurse, who had battled with breast cancer ten years earlier, knew all too well what lay ahead for Helmut and for both of them. Colon cancer is unusually vicious, a rampant malignancy for which there is, even yet, virtually no effective treatment. "Though many prayers were offered for Helmut's healing," Norma Jean says, "we were never given the assurance that Helmut would be healed." Realizing that very likely Helmut had at most two to three years, Norma Jean says, "We sat down together and prayerfully and realistically planned out our remaining time together in service for the Lord." (See August 31 reading.)

Helmut's initial response, once the awful prognosis was accepted, was keen regret that he would not have longer to serve the Lord he loved so well. Yet, he believed, God makes no mistakes and together with the precious time that remained they would literally welcome each new day as a gift from God, striving to make every hour count for His glory.

Resigning from the Missionary Church, Helmut set two prime ministry goals. First, he wanted to travel to college and seminary campuses challenging young people to unreservedly commit their lives to Jesus Christ for Christian service. Secondly, he determined to pursue a project that had long been in his mind and on which he had already done some preliminary work. He resolved to write a daily devotional book (the one you now hold in your hand), incorporating Biblical insights with practical lessons God had taught him through the course of his life and ministry.

The Schultzes then worked out an itinerary and, as Helmut's ebbing strength permitted, began to travel to key schools, college and seminaries throughout the U.S. A moving tribute came from John Wilson, who, as a seminary student, had attended the Missionary Church where Helmut pastured, and later served as dean of admissions at Wesley Biblical Seminary in Jacksonville, Mississippi. He spoke of the time Helmut came to WBS campus.

"I'll never forget that chapel service where Helmut spoke on Jonah," John said. "He preached with awful fervency, urging us not to run from God's call or to fall short of absolute obedience, to never choose our own will over His perfect will. Helmut was a man on fire, 'a dying man speaking to dying men.' When he gave the invitation at the close of that chapel service, the altar was packed. I remember his big hand on my shoulder, as he prayed that God would use me and that

I would never accept anything short of His best and perfect will for my life."

During the final months when it became increasingly clear that Helmut's pilgrimage was coming to an end, he and Norma Jean arranged visits to friends and family members for a last farewell. "Gratefully," says Norma Jean, "Helmut never experienced unbearable pain. Although increasing weakness meant that each trip had to be carefully planned so as not to place excessive strain on his limited reserves." In Canada they met with relatives for a tender, tearful but still joyous farewell. Before parting, Helmut prayed an unforgettable prayer, a kind of patriarchal benediction, and then admonished everyone to keep loving Jesus and serving Him.

Stopping at the OMS International Conference in Marion, Indiana, that summer, there were tender, final meetings with old OMS friends. Even then, Alice Huff remembers that he had not lost his sense of humor. Visiting with me at the conference, shortly before he left us," she recalls, "he ended our conversation mischievously with, 'Alice, if the Lord takes me to heaven before you, I hope you'll have something good to say about me at my funeral.'" On the phone with an old Japan missionary friend, Joanna Dyer, who was herself dying of cancer, the two wept together and then joked about which one would make it through the heavenly gates first.

Helmut passed away at their home in Wilmore, Kentucky, on August 17, 2002, their 45th wedding anniversary, with Norma Jean at his bedside caring for him to the last. Gratefully the end came quickly without excessive pain. At the time he had finished all but 80 pages of his devotional book. The remainder of the task Norma Jean would joyfully complete, drawing from Helmut's abundant sermon material.

A letter came to Norma Jean a short time later from Nozomu Kato, a former student of Helmut's at Tokyo Bible Seminary and now himself a pastor struggling with ill health. "I remember two precious moments with Dr. Schultz," he wrote. "In May 2001, at the Japanese church centennial celebration, he preached a powerful sermon in Japanese, challenging us to repent and be renewed to receive God's new blessings. I asked him to pray for me afterwards and, as I knelt down, he laid his big right hand on my head, praying for me.

"Then in August 2002, in a voice, on the phone, weaker as a result of his illness, he burst out in prayer for me. 'Praise the Lord for your continuous blessings; bless this young man; heal him and continue to use him for your kingdom's work.' I trembled before the Lord, asking that I would be a passionate pastor, preacher and missionary like Dr. Schultz. Dr. Schultz had baptized me at the age of 12 in 1972. He encouraged me as the organist at my father's church. He taught us practical theology, theology of pastoral care, liturgy, and foundations of a pastoral life. Before I go back to Japan in this spring of 2003, I want to visit you in Kentucky and pay my respects to Dr. Schultz at his gravesite. Thank God for the love of Dr. Schultz for his Lord and for the Japanese people."

Two funeral services were held for Helmut, both attended by large numbers of friends, fellow missionaries, and former parishioners. The first of these was in Wilmore, Kentucky, home of Asbury College, on August 19. The second was held on August 21 at his old pastorate in Terre Haute, Indiana, where many of his former parishioners attended. Tears flowed as tributes recounted the beloved pastor's qualities that so endeared him to the people. "Though he started out as a simple farm boy," someone recalled, "he went on to become a man of great scholarship and deep wisdom." Another called him "a man with a true pastor's heart, a tireless encourager, a friend to everyone he met, fervent in spirit, passionate in preaching, a lover of God's word, a master of the art of intercession, tireless in prayer."

For those of us who remain, Helmut has left a noble example of what it means to truly follow the Lord. Not only in the energetic, idealistic years of one's youth, but through middle age and the searing heat of the day marked by harsh disappointments, sorrow and troubles, and finally into the sunset years, to the very end, rejoicing, praising, persevering until the journey is completed and we are in sight of the gates of the eternal city.

This book goes to press with the prayer that the spirit of Helmut Schultz will somehow be perpetuated in the lives of all who read these pages.

OMS AT A GLANCE

The year was 1900. At a desk in Chicago's central Western Union office sat Charles Cowman, a young executive responsible for the supervision of 500 telegraph operators. He was hardly conscious of the incessant chatter of telegraph keys tapping out messages from every point on the globe. His mind now was occupied with another message—the call of Jesus to go into all the world with the Good News. Reaching scores of businessmen and starting cell groups in hotel lobbies, the door to Japan opened for Cowman through a friendship in Chicago with Juji Nakada.

OMS International, the agency born of Cowman's response, is sending teams to Africa, Asia, the Caribbean, Europe and Latin America.

OMS has no church denomination underwriting its work. Each of more than 450 missionaries trusts God to provide his support through the prayers and gifts of His people.

OMS exists to promote missionary outreach by mobilizing prayer, people and financial resources for evangelism, church planting and leadership training. Our purpose is to: (1) engage in culturally relevant evangelism; (2) establish organizationally autonomous, culturally indigenous and spiritually reproductive churches; (3) train servant leaders to reach their nations; and (4) partner with them to reach the world for Christ.

OMS works in partnership with more than 7,941 national workers and 5,572 organized churches whose membership exceeds one million. In 32 seminaries and institutions, 6,841 students are preparing for ministry.

Through door-to-door evangelism, 343 teams lead thousands to Christ and assist in establishing over four new congregations weekly. OMS outreach includes three radio stations and nine medical clinics.

For information regarding scholarships for seminary students, adopting a missionary or country, visiting ministry sites, sending youth teams, or personal short-term and long-term ministry opportunities, please visit or write OMS International, Box A, Greenwood, Indiana, 46142-6599, or phone 317/881/6751.

Visit the OMS web site at www.omsinternational.org

MEET NEW FRIENDS IN THESE STORIES OF OMS MISSIONARIES

A WATERED GARDEN compiled by Alice Huff and Eleanor Burr. Unique stories from missionaries "toughing it out" in the dark places of the earth. Provides fresh insight to special demands of mission work and how best to pray for today's missionaries. $5.95.

ANOTHER VALLEY, ANOTHER VICTORY, ANOTHER LOVE by Valetta Steel Crumley, with Ed Erny. The inspiring story of a courageous woman who survived three tragedies that took the lives of her husband and children. Her life continues on the mission field and homeland where she faces life threatening events, plus romance.

> English, Chinese, and Spanish $5.99.
> Japanese $12.00
> Korean $7.99
> Russian $4.00

BRIDGE ACROSS THE CENTURY by Edwin L. Kilbourne. This personalized history tells of the lives and ministries of the founders, the missionaries who followed them and the national church for which OMS was born. $10.00 soft cover. $15.00 hard cover.

FROM THE CLAWS OF THE DRAGON by Carroll F. Hunt. Miracle story of Harry Lee's China imprisonment for his faith, updated with photos and story of a long-awaited marriage. $7.00.

GOD OWNS MY BUSINESS. Story of Stanley Tam, who turned his business over to God. Profits channeled to missions are assisting church planting teams in many nations. $4.00.

HE GOES BEFORE THEM...Even into Prison by Meredith and Christine Helsby. The story of the Helsby family inside a

Japanese prison in China, as well as missionary advance in China and Taiwan. $5.00.

LET THE ROCKS CRY OUT by Rachel Picazo. Stories about Radio Station 4VEH show how God directed, gave vision, provided, protected and prospered His plan, including a Bible training institute, medical center, churches and numerous community outreaches. $7.50.

NO GUARANTEE BUT GOD by Ed and Esther Erny. By faith, with no guarantee but God, Charles Cowman, Lettie Cowman, Ernest Kilbourne, and Juji Nakada embarked on an adventure with God that began a missionary organization in Japan in 1901, which today spans the globe. Read the short biographies of each, full of answered prayers, miracles, unbelievable challenges, heartaches and victories. $5.00.

SPAIN – A TAPESTRY OF GOD'S DESIGN by Lois Miller. This book endeavors to give you a new appreciation for the Spanish people and information about the Gospel ministry of OMS among them. $6.50.

STRETCHED BUT NOT BROKEN. In this "portrait of a missionary," Lois Miller writes from her heart about experiences with OMS in Ecuador, Spain and Greece. With contagious joy she effectively communicates God's love. $8.00.

THE KEY GOOSE by Mildred Rice, with Ed Erny. An effervescent possibility thinker, well-known internationally as a speaker, Mildred talks about her life, her family and ministry, punctuated by war and transition in China, Japan and Taiwan. $4.50.

THIS ONE THING by Ed Erny. The story of a young executive, Eugene Erny, when in the Chicago business world changed his life goals and served in China, India and as mission president for 20 years. $7.00.

TO INDIA WITH LOVE, by Esther Close with Ed Erny, is a true adventure and record of a woman of unusual courage and grit. Read how God took a young farm girl in Kansas, won the total commitment of her heart, and made her His loving and humble servant to the villagers of rural India and Haiti. As a Christian midwife she delivered hundreds of babies in the villages and showed Christ's love. $5.00

WHERE STONY GROUND IS BROKEN by Lois Miller tells how the Church of Jesus Christ is becoming a force in Ecuador, South America. This book gives the reader opportunity to believe even more stalwartly that there is nothing too hard for God. $6.50.

UNDER SENTENCE OF DEATH by Ed Erny. Thrilling story of Henry Steel, dying of cancer, who changed careers to minister for the cause of missions with lasting results. $3.95.

YIPPEE IN MY SOUL by Margaret Bonnette, with Ed Erny. The story of a missionary nurse in the remote mountains of Haiti. As Margaret climbs trails, straddles donkeys, nurses patients, among the poorest of the poor, you will enjoy her humor and zest for life. $5.00.

DEVOTIONAL BOOKS BY OMS MISSIONARIES

STREAMS IN THE DESERT by Mrs. Charles Cowman, one of the founders of OMS.

Anniversary Edition	$10.00
Revised Edition	$ 5.00
Spanish Edition	$ 8.50

STORY BEHIND STREAMS IN THE DESERT by Ed Erny. How the best-loved devotional book, printed in 1924 with more than 120 editions in English alone, came to be written. $7.00.

LEGACIES OF FAITH by Ed Erny. Daily devotional readings drawn from great Christian literature both ancient and modern.

Volume I	$8.00
Volume II	$8.00
Volume III	$8.00

Books may be ordered by sending a check for listed price plus $1.50 per book for postage and handling, to the address below for USA.
Book Room, OMS International
Box A, Greenwood, Indiana 46142. Phone 317-881-6751

Prices and availability subject to change without notice. Allow 2-4 weeks for delivery.